THE EVOLUTION OF
ETHICS

THE
EVOLUTION OF ETHICS

AS REVEALED IN THE
GREAT RELIGIONS

EDITED BY

E. HERSHEY SNEATH, Ph.D., LL.D.

PROFESSOR OF THE PHILOSOPHY OF RELIGION AND
RELIGIOUS EDUCATION, EMERITUS,
YALE UNIVERSITY

"Thus saith the Lord,
Keep ye justice, and do righteousness."
Isaiah 56: 1.

NEW HAVEN

YALE UNIVERSITY PRESS

LONDON · HUMPHREY MILFORD · OXFORD UNIVERSITY PRESS

MCMXXVII

PREFACE

THIS volume includes a series of intensive studies in the ethics of the great religions. The papers were prepared, of course, by specialists. Each essay embodies, in a comparatively brief form, the results of scholarly inquiry into the ethical content of a particular religion. The combined results provide a book that may be used to advantage in courses in the History of Religion, or in a comparative study of religions. It will prove interesting and helpful, also, to the intelligent reader in revealing how fundamental in some, and prominent in all, of the religions is the conception of righteousness. The Editor desires publicly to thank the authors for their contributions to the volume.

CONTENTS

THE ETHICS OF THE EGYPTIAN RELIGION

SAMUEL A. B. MERCER

I.

STRICTLY speaking, ethics is the science of morals, concerning itself with the principles of human duty. So far as is known, the Egyptians have left us no system of ethics. The reconstruction of ethics, as the science of morals, of an ancient people, approaches the impossible. On the other hand, morals has to do with habits of life in regard to right and wrong conduct. The subject matter of the morals of any ancient people can be gleaned from their extant literature. It can be classified in the light of what was considered right and wrong conduct by the people and time under consideration. In this chapter, however, the words ethics and morals will be used interchangeably.

In a study of Egyptian ethics or morals we shall be dealing with the Egyptian idea of goodness, truth, justice, righteousness, purity, and faithfulness, on the one hand; and, on the other hand, with that of evil, falsehood, injustice, wickedness, impurity, and faithlessness.

The origin of ethical or moral ideas reaches back into prehistoric times. The earliest historic man habitually differentiated between good and bad. His "good" and "bad" doubtless differed from ours, having been probably more confused and narrower. *We* may say that "good" is that which favors human progress, and evil that which impedes it. But the Egyptians, because of their known piety, would probably have defined "good" as that which is pleasing to the gods, and evil as that which incites the anger of the gods. Egyptian "good" and "evil" may originally have been purely ritual and ceremonial, but in historic times we shall find that, although ritual right and wrong still prevailed to some extent, a positive moral distinction was made. Our own moral distinctions are based upon what we consider to be the will of God

and upon what has become customary. The same is true
of Egyptian morals. What their gods willed was right,
what they disapproved was wrong; what was customary
was right, and what was not customary was wrong.

Of course, the gods will what we *think* they will. We
think God wills justice, righteousness, purity, etc. The
Egyptians thought he willed the same, though their idea
of justice, righteousness, and purity may have been different from what ours is. They may have conceived of
sin, for example, in a more ceremonial way than we, and
may have considered it and "sickness" to be equivalent.
This we must take into consideration in our estimate of
Egyptian ethics.

Every human act is done with some end or purpose in
view. The end is always regarded by the doer in the light
of something good. If evil be done, it is done as leading
to good, or as bound up with good, or as itself being good
for the doer under the circumstances. The standard of
moral judgment is that which is considered good or bad,
wrong or right. But what is considered good or bad,
wrong or right, depends upon people and time. To the
Egyptians, human acts were right or wrong, good or bad,
not according as they were useful or harmful, nor yet according as their consequences made for or against the
end of social happiness, but according as they were pleasing or displeasing to the gods. The Egyptians aimed at
material blessings, prosperity, success in war and in private undertakings; but they also aimed at tranquillity
of soul and a happy future life, and, most of all, their
greatest concern was to please the gods.

In examining the subject matter of Egyptian ethics or
morals, allowance must be made for a wide gap between
the ideal and real. We must be careful not to confuse
what were actual practices with what were merely ideals,
although the ideals will be valuable as indications of what

the Egyptians knew to be best and of what they tried to attain.

The fragmentary nature of Egyptian literature does not at all periods allow of a complete systematization of ethics or morals, and because contemporary literature is the only reliable source for the study of the morals of any age that is past, great care has been taken in the matter of the date of our sources.

The main sources used in this study are: First, Egyptian historical, biographical, and business inscriptions; secondly, legal documents; and thirdly, religious and ethical material.

My method has been: First, to assemble all ethical materials in all Egyptian literature, classify them, so as to show what the family, social, international, transcendental, and personal virtues and vices were; and, secondly, to estimate Egyptian ethics by an examination of the moral ideals, the idea of moral evil, the question of free will, and the moral sanctions. Due care has been taken to allow for the moral determinants of the age, and to differentiate between national and individual responsibility.

Moral Materials

The earliest inscriptions reveal the family in Egypt as the social unit with its prototype in the life of the gods, and this remained true throughout the whole period of Egyptian civilization. The normal divine family consisted of father, mother, and son; such as, Osiris, Isis, and Horus.

Whether there was anything in Egyptian life corresponding to a betrothal among modern peoples cannot as yet be determined, nor can it be made out whether any contract whatever, whether expressed or understood, preceded the marriage contract.

Marriage normally consisted in the union of one man

with one woman; in other words, marriage was monogamous. The king as well as the peasant normally had but one legal wife. This may be fairly assumed from the nature of the ideal divine family, as well as from the early monuments which so often represent husband and one wife as the nucleus of the family.[1] There were, however, exceptions to this. The pharaoh not only had his queen, but he also possessed a harem (ḫnt, ḫnrt) as well. Daughters of good Egyptian families were often found among the foreign beauties comprising the royal harem. It is also certain that polygamy, or, rather, concubinage, was somewhat common, as stelas of the Twelfth and Thirteenth Dynasties show.[2] In the *Pyramid Texts* reference is found to the mistresses of the pharaoh, even in the hereafter (§ 123), and in this life it was usual to call a woman *Nebtef*, "his mistress." But these wives were never placed on the same level with a man's consort.

So far as our literary material will allow, there is no means of determining whether there were any legal impediments to marriage. At any rate, there seems to have been no degrees of consanguinity. The king could marry his sister, and commonly did so,[3] and there is no evidence that the custom was not general. Nor do our sources teach us how the average Egyptian procured his bride, whether by purchase or conquest, as among other ancient peoples, or whether the marriage was based upon mutual consent. Perhaps the normal way was to receive her freely from the hand of her father. This was true, at any rate, in the case of Ptahshepses of the Fifth Dynasty, who records that "his majesty gave to him the king's oldest daughter, Matkha, as his wife."[4]

---

[1] Poertner, *Die aegyptischen Totenstelen*, Paderborn, 1911, pp. 17 ff.
[2] Moret, *Galerie Égyptienne* (*Annales du musée Guimet*, XXXII), Paris, 1909, C 7, C 11.
[3] Rougé, *Inscriptions hiéroglyphiques*, Paris, 1877-1879, p. 153.
[4] Breasted, *Ancient Records*, Chicago, 1906, I, 257.

The Egyptian family was patriarchal. The father was the possessor, and lord in his own house. To him obedience was due. Yet there is no evidence of any such paternal power over different members of the family as was common in Sumerian times.[5] On the contrary, the earliest and latest Egyptian monuments represent man and wife as equal, and inscriptions record, again and again, that the husband treated his wife with honor and love. One of a man's chief concerns in this life was for his wife, and he was not forgetful of her future, after his death, either in this world or in the next.

In the goddess Isis was personified the fidelity of the Egyptian wife, a characteristic brought out very clearly in the stelas of the Old Kingdom, where one so often sees the wife sitting in an attitude of love and confidence with her arm about her husband. Sometimes a woman rose to a position of great importance, as in the case of Neit-hotep, who, it seems, legitimated the first Egyptian dynasty. In religious matters likewise the wife took a leading part in the cultus, and women were sometimes priestesses.

Family love seems to have been the most prominent characteristic of the home life of the Egyptians, though the birch was applied whenever necessary, and an undutiful son was disowned; but, as Ptah-Hotep taught, "a good son is the gift of God," and "a splendid thing is the obedience of an obedient son.'"[6] Again and again we read in the biographies of officials of the Old Kingdom: "Never did I judge two brothers in such a way that a son was deprived of his paternal possession. I was one beloved of his father, praised of his mother, whom his brothers and sisters loved.'"[7] So common did the senti-

[5] Mercer, "Sumerian Morals," *Journal of the Society of Oriental Research*, I, 47 ff.

[6] Gunn, *The Instructions of Ptah-Hotep*, London, 1912, §§ 43, 38.

[7] Breasted, *op. cit.*, I, 357, etc.

ment expressed by these words become that the phrase grew to be stereotyped. The parents' joy in their children is revealed in the names they gave them. It was common for a daughter to be called "beauty-comes," or for a son to be named "riches."

The most common of all family virtues was filial love. This is most beautifully illustrated in the story of the relationship between Horus and his father Osiris as well as in the solicitude with which Zau of the Sixth Dynasty made preparations for the proper burial of his father, and in the sincere filial love which prompted him to provide for a future resting place for himself beside his father. He said: "Now, I caused that I should be buried in the same tomb with this Zau, in order that I might be with him in one place; not, however, because I was not in a position to make a second tomb; but I did this in order that I might see this Zau every day; in order that I might be with him in one place."[8] It was a son's duty and privilege not only to provide a suitable burial for his father, but likewise to see to its maintenance. In this he was carrying out his father's wish, and for it he was highly praised. We can see now, on the stelas of the Old Kingdom, after a lapse of nearly 5000 years, the father and mother arm in arm, and their children standing or sitting near them. Respect and reverence were the parents' due.

Normally a man succeeded to his parental inheritance, and it was considered wrong to do anything calculated to disturb this balance. But the line of inheritance could be through the daughter, as in the case of Neit-hotep, and that is, perhaps, why Zau petitioned the king for the right of succession to his father's home, although there might have been special statutory conditions which governed the succession. But the frequency of the assertion,

8 Breasted, *op. cit.*, I, 382, 383.

"Never did I judge two brothers in such a way that a son was deprived of his paternal possession," would seem to show that filial succession was the normal one, and that a son inherited even the good name of his father, as when King Pepi II says to Harkhuf in a letter to him, "His majesty will make thy many excellent honors to be an ornament for the son of thy son forever."[9]

Family love is the ideal relationship not only between parent and child, but likewise between child and child. The characteristic of being a brother was to keep peace with one's brother. This is seen in the desired relationship between Horus and Set.[10]

Although no evidence is found for the existence of divorce in the earliest Egyptian inscriptions, the custom was probably known, for in the Middle Kingdom it is casually referred to as a well-known use,[11] and in later times it was very common. In fact, marriage being a legal contract, drawn up in the interest of the woman as well as of the man, the woman could divorce her husband and send him away just as easily as the man, who could divorce his wife and send her away.[12] The idea of divorce was never abhorrent to the Egyptian mind. It was a right which was necessary to the well-being of society, and this is illustrated by the very word which was used to express the idea, namely, _wḏā_, divorce, which means "to make right."

Egyptian society may be said to have consisted of three classes: (1) The king and the nobility; (2) lower officials; (3) laborers, peasants, and slaves. During the Middle Kingdom a feudal system was introduced, in

9 Breasted, _op. cit._, I, 352.

10 Erman, _Ein Denkmal memphitischer Theologie_, Berlin, 1911, p. 932.

11 Vogelsang und Gardiner, _Die Klagen des Bauern_, Leipzig, 1908, p. 10, l. 62.

12 Reich, "Marriage and Divorce in Ancient Egypt," _Museum Journal_, pp. 15, 50-57.

which certain nobles, called nomarchs, or barons, became
very powerful, although they were still responsible to the
pharaoh. Amenemhet I, one of the most powerful kings
of the Middle Kingdom, tried to destroy the power of the
nomarchs, but without success. The result was a spirit of
tumult and social unrest. Men became conscious of this
condition, and made a determined effort to bring about
social righteousness.[13] The interesting story of the Eloquent Peasant throws welcome light upon social conditions in the Middle Kingdom, and upon the comparative
ease with which the meanest peasant, oppressed by an
official, could effectively appeal to the grand steward of
the king, and through him to the pharaoh himself.[14] After
the feudal system passed away, its place was taken to
some extent by the priests and temple officials, who became exceedingly powerful.

At the top of the social scale stood the king. He was
considered a very god and worshiped as such.[15] As a
"great god" or "good god," the pharaoh was absolute
on earth—a wise but beneficent despot. He was the head
of his people and their representative before the gods. He
was their protector, and, as the lord of truth (*neb maāt*),
established truth. He was the law-maker and judge, the
"utterer of justice," who "judges before Rā." His
righteousness was never questioned. He was the very
image and earthly manifestation of the power, goodness, and providence of the gods. Endowed with almost
omnipotence and omniscience, the pharaoh was the bene-
factor and life-giver of his people. In short, the Egyptians considered the pharaoh to be a model of perfection,

---

[13] Erman, *Gespräch eines Lebensmüden mit seiner Seele*, Berlin, 1896,
passim.

[14] Vogelsang und Gardiner, *op. cit.*

[15] Baillet, *Le Régime Pharaonique*, Paris, 1912, I, 1 ff; Mercer, "Emperor-Worship in Egypt," *Journal of the Society of Oriental Research*, I,
10 ff.

and the favorite of the gods, the good and peaceful ruler, "whose working is in peace."

On the other hand, it must not be imagined that the king actually lived up to the people's ideal, nor that the people did not often discover his imperfections. In the *Pyramid Texts* (§ 150) we are told that the king "is the man who takes women from their husbands whenever he wills and when his heart desires," and that even in the next world the pharaoh has his mistresses (§ 123); but this was considered nothing more than a right inherent in divinity, and, therefore, pertaining to the gods and to the pharaoh as a god.

Amenemhet I, in his instructions to his son,[16] has given us an excellent picture of what the Egyptians of the Middle Kingdom thought of the duties of a king. Amenemhet himself was a reformer, his motto being to "set right that which he found ruined." He boasts that he "gave to the beggar" and "nourished the orphan," and advises his son to follow his example, treating high and low alike. But at the same time he warns his son against unnecessary weakness, and advises him to "learn to stand alone and not to depend upon others who may act treacherously." This conception of kingship prevailed in Egypt from the earliest to the latest times.

The state's duty toward the pharaoh may be summed up in the words "emperor-worship." The king was a god, and the state's duty toward him was that of reverence, adoration, and obedience. Yet the royal decrees of Egypt speak very eloquently of the rights of the people. In them we see the growth of a real democratic spirit. They teach us that the rights of each sanctuary depended upon public authority and that once a decree was made and published, granting certain rights and privileges, no law could repeal the same, not even royal authority. This idea

[16] Breasted, *op. cit.*, I, 478-483.

sprang from priestly power—the right of certain temples
to exemption from taxation, but it was nevertheless an
idea pregnant with democratic possibilities.[17]

To the people, the king was god, sovereign protector
and defender. On the other hand, the individual's first
duty to the king was that of respect and adoration. But
this duty was not irksome. The height of a man's ambition was to do what the king desired, to be beloved of the
king, and to be "more honored by the king than any servant." A common title was *mry nb-f*, "loved of his lord."
The subject believed that the virtues of his sovereign
were a reflection of the justice and goodness of the gods.

The relationship between individuals may be considered in a twofold way; first, the relation between superior
and inferior, and secondly, the relation between inferior
and superior. The duty of superior to inferior could not
be better illustrated than by quoting a part of the inscription on the tomb of a nobleman of the Fifth Dynasty: "I
gave bread to all the hungry of the Cerastes-mountain; I
clothed him who was naked therein; I filled its shores with
large cattle, and its lowlands with small cattle. . . . I
never oppressed one in possession of his property, so that
he complained of me because of it to the god of my city;
(but) I spake, and told that which was good; never was
there one fearing because of one stronger than he, so that
he complained because of it to the god.'"[18] Henku, thus,
considered it his duty to feed the hungry, clothe the
naked, defend his people's rights, and do that which was
good. In short, his rôle was that of protector and defender to those dependent upon him. Nor is this an iso-
lated example. There were many other nobles who
boasted of the same good deeds. Another asserts that
"every neighbor was supplied with water, and every citi-

17 Weill, *Les Decrets Royaux*, Paris, 1912, pp. 38 ff., 72 ff.
18 Breasted, *op. cit.*, I, 281.

zen had Nile water to his heart's desire;" another said: "I was open-handed to everyone;" and still another proclaims that he never did "aught of violence towards any person." This may also indicate a great deal of self-praise and boasting, but it is an indication of what the ideal relationship was.

The subordinate was respectful, submissive, and obedient to his superior, and the nobleman's ideal was to conduct himself in such a way as to elicit his inferiors' love, e.g., Nezemib caused to be inscribed upon his tomb the assertion that he "was one beloved of the people," that he had "never taken the property of any man by violence," and that he "was a doer of that which pleased all men."[19]

The nomarch of the Middle Kingdom was regularly expected by his fellow countrymen to be as near perfection as any human being can be.[20] He was the savior of his country, of whom justice was expected. This was the ideal, of which the actual often fell short, as we learn from the Eloquent Peasant, who complains that the "notables pillage, ravishing by force." Nevertheless, the reputation of a nomarch for justice was such that it could be said of him, "he was more unbiased than the magistrates"—a compliment not only to the nomarch but also to the magistrates. Moreover, so conscious had the official mind become to its rôle of upholder of truth and justice that "to confuse a mean mind" was considered a shameful deed.

Man with man was expected to act justly and uprightly. Cruelty, lust, murder, theft, robbery, slander, and falsehood were condemned; while love, mercy, justice, honesty, kindness, and truthfulness were commended.

The sense of individual responsibility, which became so prominent in the Empire period, was chiefly due to the

[19] Breasted, op. cit., I, 279.
[20] Newberry, The Life of Rekhmara, Westminster, 1900.

extent to which moral earnestness had developed during the time of the Middle Kingdom. The 125th chapter of the *Book of the Dead* is valuable in that it gives expression to some extent to what the individual Egyptian considered worthy of condemnation. He declared that he had not done evil to his fellow men, had not oppressed the members of his family, had not done evil in place of right and truth, had not associated with worthless men, had not ill-treated servants, had not blasphemed, had not violated property rights, had not caused pain, had not caused man to suffer hunger nor to weep, had not committed murder nor caused to commit murder, had not committed fornication, had not cheated, had not committed theft nor acted deceitfully, had not lied nor slandered, had not been angry, had not judged hastily, had not been faithless to his king and god. This formidable list shows a remarkable moral consciousness, and brings us into the presence of a civilization which was keenly sensitive to fine moral distinctions. The Egyptian official especially loved to emphasize his moral acts, and, while making due allowance for exaggeration, we are impressed by his desire to appear as good as possible. At any rate, though his intentions may not have been always realized, we have the means of forming a substantial estimate of what his ideals were. He declared himself to be "a man of truth void of deceit, useful to his lords; accurate-minded, with no lie in him, . . . turning his face to him who speaks the truth, disregarding him who speaks lies, . . . going about after truth, giving attention to hear petitions, . . . justifying the just, chastising the guilty for his guilt, servant of the poor, father of the fatherless, . . . protector of the weak, advocate of him who has been deprived of his possessions by one stronger than he, husband of the widow, shelter of the orphan, . . . who is praised on account of his character, for whom the worthy thank god.''[21] The individual was expected to be industrious, and to hold himself responsible for the safety of his neighbor: for example, he was not supposed ''to sit in a corner while one slew another.'' He prided himself on his love of learning, and he cherished his freedom of speech. The workman and official had his own house and wife, was well fed and educated, and held his position only so long as he did what was right. This democratic spirit awoke in the Old Kingdom, but did not find very fertile soil till the middle class came into its own, after the reign of feudalism, and after the Empire had well begun. Its growth may well be seen in the results of the moral teachings of the Middle Kingdom.

The king, as representative of the gods, was the source of all law and justice. A guarantee of justice was called ā nišwt, ''the king's writings,'' and decrees issued by the king were law, and should not be forgotten. The representative of the king in the administration of justice was the judge (sab), whose patron deities were Set and Maāt, goddess of truth, especially the latter, whose priests were as a rule judges. There were also chief justices (tayty), who were ''high priests of the great god.''

Judging from the mass of legal literature in later Egyptian times, it may be assumed that in early Egypt legal procedure began to be organized. But our extant material is as yet meager, though sufficient to show that the Egyptian had a tendency to regulate justice at all times.

Royal charters were common in early Egypt, and had developed into an exact form of legal contract. A typical royal charter or decree contained as many as eight separate and distinct points arranged in logical order: (1) the

[21] Breasted, op. cit., II, 768; cf. II, 343; Naville, Store-City of Pithom, London, 1903, p. 16.

name of Horus and the date, (2) general title and lists of those interested, (3) object of the decree, (4) a summons to all officers to respect and enforce the decree, (5) a statement of the irrevocability of the decree, (6) prohibition of alteration, (7) direction to be inscribed on stone and made public, (8) malediction on all violating the decree. When the decree was made and published, no authority, not even that of the king, could revoke it.[22]

There is sufficient evidence to show that legal contracts were very common in ancient Egypt. There is extant a legal document pertaining to litigation between an heir and an ancestor; and there is the testamentary enactment of an official of the Fourth Dynasty, establishing the endowment of his tomb, in which the following items follow one another logically: (1) introduction, (2) description of endowment, (3) entailment, (4) punishment for violation. The whole testament is framed in the most exact legal formulæ. A lady, Nebsent, of the Third Dynasty, made a will in favor of her children; and similar extant wills represent the Fifth and Sixth Dynasties.

The law was continually appealed to; legal trials were given all men, and a legal hearing was customary. Justice was recognized, and to be just was the source of much pride. The great judges of early Egypt never tired of the boast: "Never did I judge two brothers in such a way that a son was deprived of his paternal possessions." The nomarch, Kheti I, caused to be recorded that while he ruled "the child was not smitten beside his mother, nor the citizen beside his wife." The law must be obeyed by great as well as by small, every official must be at his post so that order may prevail and justice be done; and there must be no violence and oppression. But punishment is sure to follow disobedience, although the punishment was

22 Weill, *op. cit.*, pp. 36 ff.

extraordinarily severe, *e.g.*, the violator of a royal decree was to be sacrificed upon a block.

There seem to have been no persons especially privileged in respect to property in ancient Egypt. Anyone could possess property, and the law defended his rights. The nomarchs loved to boast that they "never oppressed one in possession of his property" or that they never took "the property of any man by violence."

Property could be acquired in various ways, but especially by inheritance; an heir, of whatever relationship, was protected in his inheritance. A woman could not only inherit property, but she could likewise leave it by will to her children.

Property was subject to taxation, but certain exemptions could be made. Religious institutions have, at almost all times, been exempted, and ancient Egypt was not an exception. We have an excellent example of a royal decree given by Pepi II of the Sixth Dynasty exempting a temple at Koptos from taxation. It is drawn up in a most precise legal manner; (1) the king's Horus name, (2) the high royal functionaries to whom it is addressed, (3) description of the sacred domain to be exempted, (4) detail of public works from which exemption is granted, (5) the prohibition to require taxation, (6) the king's dispensation, and (7) an order for execution of the decree.[23]

The high respect for law, characteristic of the Old Kingdom, continued throughout the whole of Egyptian history. Law courts were common, just judges were the beloved of the king, who were as true as the balances of Thoth, and the sense of justice was very highly developed; for example, a nomarch of Suit made a legal contract between himself as nomarch and himself as high-

[23] Weill, *op. cit.*, pp. 53 ff.

priest.[24] On the whole punishments were fair, though, from our modern point of view, some were rather severe; thus, a man's nose was cut off for robbery, and for the stealing of hides a man was punished by the loss of the hides as well as by a hundred blows and the opening of five wounds. Teachers were often severe, their philosophy being that "the youth has a back, he attends when it is beaten" (*Anast. Pap.* 5, 8, 6, in the *Select Papyri of the Br. Museum,* London, 1844-1860).

The Egyptians were not a great commercial people. Their national boundaries were such as to shut them out from very free access to foreign nations. Yet early Egyptian history records commercial expeditions to inner Africa, to Sinai, Syria, and Asia Minor. But it was in domestic business and trade that their development is to be found, and here we see the same legal precision as in their contracts.

Laborers in Egypt were of two classes; free and enslaved. Any individual short of the king may be classed as a free laborer or as a servant. Ptahshepses, of the Fifth Dynasty, prides himself on being "more honored by the king than any *servant.*" All men were servants and laborers of the king. But there were also others, whose part it was to do menial work, but who were free agents, and who could possess property.

Over against the freeman was the slave, who could not possess property. His condition of slavery may have been captivity or purchase. In the transfer of property, slaves were included as well as cattle, and the *corvée* was common in all periods of Egyptian history. During the moral period of the Middle Kingdom kindness to servants was strongly recommended, although slaves were still handed on by will from father to heir. At a later time slaves ac-

---

24 Breasted, *op. cit.,* I, 568 ff.

quired certain definite rights, and sometimes attained to great prominence.[25]

We have already had occasion to see that Egypt from the very beginning came in contact, to a certain extent, with the outside world. Her commerce and trade extended far beyond her own boundaries. Likewise the marriage relationship was sometimes extended to embrace the foreigner, for it seems that a nobleman of the Third Dynasty took a Nubian to wife, as did also a royal scribe of the Sixth Dynasty.[26]

The Egyptians were a peace-loving people, a fact to which Strabo bears witness. In a series of hymns addressed to the diadem of the pharaoh, and which have been assigned to the period previous to the Middle Kingdom, the ideal of the country is represented as decidedly peaceful (htp). The idea of peace is repeated again and again, and seems to mean not merely domestic tranquillity, but peace in the widest and most general sense.

The early Egyptians as well as other peoples, however, had their wars. The ideal divine king of Egypt, Horus, was known as the "Smiter of Barbarians." Pepi I sent Uni on a military expedition to Palestine and Phœnicia. War is always cruel, and it was not an exception in this respect in early Egypt. Uni describes in his biography how the army of Pepi I, under his generalship, "had hacked up the land of the Sand-dwellers, . . . destroyed the land of the Sand-dwellers, . . . overturned its strongholds, . . . cut down its figs and vines, . . . thrown fire upon all its troops, . . . slain troops therein in many thousands, . . . carried away there-from a great multitude as living captives." The famous slate Palette of Nar-Mer shows the king in the act of slaying his captives, and restraining them by means of a nose-hook and rope.

[25] Devéria, *Le Papyrus judiciaire de Turin*, 4, 14.
[26] Baillet, *op. cit.*, I, 201, n. 1.

Mercenaries were used, as in the case of Uni, who collected soldiers from Nubia to fight against the Asiatics. The soldiery, however, were often used in times of peace for the protection of the people. The noble, Tefibi, boasts that "when night came, he who slept on the road gave me praise, for he was like a man in his house, the fear of my soldiers was his protection."

Before the close of the Middle Kingdom Egypt was conquered by the Hyksos and was forced by cruel experience to devote herself assiduously to the arts of war, although one of the greatest kings of the Middle Kingdom, Sesostris III, long before the Hyksos, had carried Egyptian arms into Syria, and had become just as much addicted to the capture of men and women, cattle and grain, and of all kinds of spoil, as the leader of any warlike people. But the peaceful Egyptians of earlier times became the warlike Egyptians of the period of the Empire and remained so until they were conquered by the Persians.

In spite of all this, however, the Egyptians were fundamentally a peace-loving people. The desire for permanent peace pervades their whole literature, and during the Empire the art of peace and peace-making was highly developed. Thus it was during this period that the interesting treaty between Rameses II and Khetasar, the Hittite, was drawn up, in which , among other modern-sounding terms, provision was made for extradition of political fugitives from either country, and supreme emphasis was placed upon the necessity of permanent peace.

Egypt's wars were holy because they were under the protection of the gods. Horus was the vanquisher of the barbarians, and any war carried on by Egypt against a foreign power had the approval of the gods. And so it happens that on palettes and monuments which depict warfare, the symbols of the gods always find a place. The enemies of Egypt are the enemies of Egypt's gods, and against them war is a work of piety, and their death a consummation devoutly to be wished.

The early Egyptian peopled his world with gods good and bad. Everything mysterious and inexplicable to him was, or contained, a god. The most striking and mysterious phenomenon of a locality became the god of that district, and so in early Egypt each nome or district or city had its god. When the nomes united into larger districts, families of gods were formed. Thus, at Heliopolis, the center of a confederation of districts, there grew up a family of nine gods, an Ennead, which was adopted in the whole of Egypt, because of the power and influence of Heliopolis, before the Eleventh Dynasty.

Some gods proved themselves to be good, others to be evil, and it was forbidden to obey certain gods because they were bad. This idea of imperfection on the part of the gods belongs to the general conception of deity prevalent among the early Egyptians. According to this conception the gods were created, and they died, like men. Some are sinful, others are righteous, and they experience fear just as human beings do. In short, anthropomorphism of the grossest kind is ascribed to them. They were the makers of all things good and bad; they made love and hate; they gave life to the free and death to the wicked; "Atum . . . made that which is loved and that which is hated. It was he who gave life to the peaceful and death to the guilty."

But more than anything else the early Egyptian loved to think of the gods as the source of all truth, righteousness, and justice. Horus is the "lord of truth"; Rā is "the great god of truth"; Osiris is the "lord of truth"; Rā separates true from false; Rā has two barges of "truth" or "righteousness"; a god's barge is regularly called the "barge of truth"; one god is called the "expeller of deceit"; a queen is named *Ḥap-n-Maāt*, "truth is of Apis''; the daughter of Rā is the goddess of truth and righteousness; and truth was personified as the goddess Maāt.

Being the origin of truth, the gods are also the source of justice. Men are judged before the gods who are the very essence of justice and require just dealings.

The king was the direct representative of the gods to the nation. The people were servants of the king and he in turn was a servant of the gods. The king loves the gods, and the gods help the king because they know that otherwise they would lose his support. The king is the god's heir and is beloved by him. In general, the god's duty to the king is that of father to son, and the king's duty to the god is that of son to father. The gods love, help, and protect the king; and the king loves, obeys, and worships the gods.

It is the state form of religion which we know best in Egypt. The *Pyramid Texts* were inscribed in the tombs of the kings, and the other mortuary texts and biographies belong to barons and leading men of the people. We learn a good deal about the king, his nobles, and his slaves, but we know little about the great mass of the people. It is assumed on the basis of comparative religion that the average Egyptian of the early period worshiped all kinds of inanimate and animate objects, such as trees and animals; and practiced a good deal of magic. But wherever the state religion penetrated we find that the individual was conscious of his close relationship with the gods. In describing, then, the individual's relation to his gods, we shall use the extant evidence as applicable not only to the noble but also to the average Egyptian who had become conscious of the national cult.

The early nomarchs loved to boast of the honor paid them by their city-gods, and of the way in which the gods loved them. Their greatest desire was to do the will of the gods, and to be praised by them. Blasphemy was always condemned, and most severely and savagely punished.

The gods were the natural protectors of the individual, who brought his complaints before them for rectification. Henku, of the Fifth Dynasty, said, "I never oppressed one in possession of his property, so that he complained of me because of it to the god of my city," and thereby shows his respect for the individual's right to appeal to the gods.

Gods and goddesses are the object of worship in ancient Egypt. Deities were personified material phenomena, or animals; but they were likewise deified human beings. The king was worshiped as a deity and so was the mother of the king. The gods were the ancestors of the race, and their immediate descendants, the royalty, were treated as gods.

The chief religious official was the pharaoh. He stood at the head of the hierarchy. Priests were merely his representatives. He was really the priesthood in himself, and so the stereotyped phrase for making an offering by whomsoever made is *ḥtp dy nïśwt* "an offering which the king makes."

But as the king could not be present everywhere at all times, an official priesthood represented him. There were chief priests, ordinary priests (*wāb,* or *ḥm-nṯr*), of whom there were various classes, and priestesses (*dwat-nṯr*). The local noble was chief priest. The priesthood was protected and could not be drafted for forced labor, and they had specific rights which could not be alienated.

The god always had his house (*ḥ-t nṯr*) which was erected and served by the king, and in which his statue was kept. He was worshiped by sacrifices, offerings, praise, and prayer. Even human sacrifice seems to have been practiced in ancient Egypt. Great festivals were held in which the great deeds of the gods were demonstrated and when offerings and prayers were made.

That a great deal of the religion of ancient Egypt was ceremonial is to be expected. The purifications so often spoken of in the *Pyramid Texts* are as a rule to be interpreted in a ceremonial way. The commonest name for priest, namely, *wab,* means clean; and undoubtedly had a ceremonial origin. Nor was magic absent. The numerous incantations, which became so common in later times, are means whereby the actions of the gods are thought to be controlled and regulated, and the idea underlying an offering was commonly magical. The gods must help, otherwise offerings will not be made, and, conversely, an offering is made to force help from the gods. There are cases where, perhaps, the idea of cleansing was understood in a real spiritual and moral way, but the general conception was physical and ceremonial.

The early Egyptian was not adverse to proselytism, for we learn that Harkhuf, of the Sixth Dynasty, after having pacified the enemy, caused him to praise all the gods for the king's sake.

During the Middle Kingdom, along with the keener appreciation of moral values came a deeper conception of the justice and mercy of the gods. With the passage of time polytheism became less crude and anthropomorphism less naïve, in fact, a tendency to extreme henotheism, or, as some think, a kind of monotheism, developed in the reign of Ikhnaton.[27] Hymns to Amon and Aton breathe a remarkable spirit of universalism and spirituality.

The early Egyptian was exceedingly proud of his acts of kindness. Again and again we read such expressions as the following: "I was he who fulfilled his duty,"

[27] Mercer, "Was Ikhnoton a Monotheist?" *Journal of the Society of Oriental Research*, III, 70 ff.

"Never did I do anything evil towards any person," "Never have I taken a thing belonging to any person," "I give bread to all the hungry, I clothed him who was naked," "I love that which is good and hate that which is evil," "I judged brothers to their reconciling," "I saved the weak from the hands of the strong," etc.

The Egyptian individual had developed a sense of personal right which is often remarkable. The Misanthrope[28] and the Eloquent Peasant assume an individualism and sense of personal right which are eloquent of the independence of thought and action in ancient Egypt. The Eloquent Peasant, in his dispute with his antagonist, declared, "My ways are good," *i.e.*, "I have a right to the way I take": and the Misanthrope demanded that each man be responsible only for his own deeds—"sentence a man only for the deed that he has verily committed." The Egyptian's sense of truth and justice had molded him into a stern critic of personal endeavor and responsibility. "Thy tongue is the spring of a balance, thy heart is the weight, and thy two lips are its arms," declared the Eloquent Peasant; and Ptah-Hotep said, "Honor a man for what he has become, not for what he was." In keeping with this teaching, the Egyptian held himself to be upright, truthful, just, honest, frank, generous, the protector of widows and orphans, and defender of the weak; and he condemned all the opposite vices. He was warned to expect injustice and oppression and to be able to stand alone; but he was fair enough to see that "the other fellow" had his rights. These he respected, and accordingly condemned adultery, robbery, and violence, and encouraged the opposite virtues and a recognition of the rights of his fellow men.

All this was, of course, the ideal. There were many exceptions to the acts of virtue already enumerated, so

28 Erman, *Gespräch eines Lebensmüden mit seiner Seele*, Berlin, 1896.

much so that the Misanthrope could find no justice in the land, no satisfaction in the world, and nothing but evil held sway. But where there are ideals there are good intentions, and good intentions are not always unsuccessful.

Estimation of Egyptian Morals

In making an estimate of Egyptian morals, care must be taken to differentiate individual from national responsibility. The standard of judgment in our estimate must necessarily be the morals of our own day. In comparing, then, the morals of Egypt with those of our own modern Western civilization we may commend or condemn them according as they were equal or better, on the one hand; or as they were lower, on the other. But we cannot thus estimate the morals of the Egyptian individual. He must be commended or condemned not on the basis of our code of morals, but on the basis of the morals of his own nation and times. In other words, the individual Egyptian must be examined in the light of his own civilization. There is, of course, a sense in which this is likewise true of the nation. We may say that the morals of any nation should be examined in the light of the general civilization of its times. Nevertheless, it is permissible and legitimate for comparative purposes to commend or condemn its morals as a nation in comparison with any other independent standard.

Further, in our study of the morals of Egypt either in a national or in an individual way, we must bear in mind their moral determinants. This will involve a consideration of such ideas as heredity, environment, social tradition, and personal initiative. For example, in considering a perverted sense of truth or a keen sense of justice, the force of heredity must be allowed for; the force of environment should be allowed for in the case of sexual morality or immorality; that of social tradition should be allowed for in the case of monogamy or slavery; and personal rights of all kinds should be considered in the light of personal initiative.

The morals of a people can best be discovered by examining their moral ideals, their sense of moral evil, their consciousness of the presence or absence of free will, and the sanctions of their moral acts.

The Egyptians ascribed the best they knew to their gods. Hence, if we know the character of the acts ascribed to the Egyptians' gods, we shall know what their moral ideals were.

We have learned that the Egyptians ascribed to the gods, primarily, the attributes of love, goodness, righteousness, truth, and justice. But what was their idea of "love," "goodness," etc.? Did these words connote to the Egyptians what they do to us? What was their moral content? So far as we can learn from a study of the original words, *maāt* is the name of the most important of Egypt's goddesses, the daughter of Rā. Her symbol is the feather, which appears in judgment scenes weighed in the balance against the heart of the deceased. The goddess is represented sometimes with bandages over her eyes. It is evident from the part played by the feather in judgment scenes that it represents the standard of judgment. Hence, it has been rendered by the words "law," "order," "duty." The blindfolded goddess represents impartiality, and hence *maāt* has been rendered by the words "truth," "justice." Moreover, the ideal of all Egyptian gods and kings was *ānḥ n maāt*, "living according to rule, or in justice." The hall of the kingdom of the dead was called "the hall of the two truths." The expression is a very old one, indicating that the Egyptian believed in the existence of two truths, whereby a matter was looked at from both sides. The form of the original word is dual. The word *maāt* comes from the verb *maā,* "to be real," "genuine," "true." The same word appears in Coptic as ME: MHI. A common divine and royal title was *neb maāt,* "lord of truth." The word is used in conjunction with *ḥrw, maā-ḥrw,* meaning, "true of voice," the φωνὴ ἀληθής of Plutarch, or, "justified." The phrase referred to one, whether god or man, who had been found worthy, whether in this world or the next. It was sometimes used in a ceremonial way, but at the same time it connoted to the early Egyptian about what the words "truth," "justice," etc., connote to us, *e.g.,* it would be considered unjust and cruel if a citizen were "smitten beside his wife" or a "child smitten beside its mother"; it was unjust to speak untruthfully. The early Egyptian believed that justice "was born before strife of voice, blasphemy, and conflict arise": and that "sky and earth were glad when justice was done." He believed his god to be nationally just, that is, impartial as far as his people were concerned. The pharaoh was the gods' true representative, and each man's virtue was a reflection of the justice of the pharaoh.

The word *nfr,* written with a sign which resembles a small musical instrument, meant originally that which is pleasing. But there is no reason to doubt that, in the time of the Old Kingdom, it had, as well, a moral connotation. For example, the nomarch Henku, of the Fifth Dynasty, causes those who pass by his tomb to be addressed thus: "O all ye people of the Cerastes-Mountain: O ye great lords of other nomes, who will pass by this tomb, I, Henku, tell good things (*nfr-w*)." Then, he goes on to relate the "good things." He says: "I give bread to all the hungry. . . . I clothed him who was naked. . . . I never oppressed one in possession of his property. . . . I spake and told that which was good, never was there one fearing because of one stronger than he. . . . I speak no lie, for I was one beloved of his father, praised of his mother, excellent in character to his brother, and amiable to his sister." The definition of "good," here, is sufficient for any moralist.

A clear distinction was made between "good" and "evil." The word for evil, *dwt,* is written with the sign for a mountain, the probable idea being that "evil" is associated with a more or less mysterious and fearful place, the home of evil gods. "Evil" is that which a bad god does, and is that which a bad man does. The many protests against having said "aught evil," and their associations with deeds such as those described in the preceding paragraph are eloquent of the content of the Egyptian word *dwt.* Moreover, there is another word which is translated "bad," namely, *wsf,* but which is usually used in a physical and ceremonial sense. The word *dwt* was sometimes used in a ceremonial way, but there is no doubt about its moral connotation.

The gods are the source not only of good and evil, but also of "that which is loved and that which is hated." The word *mry,* to love, is contrasted with *mśdy,* to hate, in the same connection as the word *htp,* peace, is contrasted with *hbn,* guilt. The content of the Egyptian word *mry,* because of its association with "good" and its contrast with "hate," may truly be said to be a moral one.

The Misanthrope and Ptah-Hotep of the Middle Kingdom never tired in their praise of justice and truth, the former declaring that "it is breath to the nose to do justice," and the latter that "the excellence of things is their truth." Their "ought" was summed up in doing "what men love and what the gods approve," which was "what appertains to a man" (*iry-t*). Truth, justice, righteousness, and goodness were sought in family, social, international, religious, and personal life. This continued throughout the rest of Egyptian history, emphasis being placed more and more upon the word *maāt,* ."to be straight."

Trusting to the accuracy of the above interpretation of these Egyptian words, we find that family love, in Egypt, being moral, and being, as we have seen above, the family ideal, was the moral ideal of Egyptian family life. The social ideal, in Egypt, is expressed by the words "good," "right," and "just." Generosity, kindness, goodness, even to animals, and truthfulness, were the admiration of the Egyptian. Kheti II, an early nomarch, said: "When the land was in need I maintained the city. . . . I allowed the citizen to carry away for himself grain; and his wife, the widow and her son. I remitted all imposts which I found counted by my father. . . . I was kind to the cow. . . ." Justice, both legal and commercial, was demanded and democratic ideas were beginning to develop. And the ideal was a moral one, as we have seen by our study of the connotation of "good," "right," and "just." The international ideal was peace, and, being the ideal of a peace-loving people, it was a moral ideal. The transcendental ideal was truth, justice, love, and obedience. The gods were the source and fountain of truth and justice, they were models of righteousness, and they were loved and obeyed. That they were feared, we may assume; that ceremony and pure magic played a great rôle in Egyptian life there is no question; and that love and obedience often were the result of fear, we have no reason to doubt; but that the gods were the champions of justice and objects of love and obedience, we have much reason to believe. The ideal was unquestionably moral. The personal ideal was to be pleasing to one's family and friends, and its moral quality is revealed by the association therewith of excellence of character.

The word for evil, discussed above, namely, *dwt,* must be distinguished from another word which is usually translated "evil," namely, *mr-t,* but which, in reality, means "sickness" or "evil" in the sense of physical suffering. The former word, like the word *bta,* which means "evil" in the sense of "crime," is used in a moral sense. In the inscriptions of Siut, it is said: "The wicked saw it, . . . he put not eternity before him, he looked not to the future, he saw evil [*bta*]." This "evil" the Egyptian opposed and hated. Again and again, in the *Pyramid Texts,* one protests against the imputation of "evil" to him, and recommends the avoidance of "evil."

Another word for "evil" or "bad" is *byn.* Its determination would rather indicate "meanness." The same is true of the word for "lie" namely, *grg,* as well as for the general word for "sin," namely, *ysf-t.* The fundamental idea being that sin in general, including badness and lying, is small, little, mean. The determinative is a small bird, a sparrow.

The Misanthrope said: "He who makes a compact with falsehood, his portion henceforth is that truth turns away from him, for then his good is falsehood, and truth does not concern itself for him"; and Ptah-Hotep says of evil that it "never hath brought its venture safe to port." During the Middle Kingdom emphasis was placed upon the foolishness of *falsehood* and injustice, and the unrighteousness of brutal might.[29] In later periods much emphasis was placed upon the intentions of the heart and upon the idea that sin was ultimately to be traced to the thoughts of the heart.[30]

The Egyptian considered moral evil, in general, to consist in the doing of wrong and in lying. In his family life these defects were barred as thoroughly as possible. In social life injustice was considered the greatest moral evil. But harsh and needlessly severe punishments were

[29] Gunn, *op. cit.,* § 6.
[30] *Book of the Dead,* ch. 79, l. 8, etc.

tolerated. In international relations war was undesirable although not reckoned evil. In transcendental affairs impiety was the moral evil, although anthropomorphism, magic, and human sacrifice were customary and legal, and, therefore, not considered morally evil. In personal relations impiety and cruelty were especially condemned.

The Egyptians had no theory of the origin of evil other than that evil as well as everything else came from the gods, who created evil as well as good.

In Egyptian literature there is no evidence that the Egyptians speculated about free will and predestination. It would seem that their anthropomorphism and emperor-worship were too real to allow room for predestination ideas. The gods were not far-off beings, who, at the beginning of things, determined destinies, but they were ever present, super-human, beings, who lived and moved in the present. Man's destinies were in the hands of the gods, but they were being shaped in the present. It would seem, therefore, that the Egyptians believed in the reality of a freedom of the will. Their many exhortations to avoid evil and do good show that they believed in the power of making decisions, in changing courses of action, and in entering upon new experiences. There was, therefore, probably no mental conflict about the question of the compatibility or incompatibility of free will and predestination. They believed that the gods created evil as well as good, but they continually boasted of having themselves avoided the one and encompassed the other.

By the time of the Middle Kingdom, however, the idea of predestination had developed. The word *šay*, meaning "destiny," became common, and this idea is found often, especially in the story of Sinuhe, where there are found such expressions as, "Is god ignorant of what is decreed with regard to him?"; "Oh, all ye gods who predestined that I shall flee," and "The god who predestined me to this flight drew me.''[31] These ideas continued into the latest periods of Egyptian thinking.

Moral sanctions may be external or internal. External moral sanctions are low, internal moral sanctions are high. In other words, external sanctions are not ''moral'' while internal ones are. An external sanction for an action is utilitarian only and has reference, primarily, to individual comfort and advantage. If a good deed is done because of public opinion, or in order to be the object of a corresponding good deed, or to avoid punishment, or to be revered by posterity, or to enjoy a good burial, or even to gain the assurance of prosperity in the next world, it is an external sanction and cannot be called ''morally'' good. The Egyptian had an unshakable faith in the future. The resurrection, and immortality of Osiris were looked upon as a kind of assurance of the resurrection and immortality of every individual. But his idea of the future was that of an existence in the sky (*Pyramid Texts*) where life would be somewhat as it was in this world. His desire was that it might go well with him in the presence of the great god, just as in this life. There he would live forever.

On the other hand, an internal sanction for an action is moral. An internal sanction is the joy and pleasure of doing what is right; the doing of what was pleasing to the gods and to men. If this be so, the ancient Egyptian figured on ''moral'' sanctions in action. He loved to assert that he was a ''doer of that which pleased all men''; he believed that he would be justified by his good deeds, and that his worthiness was deemed valuable in the sight of the gods; he was confident that the wicked would not stand the moral test which awaited those who passed into the next world; and that even the gods must ''be justified before Geb.'' In short, the Egyptian considered the tri-

[31] Gardiner, *Die Erzählung des Sinuhe*, Leipzig, 1909, ll. 126, 155, 230.

umph of the righteous cause of Horus over Seth as typical of the triumph of right over wrong in individual life,
and that the doing of good and justice was a joy forever.
In his own way, he believed that life depended upon character here as well as in the future, where righteousness
would be built. The ferryman to the great beyond would
receive only those of whom it could be said "there is no
evil which he has done."

To sum up, it will be well to review the main features
of Egyptian morals, and to make an estimate of them. In
making this estimate we must carefully distinguish between the nation and the individual. Our standard in
judging the nation must be the morals of our own time,
but the individual must be judged in the light of the customs and laws of ancient Egypt.

In our study of the customs and laws of the ancient
Egyptians as a nation we have noticed certain defects.
Their idea of God was a very anthropomorphic one. Their
gods were created and died; they married and suffered,
and they intrigued and were coerced, just like human beings. They accepted human sacrifices, and magic words
could control them; and they were local and national. The
punishment for blasphemy was excessive. In family life,
polygamy was permissible and concubinage was common;
in social life, punishments were very severe and slavery
and forced labor were legal; and in international affairs,
cruelty to captives was common.

On the other hand, we have learned how devoted the
early Egyptians were to their gods and how sure they
were of the love, righteousness, truth, and justice of the
gods. The fundamental principle in family life was
equality and love, in social relationship, justice and kindness were always admired and encouraged, and the
growth of a real spirit of democracy is noticeable; in

international affairs, the ideal was peaceful trade, and in personal life goodness was at a premium.

In the Middle Kingdom we find one very important forward step in the development of civilization—in the advance made in social thinking. In the Old Kingdom a freeman could regularly be forced to labor; in the Middle Kingdom that was not always so. Thus there was a growing consciousness of the right of the individual. This tendency manifested itself in other ways also. In the Middle Kingdom for the first time in Egyptian history the individual is found to claim "justification" in the next world. He as well as the pharaoh is to appear individually before Thoth and Rā and be allowed to give evidence of his virtues. Along with this goes the development of the idea of predestination, which appeared as a new idea in the Middle Kingdom. Each individual was the subject of the god's forethoughtful consideration, whose fate was given its place in the whole scheme of things. While this idea was chiefly due to the growing conception of the greatness of the gods' duties in comparison with the smallness of man, it was also in part due to the emphasis placed on the individual.

The Middle Kingdom was a feudal age. The grip in which the people of the Old Kingdom were held was loosening. The power of the pharaoh was being decentralized. Small barons had sprung up all over the land, and the middle and lower classes found more opportunity for individual self-assertion. In other words, individualism was coming into its own; and, as an evidence of this new self-consciousness, the Middle Kingdom has not only furnished us with many monuments of non-official Egyptians, but has left us a literature of individualism of such a quality and quantity as no other people, at as early an age, can boast. Nor was this conception ever lost in later years.

The moral ideals of the Egyptians were: love and equality in family affairs; truth, goodness, and justice in social relationship; peace in international affairs; reverence, love, and obedience in transcendental life; and goodness in personal relationship. These were ideals, which were, however, not always attained. Moral evil was considered to be the opposite of these ideals; and a man possessed the power of choosing good or bad without being predestined to either. Sanction for right conduct was really "moral," although external or utilitarian motives were not absent.

The individual Egyptian, judged in the light of his own time and controlled by heredity, environment, and social tradition, has impressed us as a person singularly devoted to his gods and to his family within the limited sphere of his ideals; generous and just to his fellow men, although recognizing slavery and forced labor as legal institutions; peace-loving, and capable of being appealed to by lofty and unselfish ideals.

Finally, we have learned the Egyptians to have been, as a people, devoted to goodness, truth, and justice, though laboring under the limitations of their time. Their civilization was remarkably high, though limited by imperfect customs, such as polygamy, slavery, forced labor, excessive cruelty, and unworthy ideas of divinity. But there is nothing to show that the Egyptian, as an individual, controlled by the customs and ideas of his time, was lacking in the conception of moral principles. On the contrary, considering the limitations of his time, he cannot be too highly praised.

Moral sanction in Egypt of the Middle Kingdom was mostly external. There are instances of extremely utilitarian sanctions, such as in the case of the man who said, "I did that which the great ones loved, and that which was praised by the humble people, in order that Horus may extend my life upon earth.'' But the moral sanction which appealed most forcibly to the Egyptian mind was the idea of reward in the future life. He looked forward to death as a deliverance, but also as a place where his virtues would be rewarded. There the sinful would be punished, but the righteous would be gloriously rewarded. A real moral satisfaction in the future was contemplated. There eternal happiness would be enjoyed. The many stelas of this period depict the ideal family life that will ensue in the future world. But that was not the only sanction connected with the idea of the future. The Egyptians believed that to leave behind a good name in this world was most desirable, and very practical steps were often taken, by way of mortuary contracts, to guarantee this desideratum. Nomarchs were especially concerned to leave to posterity a reputation as merciful and beneficent rulers. It was firmly believed that one's name lived on in human memory.

There was also a real internal moral sanction to right thinking and pure living. Fidelity and virtue were their own reward. Not only did each person look forward to the time when his soul would be ''justified'' by Thoth in the presence of Rā, but he took keen pleasure in the idea, and it reacted upon his conduct with a restraining effect, producing a very conscious desire to think worthily, speak truthfully, and act justly.

The materialistic side of life during the Empire had made considerable headway. Consequently, external moral sanctions were very potent. But, on the other hand, the evidence of a real internal moral sanction is not altogether lacking in the later periods of Egyptian life, for when we read that ''the heart of a man is his own god, and my heart was satisfied with my deeds,''[32] we are made aware of the fact that the Egyptian could

[32] Gardiner, ''In Praise of Death,'' *Proceedings of the Society of Biblical Archæology*, 35, 165-170.

find personal satisfaction in the act of doing good itself, and was very sensitive to the inherent sinfulness of sin and goodness of good.

A CONDENSED BIBLIOGRAPHY

1. J. Baillet, *Le Régime Pharaonique*, Paris, 1912.
2. *Book of the Dead.*
3. J. H. Breasted, *Ancient Records of Egypt*, Chicago, 1906.
4. J. H. Breasted, *Development of Life and Thought in Ancient Egypt*, New York, 1912.
5. A. Erman, *Life in Ancient Egypt*, London, 1894; *Aegypten und aegyptisches Leben im Altertum*, Tübingen, 1922-1923.
6. A. Erman, *Ein Denkmal memphitischer Theologie*, Berlin, 1911.
7. A. Erman, *Gespräch eines Lebensmüden mit seiner Seele*, Berlin, 1896.
8. A. Erman, *Hymnen an das Diadem der Pharaonen*, Berlin, 1911.
9. A. H. Gardiner, *The Admonitions of an Egyptian Sage*, Leipzig, 1909.
10. A. H. Gardiner, *Literary Texts of the New Kingdom*, Leipzig, 1911.
11. A. H. Gardiner, *Die Erzählung des Sinuhe*, Leipzig, 1909.
12. B. Gunn, *The Instructions of Ptah-Hotep*, London, 1912.
13. A. Mariette, *Les Mastabas de l'ancien empire*, Paris, 1881-1887.
14. S. A. B. Mercer, *Growth of Religious and Moral Ideas in Egypt*, Milwaukee, 1919.
15. P. E. Newberry, *The Life of Rakhmara*, Westminster, 1900.
16. A. Moret, *Galerie Égyptienne*, Paris, 1909.
17. W. M. F. Petrie, *Royal Tombs*, London, 1900-1901.
18. B. Poertner, *Die aegyptischen Totenstelen*, Paderborn, 1911.
19. K. Sethe, *Die Altaegyptischen Pyramidentexte*, Leipzig, 1908 ff.
20. F. Vogelsang und A. H. Gardiner, *Die Klagen des Bauren*, Leipzig, 1908.
21. R. Weill, *Les Decrets Royaux*, Paris, 1912.

THE ETHICS OF CONFUCIANISM

HARLAN PAGE BEACH

II.

In discussing this theme, one needs to acknowledge at the outset what Professor Henry S. Nash has said of Christian ethical teachings: "There is no system of ethics in the New Testament, not even a conscious suggestion of the need for system."[1] And yet the Classics of Confucianism are predominatingly ethical. Its founder is accurately described by a former professor of Chinese at Oxford, T. L. Bullock, M.A., in these words: "Of an eminently prosaic and practical turn of mind, he was never weary of describing the characteristics of virtue, or of drawing distinctions between right and wrong in actual life; but he cared little to speculate upon the moral faculty, or any such questions."[2] It is true that Mencius, the Plato of the early Confucian School, comes nearer to a systematic discussion of the subject; yet his writings are far from being like those of his contemporary, Aristotle, as we find the Greek philosopher setting forth virtue in his *Nicomachean Ethics*.

Since the Chinese Classics do not discuss the theme systematically, in the present treatment of the subject data will be used indiscriminately from the *Canon of History,* probably the oldest[3] of the *Nine Classics,* to the *Record of Rites,* the latest, dating from our second century in its present revision. This mingling of the ethical statements of writings so widely variant in the time of their composition is less objectionable than it would be in modern discussions of ethics, since a basal claim of Confucius is his statement in the *Analects,* Book VII: "A transmitter and not a maker, believing in and loving the an-

---

[1] *New Schaff-Herzog Encyclopædia of Religious Knowledge,* IV, 192.
[2] *Encyclopædia of Religion and Ethics,* V, 466.
[3] "The earliest chapters were not contemporaneous with the events which they describe, but the others begin to be so in the twenty-second century B.C." *Sacred Books of the East,* vol. III, *Sacred Books of China,* p. xv.

cients." Couvreur's translation is even more true of Confucius than Legge's, just quoted: "Je transmets (les enseignements des anciens), et n'invente rien de nouveau. Je m'attache à l'antiquité avec confiance et affection."[4] Nothing is more obvious than that Confucius desired his disciples to be governed by the examples and teachings of the sage rulers of primal antiquity of more than four millenniums ago, and of those paragons of his own Dynasty of Chou who founded it in 1122 B.C. As all the writers of the Classics seek conformity with these ancient teachings, and as they succeeded in producing a series of writings wonderfully homogeneous in their ethical standards, our position is justifiable, even though it disregards modern methods of historical exposition.

One other preliminary word should be added. Owing to the official ban placed upon heterodoxy in the Confucian civil service examinations, the *Nine Classics* and their official commentaries have been in recent centuries the only authoritative source for the study of ethics. And since the time of Chu Hsi,[5] who died in 1200 A.D., his commentaries have been regarded as the standard of orthodoxy. Hence we follow these sources, which are so important that Confucianism is sometimes called Chucianism. In so doing one loses the richness and modernity of other eminent Confucian scholars, like Wang An-shih, the social reformer of our eleventh century, and especially Wang Yang-ming (1472-1528 A.D.), the most highly esteemed exponent of Confucianism at the present day, both in Japan—called there Ō Yō-mei—and among the advanced younger scholars of China.

I. Man's Ethical Nature

So important is this item in the estimation of Confu-

---

[4] *Les Quatre Livres*, p. 136.

[5] Here and elsewhere in this chapter the romanization of Chinese words follows the system of Sir Thomas Wade as being the standard.

cianists that the orthodox belief stands at the very opening of Wang Ying-lin's *Three Character Classic,* quoted
in part from the Sage's own dictum, and since then
memorized by untold millions of schoolboys as their first
bit of Confucian lore:

Men at their birth are naturally good.
Their natures are much the same; their habits become widely
       different.[6]

Though Confucius states it as an axiomatic truth and
never fully discusses it, it is different with Mencius. Both
philosophers held as true the assertion of the Sage Emperor Shun (2255-2205 B.C.), who asserts that "the mind
of man—human heart—is restless, prone to err; its af-
finity for the right way—wisdom heart—is small.'"[7] Yet
the officially accepted commentary of Chu Hsi in explaining here the difference between the "human heart" and
the "wisdom heart," says that if the former is regulated
and controlled, it becomes the wisdom heart; whereas the
latter, if left uncared for, becomes the human heart. A
few other passages echo Shun's sentiment, but the great
majority hold to the axiom of Confucius.

In Mencius' work objectors appear, both from before
his day and among his contemporaries; and hence the
moral quality of human nature became a principal subject of discussion. Kao Tzŭ, a contemporary, maintained
that human nature is destitute of any moral tendency and
is wholly passive under the plastic hand of education.
"Nature," said he, "is a stick of timber, and goodness is
the vessel carved out of it." To which Mencius replied:
"The wooden bowl is not a natural product of the timber; but the tree requires to be destroyed in order to produce it. Is it necessary to destroy man's nature in order

---

[6] Giles, *San Tzŭ Ching,* pp. 2-3. *Cf. Analects,* Bk. XVII, ii.
[7] *Shu Ching* Pt. II, Bk. II, 15.

to make him good?'' Using another illustration, Kao rejoined: ''Then human nature may be compared with a stream of water. Open a sluice at the east, and it flows to the east; open one to the west, and it flows westward. Equally indifferent is human nature with regard to good and evil.'' ''Water,'' insisted Mencius, ''is indifferent as to the east or the west; but has it no choice between up and down? Now human nature inclines to good, as water does to run downward. The evil it does is the effect of interference, just as water may be forced to run up hill. Man inclines to virtue, as water does to run downward.''[8] Dr. Legge, in his Prolegomena to *Mencius,* pp. 56-57, says that Bishop Butler's views and those of this philosopher ''are, as nearly as possible, identical. There is a difference of nomenclature and a combination of parts, in which the advantage is with the Christian prelate. Felicity of illustration and charm of style belong to the Chinese philosopher.''

A few years later, Hsün Tzŭ strongly opposed the Mencian doctrine by his assertion that human nature is evil. Education was given an even more influential place in relation to this nature than Kao had granted it, holding that whatever good man does is a triumph over his nature. Virtue is the slow result of teaching, while vice is the spontaneous fruit of neglected nature. Yang Tzŭ, about the commencement of our era, tried to combine these opposite views, each of which was a partial truth only. Though human nature possessed benevolent affections and a conscience approving of good, it also had perverse desires and a will to choose evil. A man, therefore, was virtuous or vicious according to the qualities most cultivated. In the end these heterodox views yielded to the Mencian doctrine, and the works of Hsün and Yang

8 Dr. Martin's summary of the argument, as found in his *Lore of Cathay,* 216. For a translation, see Legge's *Mencius,* Bk. VI, Pt. I, i, ii.

were placed on the *Index Expurgatorious* of Confucianists.

The heart is a prominent factor in the ethical nature of man, as already hinted. A common chart of Confucian ethics, anonymous yet none the less authoritative, makes this central in one of its main divisions.[9] The late Dr. Ernst Faber describes it in minute detail in his *Mind of Mencius,* pp. 60-69. His main headings will suggest its place in psychology and ethics. They are as follows, psychologically considered: "Its office is thought; its contents, the will and the motives; ideas and righteousness; benevolence and righteousness; elementary motives of four kinds." The moral definition of the heart, which chiefly concerns us, is thus given, subjectively considered: "Development of the four germs; cultivation needed on account of the desires; diminution of the desires; there must be neither negligence nor incautious interference; of seeking to recover that which has been lost; sincerity in endeavor; error and need serve the best ends; activity is required, passivity is prejudicial; motion results in commotion." Considered objectively: "Sympathy in the heart leads to general beneficence in the Government; consistency in the heart tends to general consistency of conduct; of the influence exerted upon political life by a corrupt heart; hearts may be won; satisfaction of the heart concerning the dead." When this skeleton is clothed with the flesh of Mencian illustrations and its concrete relation to real life, the heart and its important place in ethics will be seen.

One of its functions is of especial interest through Western theories of the conscience. Three phrases used in the Classics and signifying what Occidentals denominate as conscience, are *shih fei chih hsin,* right and wrong

---

[9] For the original text and an excellent translation, see Martin, *Lore of Cathay,* pp. 207-210, 230-233.

heart, *tao hsin,* heart of the way or law, and *liang chih,* good or intuitive knowledge. Two other phrases in common non-classical use are *T'ien liang,* heaven's good, or heavenly intuition, and *liang hsin,* good or intuitive heart.

Three quotations will be explanatory here. The first is an utterance of the Emperor T'ang in his coronation address, delivered in 1766 B.C. "The great God has conferred even on the inferior people a moral sense, compliance with which would show their nature invariably right."[10] The ideograph rendered "a moral sense" by Legge, is translated by Gaubil as "la raison"; while Wieger, in his character studies, says that the original sense was the undergarment, and by extension the inside of man, the feelings of his heart.

Later, the Duke of Chou (died 1105 B.C.), the ideal of Confucius, in speaking of the blackly infamous Chou Hsin, last emperor of the Hsia Dynasty, then just at an end, says: "God sent down correction on Hsia, but the sovereign only increased his luxury and sloth and would not speak kindly to the people. He showed himself dissolute and dark, and would not yield for a single day to the leadings of God."[11] "Leadings" is the translation of an ideograph suggesting by its composition the idea of "following in the footsteps" of God. Chinese commentators understand by the phrase the unceasing monitions of conscience. One of them writes: "In the daily business of life and the most common actions, we feel, as it were, an influence exerted on the intelligence and emotions of our hearts. Even the most stupid are not without their gleams of light. This is the leading of God, and there is no place where it is not felt."[12]

The third person quoted is Mencius. Translating some-

10 *Shu Ching,* Pt. IV, Bk. III, ii.
11 *Ibid.,* Pt. V, Bk. XVIII, i.
12 *Chinese Recorder,* 1911, p. 582.

what literally, he says, "Conscience all men have." And again, "Conscience is wisdom's principal source." Elsewhere he asserts, "A man who has no conscience, is not a man." Genähr, in his discussion of the subject,[13] concludes that Mencius believed in an innate and essential faculty in man, by obedience to whose monitions he may become perfect.

II. Heaven and Ethics

Shang Ti, commonly translated God, and *T'ien*, Heaven, are practically synonymous terms, possessing many of the connotations which we apply to God. This superhuman power and wisdom is deeply concerned in human conduct. As already stated, conscience is God's gift. The sage emperors of primal antiquity sought the guidance of Heaven, and its indications later became the norm for official conduct. "Its will is the destiny of men and things; it forms their disposition and ethical tasks. But man stands, nevertheless, free in regard to it. Will and desire are in the power of man, and cannot be taken away from without."[14] "He who has fathomed his own heart knows his nature; if one knows his nature, he knows Heaven," is a Mencian statement (Bk. VI, Pt. II, xvi) which would seem to indicate that one had only to look within to know God's will for human conduct. It was the holy man, however, who was thus endued. Man's heart was the oracle by which his nature and duty stood revealed. "From this point of view, human nature passes as the image and, at the same time, the oracle of Heaven."[15] Holy men and sages were used by God to arouse and quicken ethical action among men. Thus the border-warden at I said of Confucius: "The kingdom has long been without the principles of truth and right;

[13] *Chinese Recorder*, 1911, pp. 577-584.
[14] Faber, *Systematical Digest of the Doctrines of Confucius*, p. 30.
[15] Faber, *Mind of Mencius*, p. 51.

Heaven is going to use your Master as a bell with its wooden tongue''[16] to summon people to hear truth and righteousness.

But how might the leaders of men be sure of right action in special cases?—how might even sage emperors know Heaven's will? From the earliest pages of the *Canon of History* we find rulers resorting to the use of the shell of the tortoise which was subjected to heat, the resultant cracks and spots thus indicating the divine will; or else milfoil was manipulated in a complicated sortilege. Chu Hsi, the foremost Confucian commentator, thus explains: ''The tortoise, after great length of years becomes intelligent; and the milfoil will yield, when a hundred years old, a hundred stalks from one root, and is also a spiritual and intelligent thing. The two divinations were in reality a questioning of spiritual beings, the plant and the tortoise being employed, because of their mysterious intelligence, to indicate their intimations.''[17] If both methods coincided in their indications, as well as the voice of the nobles, officers, and the common people, by this ''great concord'' the course of action became perfectly clear. Precisely how Heaven made its will known to Confucius, guiding him in the path of duty, we do not know beyond the indications of the usual methods just named. In the *Analects,* Bk. XVII, xix, he asserts that Heaven does not speak. It operates, and man must be attentive. According to the *Canon of Odes,* ''The doings of Heaven have neither sound nor smell''[18]—*i.e.,* its leadings are usually imperceptible. It should be added that in imperial inquiry into the wishes of Heaven, ancestral spirits—the manes of dead emperors of the line—were an important intermediary, supplying the desired nexus with those who

16 *Analects*, Bk. XII, xxiv.
17 *Shu Ching*, Pt. V, Bk. IV, 24.
18 *Ode* III, i; *Ode* I, 7.

were naturally interested in their descendants and former subjects.

Heaven, it is further taught, determines the *ming,* or destiny, of man—the divine plan affecting his life. To know Heaven's decree was one of the marks of the Superior Man, according to the *Analects,*[19] where we read the comment: "Here it means not only knowing, but believing and resting in the will of Heaven regarding right and wrong, of which man has the standard in his own moral nature. If this is not recognized, a man is the slave of passion, or the sport of feeling." In summarizing his own moral progress, Confucius said: "At fifty, I knew the decrees of Heaven,"[20] a statement which offends those Confucianists who hold that the Sage was "born with knowledge." While the Confucian conception of destiny is widely removed from the Mohammedan idea of *kismet,* still Faber gives no optimistic view of it in his remarks on the subject: "The heavenly destiny is given to each man; it forms the innermost quintessence of human nature; again, it stands on the outside of him and above him as the infinite Heaven, as the destining power opposed to men, the destined. . . . Man has to stand by himself; he can expect nothing extraordinary, no favor from above. . . . Man must look to himself,—how he can get on with what he has received, once for all, from Heaven, and what is at his disposal in the world."[21] Yet Faber is not more cold here than is Chu Hsi in his comment upon the *Analects,* Bk. II, iv: "By the decree of Heaven is meant the promulgation and bestowal of the laws of Heaven in nature, *viz.,* that whereby all creation obtains its order."[22]

Another commonly occurring word indicating the ethi-

19 Bk. XX, iii.
20 *Analects,* Bk. II, iii.
21 *Systematical Digest of the Doctrines of Confucius,* pp. 30-31.
22 Soothill, *Analects of Confucius,* p. 109.

cal course which Heaven would have men follow is *Tao*,— way, path, truth, etc. Quoting Chu Hsi once more: "Every reference to Tao always means the law of the right and proper, the ought-so-to-be in regard to man and things, that which is for all men to follow."[23] One would hardly agree with this official interpretation in its inclusive meaning; yet compared with its omnibus use in the writings of Confucius' elder contemporary, Lao Tzŭ, founder of Taoism, this is its relatively simple signification. A few typical statements concerning it will show its place in ethical action. "Truth is the Tao of Heaven; the attainment of truth is the Tao of man."[24] "The superiors have lost their Tao; the people consequently have been disorganized."[25] "The Tao which the superior man pursues reaches wide and far, and yet is secret. Common men and women, however ignorant, may intermeddle with the knowledge of it; yet in its utmost reaches, there is that which the sage does not know. Common men and women, however much below the ordinary standard of character, can carry it into practice; yet in its utmost reaches, there is that which even the sage is not able to carry into practice."[26] "If a man in the morning hear Tao, he may die in the evening without regret."[27]

III. *The Reputed Confucian Foundation of Ethics*

Some writers[28] upon our theme regard the *Great Learning* as the foundation upon which the Confucian ethical system is built. The so-called "text" of that work contains the very words of Confucius, the illustrious Chu

23 Commentary upon the *Analects*, Bk. I, xiv.
24 *Doctrine of the Mean*, XX, 18.
25 *Analects*, Bk. XIX, xix.
26 *Doctrine of the Mean*, XII, 1-2.
27 *Analects*, Bk. IV, viii.
28 *E.g.*, Faber in his *Systematical Digest of the Doctrines of Confucius*, p. 36, a wholly competent German scholar, and M. M. Dawson, an Occidental *littérateur*, not a Chinese scholar, in his *Ethics of Confucius*, p. ix.

Hsi declares—with many dissentient voices among later commentators. At any rate, Dr. Legge's translation of part of it, reminding us of an incomplete sorites of both the progressive- and regressive-comprehensive types, deserves full citation.

The ancients who wished to illustrate illustrious virtue throughout the kingdom, first ordered well their own States. Wishing to order well their States, they first regulated their families. Wishing to regulate their families, they first cultivated their persons. Wishing to cultivate their persons, they first rectified their hearts. Wishing to rectify their hearts, they first sought to be sincere in their thoughts. Wishing to be sincere in their thoughts, they first extended to the utmost their knowledge. Such extension of knowledge lay in the investigation of things.

Things being investigated, knowledge became complete. Their knowledge being complete, their thoughts were sincere. Their thoughts being sincere, their hearts were then rectified. Their hearts being rectified their persons were cultivated. Their persons being cultivated, their families were regulated. Their families being regulated, their States were rightly governed. Their States being rightly governed, the whole kingdom was made tranquil and happy.

Of this program, called the "Tao of the Superior Man," the first five items in the preceding paragraph refer to the individual; the last three have to do with the efficiency and well-being of the family, the state and the whole empire. The phrase, "Superior Man," occurs almost two hundred times in the first three of the *Four Books*. For all who are not holy by nature, the way here pointed out stood open. Often the words merely mean the ethical ideal of the system.[29]

From a modern point of view the four outstanding teachings of this reputed utterance of the Sage are these: (1) The noble conception of government as that of mak-

[29] For an exposition of these eight particulars, see Faber, *Systematical Digest of the Doctrines of Confucius*, pp. 36-66.

ing its subjects happy and good. Before Chu Hsi's authorization of a substituted character in the opening sentence of the *Great Learning,* it read: "What the *Great Learning* teaches is—to illustrate illustrious virtue, to love the people, and to rest in the highest excellence." The redacted text has another character, meaning to renovate the people. It is the general teaching of Confucius that rulers should love their subjects if they would effectively govern. (2) The insistence upon a personal character that is wholly ethical is the *sine qua non* of fitness to rule in family, state, and empire. (3) Going a step farther, the state of the heart and internal sincerity are the primary elements in personal character. (4) "The principle with which as with a measuring square to regulate one's conduct," as stated in the commentary section of ch. X, 2, is an amplification of the Confucian Golden Rule and hence is of unusual interest.

IV. *The All-Inclusive Rule and Key-Word*

Looking more particularly at this dictum, often called "The Silver Rule of Confucius," we shall find that, while stated negatively in every case, in one instance its context proves that the Sage had in mind the positive form of the rule. We quote this exception, found in the *Doctrine of the Mean,* XIII, 3-4: "When one cultivates to the utmost the principles of his nature and exercises them on the principles of reciprocity, he is not far from the path. What you do not like when done to yourself, do not do to others. In the way of the Superior Man there are four things to not one of which have I as yet attained. To serve my father as I would require my son to serve me, to this I have not attained. To serve my prince as I would require my minister to serve me, to this I have not attained. To serve my elder brother as I would require my younger brother to serve me, to this I have not attained. To set the example in behaving to a friend as I would require him to behave to me, to this I have not attained.'' Surely, one is not justified in asserting that Confucius held only to a negative sense of the rule when this statement is read.

But another item is even more central, namely, the single word of all-comprehensive significance which the Sage used in the passage just quoted, and also in the *Analects,* XV, xxiii, as the summary of all ethical conduct. In the latter paragraph we read: ''Tzŭ Kung asked, saying, 'Is there one word which may serve as a rule of practice for all one's life?' The Master said, 'Is not reciprocity such a word? What you do not want done to yourself, do not do to others.' '' This keyword *shu* is an ideograph made up of two others meaning ''as'' and ''heart.'' The implication is that as one's heart would wish for oneself, so ought one to do to others. It is positive, quite as much as negative; and hence the rule, of which *shu,* reciprocity, is an epitome, is also positive.

V. The Five Relations of Confucianism

Confucian ethics is a system of relations and their respective duties. The *Wu Lun,* Five Relations, and their ''ten obligations,'' constantly on men's lips, are thus given in the universally used Confucian primer previously quoted.

> Affection between father and child;
> Harmony between husband and wife;
> Friendliness on the part of elder brothers;
> Respectfulness on the part of younger brothers;
> Precedence between elders and youngers,
> As between friend and friend;
> Respect on the part of the sovereign,
> Loyalty on the part of the subject.[30]

In a briefer form and a different order they are given as

[30] Giles, *San Tzŭ Ching,* pp. 45-48.

the appropriate relations between sovereign and minister, husband and wife, father and son, elder and younger brother, friend and friend. It will be remembered that four of these—all except the relation of husband to wife —were instanced in the confession made by Confucius as to his own failures in reciprocity. His omission of that relation may be accounted for by the reticence of all Chinese with regard to their women folk, which would forbid any mention of his wife. Moreover, a common though dubious tradition is that the Sage's wife was a veritable Xanthippe, and that he divorced her.

A common criticism of these relations, both as they are discussed in Confucian literature and as they work out in Chinese life, is that by the emphasis laid upon superiors in age and in rank or honor, the lower member in each pair bears the heavier burden and is subservient to the higher member. Until the child is mature, the parent bears the greater burden, an exception to the statement just made; yet in later years children more than make up for the inequality of service in childhood. Thus our Occidental theory of *noblesse oblige* does not hold in Chinese ethics; though in the literal meaning of the phrase, as indicating the obligations of the higher classes to the lower, Confucius would have held to its binding quality. Substituting the word ruler for nobleman, he would have approved of Emerson's saying: "I think I see a place and duties for a nobleman in society; but it is not to drink wine, or ride in a fine coach, but to guide and adorn life for the multitude by forethought, by elegant studies, by perseverance, self-devotion and the remembrance of the humble old friend—by making his life secretly beautiful."[31] This quotation may have been one of the evidences for President Eliot's statement: "Plato, Confucius, Shakespeare and Milton were of his [Emerson's] teach-

31 *Emerson as Seer,* an address at Symphony Hall, Boston, 1903.

ers. . . . All those materials he transmuted and molded into lessons, which have his own individual quality, and bear his stamp.''[32] The Confucian relation which is most widely known in the Occident is that of father and son—filial piety—which later will be discussed separately.

VI. The "Five Constants"

Another phrase of Confucian ethics is not as well known as the "Five Relations." It is *Wu Ch'ang,* or the "Five Constant" virtues known to all. While Plato and Cicero taught that the cardinal virtues were four,—justice, prudence, fortitude, and temperance,—Confucianism holds them to be five,—benevolence, righteousness or justice, order or propriety, wisdom, and good faith or sincerity.

Of these, Chinese Confucianists have always held that the first is the fundamental one. So, also, do the Japanese, who discuss it more broadly as humanity. The eminent American Sinologue, the late Dr. Martin, thus writes of Confucianism's view of virtue:

Benevolence and good faith, which are quite subordinate in the heathen systems of the West, in that of China are promoted to the leadership of a grand division. In fact, the whole tone of Chinese morals, as exhibited in the names and order of their cardinal virtues, is consonant with the spirit of Christianity. Benevolence leads the way in prompting to positive efforts for the good of others; justice follows, to regulate its exercise; wisdom sheds her light over both; good faith imparts the stability necessary to success; order, or a sense of propriety, by bringing the whole conduct into harmony with the fitness of things, completes the radiant circle; and he whose character is adorned with all these qualities may be safely pronounced *totus teres atque rotundus.*[33]

[32] *Emerson as Seer.*
[33] Martin, *Lore of Cathay,* p. 221. The order found here is not that usually given, nor that which the author himself follows on p. 220.

In a summary of the Sage's work for his disciples, we read: "There were four things which the Master taught, —letters, ethics, devotion of soul and truthfulness." Chu Hsi thus comments upon this text: "He taught literature, amendment of life, and the maintenance of conscientiousness and veracity,—and the last two are the foundation of all." As the character translated "ethics" above is thus defined in another authoritative commentary, "daily action in human relations,"—*lun* of *Wu Lun* or "Five Relations" is here used,—one might hold that Confucian orthodoxy regarded veracity, or good faith, and conscientiousness as inclusive of all the great five.

Another comprehensive word is even more commonly used to include all forms of virtue, namely, *tê*, an ideograph composed of "short steps," "straight," and "heart." That is, virtue of the ethical man is gained by a continued process, not necessarily rapid, in which he steadily sets his heart upon straight ways, avoiding all crookedness. One of these component parts, translated "straight," is in turn composed of "ten," "eyes," and "deviation," which an ancient gloss thus interprets: "When ten eyes looked at something, any deviation, when existing, may certainly be discovered."[34] Here the added element of careful personal scrutiny of courses of action is suggested, as well as the corroboration of others. Chu Hsi, in his comment upon the text, "The Master said, 'He who exercises government by means of his virtue [*tê*], may be compared to the north polar star, which keeps its place and all the stars turn toward it,' " asserts that this character may be interpreted as "something acquired; that is, by the practice of truth to have obtained possession of it in the heart." Hence it is something more than mere outward morality of conduct; it is also an inward grace of soul.[35]

---

[34] Wieger, *Caractères chinois*, p. 44.
[35] Soothill, *Analects of Confucius*, pp. 109-110.

VII. Chinese Filial Piety

Turning now from these summary statements concerning ethical ideas occurring in groups, we shall consider separately two which are of especial importance. The first of these is filial piety. Its Chinese equivalent is *hsiao*, an ideograph composed of "old," or "aged," and "son." The *Shuo Wên*, an old dictionary of our first century, says that it represents a son bearing up an old man, that is, a child supporting his parent,—a prominent idea of Chinese filial piety today. As previously stated, it is one of the "five relations"—commonly placed third in the list. Its importance is seen from the place given a pseudo canonical work, the *Hsiao Ching—Filial Piety Canon*— often ascribed to Confucius himself. Its final paragraph illustrates its style and sums up the main teachings: "The service of love and reverence to parents when alive and those of grief and sorrow for them dead—these completely discharge the fundamental duty of living men. The righteous claims of life and death are all satisfied, and the filial son's service of his parents is completed."[36]

In a more popular way, this virtue is inculcated in a widely known children's picture book entitled, *Twenty-four Paragons of Filial Piety*,[37] whose authorship has been very doubtfully attributed to Chu Hsi. Eleven of the twenty-four stories relate to the duty of son to mother; four, of son to father; five, of son to both parents; two, of son to stepmother; and two, of daughter-in-law to mother-in-law. It is worthy of note that nearly one-half of the paragons are immortalized because of devotion to their mothers, a partial offset to the common presentation of woman's position in China. The mother ranks highest among females, the wife less high, and the daugh-

[36] *Sacred Books of the East*, vol. III, *Sacred Books of China*, p. 488.

[37] For an abridgement and description, see Mac Gillivray in the *Chinese Recorder*, 1900, pp. 392-402.

ter lowest of all. No daughter appears in the above booklet, and only two are daughters-in-law.

In the canonical writings, filial piety is strongly emphasized. Here are a few definitions.

Mêng I asked what filial piety was. The Master replied, "It is not being disobedient. . . . The parents, when alive, should be served according to propriety; when dead, they should be buried according to propriety; and they should be sacrificed to according to propriety. . . . Tzŭ-Yu asked what filial piety was. The Master said: "The filial piety of nowadays means the support of one's parents. But dogs and horses likewise are able to do something in the way of support; without reverence, what is there to distinguish one from the other?"

In amplifying the statement of Confucius concerning his favorites, "How far extending was the filial piety of King Wu and the Duke of Chou!" he gives as the climax of their piety:

They reverenced those whom they honored and loved those whom they regarded with affection. Thus they served the dead as they would have served them alive; they served the departed as they would have served them had they continued among them. By the ceremonies of the sacrifices to Heaven and Earth they served God; and by the ceremonies of the ancestral temple, they sacrificed to their ancestors.[38]

On the parent's part love is supposed to be present. Thus a disciple asked Mencius: "When his parents love him, a son rejoices and forgets them not. Was Shun, then, murmuring against his parents?" In the philosopher's reply we read: "Shun would say, 'I exert my strength to cultivate the fields, but I am thereby only discharging my office as a son. What can there be in me that my parents do not love me?'" In this most explicit classical refer-

[38] *Analects*, Bk. II, v, vii; *Doctrine of the Mean*, XIX, 1, 5.

ence to parental love, the ancient Sage Emperor in his younger days is thus described in the sectional heading, "Shun's great filial piety: how it carried him into the fields to weep and deplore his inability to secure the affection and sympathy of his parents."[39] The further context shows that the primal duty is for the son to seek his parent's love, and not for the parent to love the children.

In another passage we read: "Why is it that the superior man does not himself teach his son?" Mencius' view is thereupon set forth:

The circumstances of the case forbid its being done. The teacher must inculcate what is correct. When he inculcates what is correct and his lessons are not practiced, he follows them up with being angry. When he follows them up with being angry, then, contrary to what it should be, he is offended with his son. At the same time the pupil says, "My master inculcates in me what is correct, and he himself does not proceed in a correct path." The result of this is that father and son are offended with each other. When father and son come to be offended with each other, the case is evil. The ancients exchanged sons, and one taught the son of the other. Between father and son there should be no reproving admonitions to what is good. Such reproofs lead to alienation, and than alienation there is nothing more unauspicious.[40]

These statements are practically all that Mencius has to make concerning the parent's obligations to children.

Of the son's filial obligations all Chinese classical writers have much to say. In *Mencius*, Bk. IV, Pt. II, xxx, we find a summary statement concerning conduct notoriously unfilial. The reference is to an official whose mother had been slain by his father on account of a crime and who had then buried her in a very simple way. The official's prince ordered him to bury her with more ceremony, but he declined to obey without the consent of his father—a

[39] *Mencius,* Bk. V, Pt. I, i.
[40] *Ibid.,* Bk. IV, Pt. I, xviii, 2-4.

conflict between duties owed a father and a prince. In the discussion Mencius remarks:

There are five things which are said in the common practice of the age to be unfilial. The first is laziness in the use of one's four limbs, without attending to the nourishment of his parents. The second is gambling and chess playing and being fond of wine, without attending to the nourishment of his parents. The third is being fond of goods and money and selfishly attached to his wife and children, without attending to the nourishment of his parents. The fourth is following the desires of one's ears and eyes, so as to bring his parents to disgrace. The fifth is being fond of bravery, fighting and quarreling, so as to endanger his parents.

While the official was not guilty in any of these respects, Mencius adds:

Now between Chang and his father there arose disagreement, he, the son, reproving his father, to urge him to do what was good. To urge one another to what is good is the way of friends. But such urging between father and son is the greatest injury to the kindness which should prevail between them.

A feature of filiality very strongly insisted upon is thus expressed by Mencius. "There are three things that are unfilial, and to have no posterity is the greatest of them."[41] He is speaking from the point of view of the Superior Man, for whom this and the other two unfilial courses were reprehensible. The other two, according to the commentator Chao, are: "By a flattering assent to encourage parents in unrighteousness, and not to succor their poverty and old age by engaging in official service. To be without posterity is greater than those faults, because it is an offence against the whole line of ancestors and terminates the sacrifices to them." The proper person to offer these sacrifices is the eldest son, daughters

41 *Mencius*, Bk. IV, Pt. I, xxvi.

not being allowed to officiate here. This particular duty is responsible for divorces when the wife does not bear a son, for plural wives and concubinage, and for a view of marriage which greatly lowers that relation.

Filial devotion after a parent's death is quite as binding as in life, and it is more responsible than any other cause for the heavy financial obligations so commonly burdening poor families. An expensive funeral often plunges the survivors into debt; and with interest ranging from thirty to one hundred per cent per annum, according to the security offered, the extent of such a calamity is easily understood. Happily the ancient rule, according to which the period of mourning extended through three years, has been shortened and less expense is incurred.

An axiom prevailing in Chinese society, "A man may not live under the same heaven with the slayer of his father, nor in the same state with the slayer of his elder brother," is based on Confucian teaching as to filial piety, and in times past has led to much blood revenge. The statement of Mencius is as follows:

From this time forth I know the heavy consequences of killing a man's near relations. When a man kills another's father, that other will kill his father; when a man kills another's elder brother, that other will kill his elder brother.[42]

Only one other item needs mention here. Werner says of the relation of parents to children during the last historical period:

The relation of parents and children seems to have undergone considerable improvement since the earliest times; but the power of the father over his children, whether real or adopted, was still unlimited. He; or after his death, the mother, could chastise, sell, expose, or kill them; but the selling or killing of a grown-up

42 *Mencius,* Bk. VII, Pt. II, vii.

son was strongly reprobated by public opinion and practically an impossibility. Toward the end of this period chastisement causing the death of a child was a statutory offence.[43]

VIII. *Li in Confucian Ethics*

Inclusive of filial piety, and even more pervasive in Chinese ethics, is another term, *li,* which has already been mentioned as the third of the "Five Constants." One of the *Five Classics,* the *Li Chi,* or *Record of Rites,* is not only what Callery, seconded by Legge, calls "the most exact and complete monography which the Chinese nation has been able to give of itself to the rest of the human race,"[44] but it is also as dominating an element as "custom"—ἔθος—is in the ethics of the world at large. What is authorized in the *Li Chi* has constituted good form for the rulers and scholars of two and a half millenniums; and from them its multitudinous details of correct living have filtered down through the masses to the present time.

But what does *li* connotate? Callery, in the Introduction to his *Mémorial des Rites,* gives twenty-nine equivalents of the term in its varying significance, though his general translation of it would be "rite." Dr. Legge calls attention to the ideograph, composed of a character "employed to indicate spiritual beings and entering into characters denoting spirits, sacrifices and prayers," and of a second element, signifying "a vessel used in performing rites. . . . Next the character is used, in moral and philosophical disquisitions, to designate one of the primary constituents of human nature. . . . Thus the character *li,* in the concrete application of it, denotes the manifestations, and in its imperative use, the rules, of propriety. . . . A life ordered in harmony with it would realise the

43 Werner, *China of the Chinese,* p. 54.
44 Quoted in *Sacred Books of the East,* vol. XXVII, *The Li Ki,* p. 12.

highest Chinese ideal, and surely a very high ideal, of human character."[45] Perhaps the opening sentence of *The Li Chi* will best suggest what *li* aims at in producing the ethical man. "The Summary of the Rules of Propriety says: Always and in everything let there be reverence; with the deportment grave as when one is thinking (deeply), and with speech composed and definite." The character here translated "reverence," according to Wieger's statement, means "etymologically, to restrain one's mouth and to stand like a sheep. . . . Deferential behavior, reverence, reserve, modesty in the presence of authority (the hand holding the rod.)"[46] Dr. Williams, in his *Dictionary of the Chinese Language,* defines it thus— in part: "Reverent, sedate, attentive, respectful; that feeling of the heart which springs from self-respect and a due regard to all positions; to worship, to venerate, to stand in awe of; to watch one's self; self-poised." These varying conceptions of *li* are discussed in detail, with reasons for their importance in ethical training in the *Li Chi* and in two other rituals, non-canonical but hardly less important, the *I Li* and *Chou Li.* The casual Occidental reader and Oriental traveler will ridicule the formality and meticulousness of such a system; but he fails to realize that what he notes in a few Chinese survivors of the old régime and what the Classics so strongly emphasize is an attempt to reach idealism in conduct and that it is Confucian religion in action.

IX. *Ethical Paragons*

Quite as outstanding as filial piety and propriety in Confucian ethics is the rôle which theoretical and living paragons play in this system. Reference to the Superior Man has already been made, a phrase which constantly

45 *Sacred Books of the East,* vol. XXVII, *The Li Ki,* p. 10.
46 *Chinese Characters,* vol. I, 142.

recurs in the *Four Books*. Pages might be filled with his various attributes.[47] But there are gradations of idealism in moral realms. Seen in actual life, the Chün Tzŭ, or Superior Man—Princely Man, more literally—is thus differentiated from other good persons: "When Shun was living amid the deep retired mountains, dwelling with the trees and rocks, and wandering among the deer and swine, the difference between him and the rude inhabitants of those remote hills appeared very small. But when he heard a single good word, or saw a single good action, he was like a stream or a river bursting its banks, and flowing out in an irresistible flood."[48] And again:

The great Shun had a still greater delight in what was good. He regarded virtue as the common property of himself and others, giving up his own way to follow that of others and delighting to learn from others the practice of what was good. From the time when he plowed and sowed, exercised the potter's art and was a fisherman, to the time when he became emperor, he was continually learning from others. To take example from others to practice virtue is to help them in the same practice. Therefore, there is no attribute of the Superior Man greater than his helping men to practice virtue.[49]

The sort of man just described, with added elements of ethical and spiritual goodness, is the Sage, or *Shêng-Jên* —"Holy Man." "There is the unicorn among quadrupeds, the phœnix among birds, the T'ai mountain among mounds and anthills, and rivers and seas among rainpools. Though different in degree, they are the same in kind. So the sages among mankind are also the same in kind. But they stand out from their fellows and rise above the level; and from the birth of mankind till now, there

[47] For a brief summary of such an exhibit, see Faber's *Systematical Digest of the Doctrines of Confucius*, pp. 69-74, and pp. 135-141 of his *Mind of Mencius*.
[48] *Mencius*, Bk. VII, Pt. I, xvi.
[49] *Ibid.*, Bk. II, Pt. I, viii, 3-5.

never has been one so complete as Confucius.''[50] The oft-quoted sentence, "His knowledge is innate, and he pursues the right course without effort," describes sages in a general way. They apprehend clearly, and there is nothing they fail to comprehend. In the eulogium of Confucius as "the beau-ideal of the perfectly sincere man, the Sage, making a ternion with Heaven and Earth," found in the *Doctrine of the Mean*, XXX-XXXII, we read: "All embracing and vast, he is like Heaven. Deep and active as a fountain, he is like the abyss. He is seen, and all the people reverence him; he speaks, and the people all believe him; he acts, and the people all are pleased with him. Therefore his fame overspreads the Middle Kingdom and extends to all barbarous tribes. Wherever ships and carriages reach, wherever the strength of man penetrates, wherever the sun and moon shine, wherever frosts and dews fall—all who have blood and breath unfeignedly honor and love him. Hence it is said, 'He is the equal of Heaven.' " Posterity down to the present century has re-echoed the sentiment of this panegyric; but what is more to our present discussion, Confucius has been the model of all who seek to be good and become duty-doers. It is no empty phrase often applied to him, "The Throneless King"; for he has ruled the lives of millions who have believed him to be the truest ethical exemplar of their nation.

Yet Confucius and Mencius regarded the imitation of other sages than themselves as also important, if men were to be perfect in their life. The Sage himself was perpetually quoting the examples of the ancient sage emperors, Yao, and Shun, and Yü, and T'ang the Completer. His affections went out most to the sage founders of his own dynasty, Kings Wên and Wu and the matchless Duke of Chou. His ceasing to dream of Chou Kung was to Con-

[50] *Mencius*, Bk. II, Pt. I, ii, 28.

fucius a portent of his own approaching demise. In addition to the foregoing, Mencius describes four types of holy men, like Carlyle in his *Heroes and Hero Worship,* under characterizations. They are: the Holy Man as an official, with I Yin, minister under the Emperor T'ang in the eighteenth century B.C., as the type; Baron Po I, the Pure, who lived six centuries later, and whose unsullied conscience would not permit him to appear at the court of a bad man nor converse with an evil man, as it would be like "sitting amidst coals or filth in one's festal attire"; a probable contemporary of Confucius, Hui of Liuhsia, the sage who "accommodated" himself to all—a "mixer" who became the teacher of a hundred generations, making "the mean become generous and the niggardly become liberal"; and Confucius, the "Timeous one," as Legge translates, Faber, much better, "the man suited to his age."

While conduct can be perfected by following examples such as are theoretically presented in the Superior Man and whose historical foundations are the sages and especially The Sage, the final ideal of men is found in the fullness of Heaven, or God.

The highest ethical development fulfils the destiny of the creature, the idea of Heaven. Thus man walks in fullest intercourse with the highest Being and is able to coöperate in accomplishing in the world the yet unexecuted purposes of God. We perceive how closely this conception approaches to that of the God-man. The high significance of individuality is set forth in these extracts from Mencius in a way that deserves our attention. . . . Mencius only knew of a rigid morality, a purifying of the heart and nourishment of every germ of good, and the exercise of wisdom, humanity, righteousness and propriety:—in one word, the subjugation of the appetites and passions by means of the ideal of human nature, and the gradual perfection and final sovereignty of this latter.[51]

[51] Faber, *Mind of Mencius,* pp. 158-160.

Confucian ethics may be described very briefly as a system of imitation. All Confucianists ought to imitate Confucius and the sages in whose footsteps he walked. And beyond,—there is heaven, Shang Ti. St. Paul expresses a similar idea when he writes: ''Be ye imitators of me, even as I also am of Christ.'' ''Be ye therefore imitators of God.''[52] The practically contemporaneous philosophers of Greece, to whom we owe our first sketch of a complete moral philosophy, held to a modified form of the same view. Professor Muirhead of the University of Birmingham writes: ''To live the good life was not simply to be a citizen; it also expressed the true nature and purposes of the world in general, and thus united the human to the divine. To Plato the highest form of human life could only be the outcome of a vision of the eternal God; to Aristotle (herein out-Platoing Plato) it was itself that vision—a putting aside our mortality that we may ourselves live in the Eternal.''[53] Yet neither Confucius nor Mencius ever attained to the heights of Aristotle in this conception of ethics.

X. Confucian Ethics and the State

The Confucian ethical system as found in the *Nine Classics* was primarily intended for the state, rather than for the individual. Most of the traditional three thousand students and disciples whom Confucius taught through his conversations were either officials or young men hoping to enter official life. And for centuries before 1905 the Classics were the basis of the civil service examinations. The first of the *Wu Lun*, Five Relations, it will be remembered, had to do with duties owed to the higher official by the lower servant of the state. If duties between the common people were being discussed, most of the illustrations were drawn from official dicta or life.

52 I Corinthians 11: 1, Ephesians 5: 1, Revised Version.
53 *Encyclopœdia of Religion and Ethics*, V, 416.

But aside from the application of such ethical material to the common life of the masses, Confucianism has especially provided for the common people a summary of its teachings. The two most commonly and semiofficially used are the *Hsiao Ching,* or *Filial Piety Classic,* already referred to, and a later production, the *Shêng Yü Kuang Hsün Chih Chieh,* literally, *Holy (i.e.,* Imperial) *Command Broad Instruction Straight Explanation.* This book is commonly known as the *Sacred Edict* of K'ang Hsi, perhaps the most able emperor in all China's history. When it was issued in its original form in 1670 A.D., it consisted of sixteen maxims intended for the guidance of officials, each seven words in length, written in the highest literary style. It was hortatory and was hung up in prominent positions in the national law courts. His son and successor, the Emperor Yung Chêng, republished the *Edict* in an enlarged form, expounding his father's texts in a simple literary style. To make this imperial summary of ethics more practically useful to the common people, a high official, named Wang Yu-p'u, rendered this latter version into the colloquial, enlarging and illustrating the thoughts contained in it and interspersing it with proverbs and homely sayings. This rendering is "useful as giving a comprehensive view of Chinese life and character, and showing the value of merely moral teaching. In every chapter may be seen the importance attached by this people to respect to parents and seniors, and deference to rulers,—principles which probably have done much toward securing that long continuance as a nation, of which China is justly proud.'"⁵⁴ An outline of the ethical character of this famous compend of Chinese ethics may be seen in a free translation of K'ang Hsi's original maxims, as rendered by Mr. Baller.

⁵⁴ Baller, *The Sacred Edict,* p. iv.

1. Enforce duteousness and subordination, so as to emphasize social obligations.

2. Give due weight to kinship, with a view to the display of concord.

3. Pacify the local communities, in order to put an end to litigation.

4. Attach importance to farming and mulberry culture, that there may be sufficient food and clothing.

5. Set store by economy, as a means to the careful use of property.

6. Attach importance to academies, in order to improve the habits of scholars.

7. Extirpate heresy, and so exalt orthodoxy [*i.e.*, Confucianism].

8. Explain the law, to warn the foolish and the wayward.

9. Elucidate courteousness, with a view to improving the manners and customs.

10. Let the people attend to their proper callings, that they may have settled determination.

11. Instruct the rising generation, with a view to prevent evil doing.

12. Prevent false accusations, and so shield the law-abiding.

13. Prohibit giving shelter to deserters, in order to prevent others from sharing their fate.

14. Pay taxes, and so avoid being pressed for payment.

15. Unite the tithings [a ward system with headmen], in order to suppress crime.

16. Make up quarrels, and so respect the person and life.

So important was this summary deemed that it was required by law to be proclaimed throughout the empire by local officers on the first and fifteenth day of every month in a public hall set apart for the purpose, where the people were requested and encouraged to attend. Yet this political teaching of ethics soon became a dead letter except in the largest cities, or under an official who was personally devoted to Confucianism. The present writer has never known it to be so taught except by one official, who was spurred on by the example of Christian teachers and preachers.

XI. Confucian Ethics in Proverbs

If the teaching of ethics through imperial edict was largely a failure, the ever present and constantly used proverb has done much to popularize Confucian views of right. As all proverbs are deemed axiomatic statements of universal truths, they have great weight. Though Taoism and Buddhism have issued some of the most widely used collections of this sort, very many proverbs are taken from the Confucian Classics. Here are a few samples of such maxims.

From the *Four Books:* "All within the four seas are brethren." "Riches adorn a house, and virtue adorns a person." "It is not gain that is gain; it is upright conduct that is gain." "There is no calamity and happiness which is not of one's own seeking." "When Heaven sends calamities, it is possible to escape; when one occasions the calamity himself, it is no longer possible to live." "Those who follow that part of themselves which is great, are great men; those who follow that part which is little, are little men." "Without rules there can be no perfection."

From the *Five Classics:* "The family which stores up virtue, will have an exuberance of happiness; the family which stores up vice, will have an exuberance of calamity." "A flaw in a scepter of jade may be ground away; but for a flaw in speech nothing can be done." "The Superior Man guards his body, as if holding jade." "Heaven and Earth is the parent of all creatures; and of all creatures, man is the most highly endowed." "The way of Heaven is to bless the good and punish the bad." "Good and evil do not wrongly befall men, because

Heaven sends down misery or happiness according to conduct.'"[55]

Though scarcely proverbial, the closing sentence of the *I Ching—Classic of Changes*—may be quoted as summing up the general ethical teaching of the Confucian Classics. It is in the final appendix—ascribed to Confucius—of a work concerning which tradition says that the Sage had worn out through use three sets of leather thongs binding his edition together, and of which we read in the *Analects,* Bk. VII, xvi: "The Master said, 'If some years were added to my life, I would give fifty to the study of the *I,* and then I might come to be without great faults.' '"[56] Literally this "Finis" reads: "The Superior Man's way grows; the small man's way ends in sorrow." Dr. Legge poetically renders it: "Prospers the good man's way; to grief all small men go."

XII. *The Future of Confucian Ethics*

To attempt to prognosticate as to the future of Chinese ethics may be as futile as was the work of two famous and very expert Chinese diviners and prophets living at the time of the break up of the Sui Dynasty and the early struggles of the T'ang (618 A.D.). Their booklet, called *T'ui Pei T'u,* is sometimes designated as *Tui Pei T'u,* or *Chart of Opposing Backs,* because of its origin. The two prophets, Yüan T'ien-kang and Li Ch'un-fêng, sat down back to back to evolve their theory of history, described as "the evolution of revolution." Yüan with his pen drew pictures, while Li with his wrote sentences, neither seeing the work of the other. The two sets of prophecies as to the T'ang Dynasty thus resulting were made to coincide by a sort of juggling, until an old man from heaven de-

[55] See A. H. Smith, *Proverbs and Common Sayings from the Chinese,* pp. 41-47.

[56] Thus Legge translates; but see his note and also other different translations by Soothill, Zottoli, and Couvreur.

scended and rebuked them, when they broke up their pens and retired.[57] This might be the fate of any two students of Confucian ethics prophesying today; yet a few paragraphs may be written on the basis of what has recently happened and what is now in progress.

As in the case of the average Christian's failure to live up to the ethics of Jesus, so Confucianists may be said to have followed their Sage afar off, almost from the beginning. Hence during two millenniums the system has had relatively little power in the ethical life of China. From the year 1905, when one stroke of the vermilion pencil signed the doom of the imperial examination system, the *Nine Classics* have languished more and more. The new scholar there is so busied with learning the science of the West and usually the English language as a medium of education and of intercourse with Occidentals, that he has not had time to learn to read the classical texts even. This handicap of an analphabetical language and the jejuneness of much of that literature, especially of the *Doctrine of the Mean,* have inclined the newer scholars to turn to the ethical teachings of the Occident.

Those interested in the modern scheme of education have noted certain ethical trends in Japan. As the board of education there has been seriously disturbed by the decadence of ethical living to the extent that a number of conferences have been called that the Government might get the best views of Shintoists, Buddhists, and Christians, as to some ethical remedy for epidemics of suicide due to despair and other national forms of moral laxity, so Chinese educators are realizing the absolute necessity of an emphasis upon ethical studies. This has resulted in the issuance of small books of ethical extracts, largely classical, which pupils in the lower grades are supposed to learn and practice. As for the more advanced students,

[57] Smith, *Proverbs and Common Sayings from the Chinese,* p. 326.

writings of a group of modern Chinese educators, headed
by Professor Su Hu of the Peking Government University, are being read by college and university men.

Many readers who are not scholars are also heed-
ing the exhortations of certain high officials who have
sounded out the cry, "Confucianism in danger!" as did
the famous viceroy, Chang Chih-tung, in his epoch-
making volume, whose English translation bears the
title, *China's Only Hope*. Though that is now a "far
cry," other moderns, like the present Governor Yen of
Shan-hsi, in his very widely read *Jên Min Hsü Chih
(What the People Ought to Know)*,[58] are emphasizing
the absolute necessity of moral education and living.
Written for the people, the significant section is the one
entitled "The Three Fears." These are God, the law, and
public opinion, as over against the three things which
Confucius bade men to fear, the ordinances of Heaven,
great men, and the words of sages (*Analects*, Bk. XVI,
viii, 1). On the back cover of this brochure is an account
of the governor's "Heart Cleansing Society," the purpose of which is to exalt Confucianism. It emphasizes
public and popular lectures, usually held on Sunday and
often with avowed Christians as speakers. In the villages,
temples are often used as the meeting place. An idea of
the tractate may be seen in a brief quotation from his discussion of Shang Ti, God.

Consider the heavens and the earth, how mysterious they are;
every possible wonder is in them. Were there no vital principle
here, how could this great creation be? All you people worship
a tablet of the true ruler of heaven and earth. . . . The words
"true ruler," what do they mean? They mean God. The words
in the *Book of Poetry* which say, "God is with you; have no
doubts in your hearts," mean that God is above men, and that

[58] The first edition was of 2,700,000 copies. See *Chinese Recorder*, 1819,
pp. 743-748.

no thought or deed of any man can be hid from the eyes of God. The *Four Books* and the *Five Classics* speak frequently of God. This was the truth that Confucius taught men.[59]

The last sentence is characteristic of writings of modern Confucianists—the attempt to find Christian teachings in the Chinese Classics. Perhaps Dr. Chên Huan-chang is the best known of such writers to English readers. He signs himself a Chin Shih, or Ph.D., of 2455 A.K., *i.e.*, Anno Konfucii, our 1904 A.D. In his *Economic Principles of Confucius and His School* are many instances of this tendency, as well as of his desire to read into the Classics the latest modern scientific and sociological ideas.[60]

In a word, judging from interviews with prominent Confucianists during a visit to China in 1919, and from the writings of a number of others, the present writer would say that Confucian ethics are being modified in the direction of bringing them more into accord with Occidental ideals; in elevating them from the merely ethical realm into that of religion; and of adopting a wider conception of obligations, so that the family and Chinese state will be broadened to include the family of nations where "all within all seas will be brothers"—to alter by a word Tzŭ-hsia's quotation,—from Confucius probably, —thus constituting part of Tennyson's "parliament of man, the federation of the world." Before that consummation can be reached, Confucian ethics and all other ethical systems are likely to acknowledge what the real leader of Governor Yen's "Heart Cleansing Society" publicly declared, that he believed Christianity to be the true religion; and hence—our corollary, not his—all ethics will be infused with the spirit and the power of the Sage of Galilee, Son of Man and Son of God.

[59] *China Mission Year Book,* 1919, p. 91.
[60] See especially vol. I, ch. II, and vol. II, ch. XXXVI.

ETHICS OF THE BABYLONIAN AND ASSYRIAN RELIGION

GEORGE A. BARTON

III.

THREE nations of the ancient world developed high civilizations before they had emerged from the animistic stage of culture; they were the Babylonians, Egyptians, and the Chinese. While in each the civilization crystallized the nation's idea of deity and the supernatural in a very primitive state, and through its literature transmitted that form to subsequent generations, in each a comparatively high code of ethics was developed. This is not strange, since it is now a well-recognized fact in the history of religion that taboos, which in some form are universal, develop in men the sense of duty and a conscience. The herd instinct also helps this development. To so organize as to subdue the forces of nature to the service of man, as the nations mentioned did, presupposes a considerable ethical achievement.

Of the three, the Babylonians were probably the first to develop; at all events, they were in some important respects nearer than the others to the primitive type. Professor William James once said, "You cannot turn on the light quickly enough to see the dark," but in some respects in Babylonia you can almost see the dark. In other respects her ethical life was of an advanced character. True, we have not yet recovered from Babylonia any considerable body of ethical sayings, such as are found in the Precepts of Ptah-Hotep or in the *Analects* of Confucius, though ethical precepts in Babylonia are not wanting. Nevertheless, we have the evidence of Babylonian law and practice that her ethical development was in many respects of no mean order, and practice is better than precept.

Two races were mingled in Babylonia, the Sumerians and the Akkadians. The Akkadians were Semites from Arabia; the racial affinities of the Sumerians are not yet determined, though it seems certain that they entered the country from the eastern mountains. Pottery found in recent excavations at Abu Sharain, the site of ancient Eridu, makes it probable that before the entrance of the Sumerians, a civilized people kindred to those of ancient Elam and of ancient Anau, east of the Caspian Sea, had settled in the land. Probably, therefore, Babylonian civilization was originated neither by the Sumerians nor the Semites. It is, however, true that these two peoples constituted the principal inhabitants of the country during the historical period and molded its institutions and ethics.

Before attempting to outline their ethical conceptions, it will be convenient to ascertain what terms they employed for the expression of ethical ideas. The Sumerian word which is most often employed to express the idea of right is *di*, which means "wholeness," "health," and then "welfare," "peace." As a verb it was used in the sense of "helping one to his rights," and so came to express the idea of "judge" and "judgment." The ideogram employed to write the sign was derived from a hieroglyphic picture of the sun-disc. With the word *di* the word *si*, "be full," was often combined. Thus Sumerian *si-di* meant in Akkadian *ašâru*, "be straight," "go straight," "prosper," "thrive"; then *išâru*, "straight," "right," "just"; also *mêšâru*, "justice," "righteousness." These words show that in the minds of the Sumerians ethical conduct was associated with well-being, and in the minds of the Akkadians, with straightness, uprightness.

The Assyrians were, as is well known, a different people from the Babylonians. They were a composite race, but the main element in their composition appears to have been Akkadian. They developed after 2500 B.C., some fifteen hundred to two thousand years later than the Babylonians, and derived their civilization from the older country. The Assyrians worshiped for the most part Babylonian gods and looked to Babylonia as to a mother country. With these few facts in mind, we shall take a brief glance at the individual morality of the Babylonians and Assyrians, their social morality, business morality, public morality, and the relation of their religion to morality.

1. *Ethics of the individual.* In the eyes of Babylonian law the family, rather than the individual, was, from some points of view, the ethical unit. Thus the record of a lawsuit from the reign of Nabonidos, 555-538 B.C., in the last period of Babylonian national life, presupposes the solidarity of the family. A woman, Belilit, brought suit to secure payment for an obligation; the defendant produced documents which showed that he had paid the debt to her two sons, who had embezzled the money. As the family was regarded as an ethical unit, Belilit was fined a sum equal to that for which she had brought suit.[1]

While such a case shows that in some respects the family was the ethical unit, the laws and the religious literature show that, at least from before 2000 B.C. onward, the individual alone was often held responsible for his deeds. In the Code of Hammurabi the adulterer, the adultress, the false witness, the thief, the murderer, are held individually responsible. The Assyrian code, in so far as it has been recovered, indicates that the same was the case in that country. In spite of this fact, the laws also make it clear that individual responsibility had not altogether superseded the idea of the solidarity of the family. Such regulations as that of the Code of Hammurabi, §§ 229, 230, to the effect that, if a house-builder builds a house for a man and does not make its work strong and it falls and causes the death of the son of the

---

[1] See *Babylonian and Assyrian Literature*, Aldine ed., edited by R. F. Harper, New York, 1901, p. 276.

owner, the son of the builder shall be put to death, presupposes either the solidarity of the family or that the son was simply a possession of the father. The son suffered for that which was no fault of his own.

In spite of this failure to recognize fully individual responsibility, the ideal of personal righteousness was, at least in the later time, high. In an incantation text it is provided that, when a person appears before a god or goddess to call upon it, the following questions shall be put:

Has he pointed the finger at (any one); has he spoken that which is forbidden; has he spoken evil; has he spoken that which is unclean; has he caused unrighteousness to be spoken; has he nullified the decision of a judge; has he trodden down the fallen; has he oppressed the weak; has he separated son from father, father from son, daughter from mother, mother from daughter, daughter-in-law from mother-in-law, mother-in-law from daughter-in-law, brother from brother, friend from friend, neighbor from neighbor? Has he let no prisoner go free or loosed one who was bound; has he caused a prisoner to see the light? Has he despised father or mother, given to a younger sister and withheld from an elder? For yes said no, for no, yes; uttered what is unseemly, what is wicked? Used false weights, received dishonest gold, refused honest gold? Has he removed a faithful son; established an unfaithful? Has he established a false boundary-stone instead of establishing a true one? Has he removed a boundary, a border, or a boundary-stone? Has he entered the house of his neighbor, approached his neighbor's wife, shed his neighbor's blood, stolen his neighbor's garment? Through his fault has he destroyed a noble man, forced a brave man from his family, separated a united kin, unto an overseer delivered them? Was he in mouth upright, but in heart untrue? In his mouth this; in his heart that? In anything did he speak what was untrue?[2]

In this passage a high standard of personal morality

2 Translated from Zimmern's *Beschwörungstafeln Šurpu*, II.

is held up. It not only is a standard which enjoins obedience to the government, honesty between man and man, a clean social life, and honesty in business, but which urges mercy to the unfortunate and the possession of a true and loyal heart. Mere lip-honesty was despised and condemned.

While this was the high standard of personal conduct held before a worshiper, in the humdrum routine of everyday life, considerations of expediency often asserted themselves. If we may judge from Babylonian proverbs prudential motives were as powerful as the requirements of the gods, and often prevailed. Thus one proverb ran: "If thou goest and takest the field of an enemy, the enemy will come and take thy field."[3] Again: "A hostile act thou shalt not perform that fear of vengeance shall not consume thee." Another: "Be gentle to an enemy as to an old oven." Still another: "If I do more than is expected, who will repay me?" Then as now men sometimes felt that goodness did not pay, for another proverb says: "He is altogether good, but he is clothed with darkness." The perplexity caused by those counter currents of life which often thwart all one's best efforts also found expression in the following: "My knees go, my feet are unwearied, but a fool has cut into my course." Then as now men became weary in well-doing and lost the glow of ethical endeavor in the dull struggle for existence, as this proverb proves: "His ass I am; I am harnessed to a mule; a wagon I draw; to seek reeds and fodder I go forth."

Not all the proverbs reflect, however, this prudential and disillusioned point of view. Some of them are as cheerfully ethical and idealistic. Here are some of them:

Thou shalt not do evil, that life eternal thou mayest obtain.

[3] The proverbs quoted here are selected from those translated in the writer's *Archæology and the Bible*, 4th ed., pp. 467, 468.

The face of the toiling ox thou shalt not strike with the goad.
Upon a glad heart oil is poured out of which no one knows.
When thou seest the gain of the fear of the god, exalt the god
    and bless the king.
Thou shalt not slander, but speak kindly,
Thou shalt not speak evil, but show mercy,
Him who slanders and speaks evil—
With its recompense shall Shamash visit his head.

A number of the proverbs reveal a wistful perception
that high ideals do not rule everywhere. Such are the
following:

There is strife where servants are; slander where anointers
    anoint.
An ass, in another city (than his own), becomes its head.

In ethical ideals, then, the Babylonians compare favorably with other nations of antiquity, such as the Egyptians and Hebrews. These ideals the Assyrians shared.
The texts we have quoted, though based on Babylonian
originals, come to us from the library of the Assyrian
king Ashurbanipal, by whom they were cherished.

2. *Social morality.* Our knowledge of the social morality of the Babylonians and Assyrians is derived from
their institutions and laws. The laws of a people reveal
not only their institutions, but their faults—those lapses
from ethical rectitude which society found it necessary
to correct by punishment. At the center of the social
structure is the family, and the laws of Babylonia and
Assyria enable us to form a fairly clear idea of their
family life. As the Assyrians were less civilized than the
Babylonians, it will be necessary to treat the family ethics of the two peoples separately. In neither country were
the sexes on an equality, but in this regard they did not
differ materially from other countries of the ancient
world. In Assyria the wife was considered the possession
of her husband. If she committed a fault, her punishment

was wholly within his power; he could cut off her nose or ears, or even put her to death. While in Babylonia the husband had no such absolute power over the wife, she was by no means his equal. She must be thoroughly loyal to her marital obligations, while he might be lax; he could divorce his wife at will, while if she instituted divorce proceedings, she must prove that he had abused her and had not provided for her, on pain of being thrown into the river if she failed to prove her assertions.

Nevertheless, Babylonian women had many advantages. They went unveiled; they could engage in business, sometimes forming business partnerships with men not their husbands. This liberty was enjoyed by free women of all ranks. If they brought dowries to their husbands, such dowries remained their own property, to be inherited by their children, or, in case of divorce, to be returned to the wife or to her family. Marriage was usually monogamous. The Code of Hammurabi presupposes that the normal marriage will be monogamous, though it recognizes the right of a husband to have slave concubines. The purpose of marriage was to beget children; this Code accordingly provides that, if a wife, either because of physical infirmity or other reasons, does not present her husband with children, he may take another wife. In that case he might not divorce the sick wife; he was to support her in a separate house. Sometimes by private agreement marriages were made on conditions other than those laid down in the Code. Two documents have survived which certify to the marriage of two sisters to one man; they stipulate, however, that the elder sister shall be the chief wife, and that the other shall perform certain duties for her. Similarly marriage contracts sometimes modified the provisions of the Code as to divorce. In some cases the penalty for attempted divorce was made as severe for the man as for the woman; in other cases the penalty for the woman was made even more horrible than that in the Code.

In Assyria women were allowed less freedom than in Babylonia. There is no reason to think that they were permitted, after marriage, to engage in business. Men's wives, daughters, and slave-girls were compelled to go veiled on the street. An unmarried hierodoule and a prostitute were to go unveiled. Women captured from foreign countries were slaves; if they walked abroad with a mistress, they were to be veiled.[4]

Prostitution was practiced in both Babylonia and Assyria. The Assyrian code recognizes that such houses existed and enacted severe penalties for a man's wife, if she entered such an establishment. An old Sumerian law quoted in a lawyer's manual which has come to us in a fragmentary condition from the library of Ashurbanipal, recognized that, under certain conditions, a divorced woman might practice this profession on the street.[5] Such women sometimes adopted girls to bring them up to the profession.

Probably it was experience with women of that type that gave some ancient Babylonians as poor an opinion of women as that entertained by some of the makers of Old Testament proverbs. Thus we find embedded in a Babylonian ritual the statement: "Woman is a well, a well, a grave, a ditch; woman is a sharp iron dagger which cuts man's neck."[6] In a curse the wish is expressed that the gods would change a certain man into a woman. Notwithstanding all this, in Babylonia women held a position of greater freedom and respect than in many Oriental countries.

Marriages in both Babylonia and Assyria were usually

[4] G. A. Barton, *Archæology and the Bible*, 4th ed., p. 393.
[5] *American Journal of Semitic Languages*, XXXVII, 62-71.
[6] Reisner, *Sumerisch Babylonische Hymnen*, Nr. VI, 11, 12.

arranged by the parents and were controlled by family and economic considerations. A bride-price was often given and a dowry received. Second marriages of full-grown men and women were made often from personal choice, and love letters and various expressions of the tender passion have come down to us. Children were under the complete control of the parents and yet it was recognized that there were mutual bonds. Stringent demands were made upon filial obligation. If a child attempted to renounce his father an old Sumerian law provided that he should be branded, fettered, and sold into slavery. If he tried to renounce his mother, he was to be branded, cast out from the house, and belittled in the city. The regulations on this point were, however, not uniform, for another fragment of a Sumerian code provides that, if a child shall repudiate his parents, he shall leave the house and neighborhood, but his father must first give him his share of the estate. The same principle applied to adopted children. To children of sacred harlots which had been adopted by respectable families, they applied with great severity. Thus the Code of Hammurabi provides that, if the son of a temple servant or of a sacred harlot shall say to the father or mother that brought him up, "Thou art not my father" or "Thou art not my mother," they shall cut out his tongue. If such a person identified his father's house and returned to it, they were to pluck out his eye. A proverb—"The strong live by their own wages; the weak by the wages of their children"—certifies that filial obligations were often turned to economic advantage.

Fathers, on the other hand, were not without obligations to their children. A son had a right to inherit his proportion of a father's property; from this right the father could not cut him off without consent of the court. Such consent was not granted unless the son had committed some grave crime against the father, and then the Code of Hammurabi provided that the first offense must be pardoned by the father. This applied to children of legitimate wives only; children of slave-girls could not inherit unless the father had recognized the child as his. If he recognized it as his the child had the same rights as children of a legitimate wife.

A considerable fraction of the population of Babylonia and Assyria during all periods of the history were slaves. How large this fraction was we have no means of knowing. The slave class was perpetuated by birth, capture, purchase, and disinheritance. Slaves were freely bought and sold, and many documents recording such transactions have come down to us. An unskilled slave could be purchased for about the price of an ox or an ass, though in Assyria, during the last period of her history, a skilled worker brought five or six times as much. In spite of the fact that in the eyes of the law a slave was a chattel, Mesopotamian slaves had many privileges and their condition was far less unfortunate than that of slaves in many countries. They could own property, engage in business, and make the money with which to purchase their own freedom. A slave could marry a free woman, who did not thereby lose her freedom, and her children were also free. In Assyria a slave could own slaves. These could not be separated from him. It does not appear that he could sell them, but, if he were sold, his slaves went with him. The one law concerning slavery that has survived from the old Sumerian codes is a law for the protection of the slave. It provides that, if a man attack a slave and injure him, he shall give the slave a certain allowance daily until the slave recovers.

Something of the ethical feeling of a people is revealed by the punishments that they inflict. Many of the penalties prescribed by the Babylonian and Assyrian laws were monetary, but a number of them were applications of the law of blood revenge. If a man killed a man, he was to be killed; if he killed a man's son, his son was to be killed; if he knocked out a man's tooth, his tooth was to be knocked out. Mutilation in various forms was also practiced as punishment. It has already been pointed out that the laws of Hammurabi prescribed the cutting out of the tongue and the putting out of an eye as a penalty in case children of certain parentage, who had been adopted, tried to renounce their adopted parents. A physician who operated on a patient with a lancet, after which the patient died or lost an eye, was to have his hand cut off. In Assyria, where both men and women engaged in fights, they suffered, as a penalty for inflicting certain injuries, the cutting off of a finger. In that country a husband could cut off his wife's nose for unfaithfulness or could kill her. If he killed her, her paramour was to be killed; if he cut off her nose, the paramour was to be made a eunuch and have his whole face mutilated. Such punishments are, however, not more barbarous than many that were enjoined by English law as late as the Tudor period.

3. *Business morality*, as revealed in the laws of Babylonia and Assyria, was in principle well developed. In both countries individual property in land was recognized. The transfer of a lot of land from one owner to another in the city of Assyria was a grave matter attended by serious formalities. A month's notice had to be given; advertisement of intention must be proclaimed three times through a public crier, and the transfer must in the end be made in the presence of the city scribe, recorder, and magnates—all of which indicates a highly developed sense of property rights. In Babylonia, where the fields were separated by irrigating ditches and all abutted against a large irrigating canal, severe penalties were in-

flicted upon a man who left the gate of his dyke open and ruined his neighbor's crop by flooding. Land was often rented and the laws well protected the interests of land-lord and tenant. The temples and nobles owned large tracts of land and many flocks and herds. The last-mentioned were placed in the care of shepherds and sent out to pasture for the season. When the season was over the shepherds had to give an account of all the animals, but the law exempted them from responsibility for ani-mals killed by lightning or by wild beasts, such as lions. On the canals and rivers of Babylonia and Assyria many boats plied, carrying merchandise; collisions sometimes occurred in which boats were sunk and valuable property was lost. Laws fixed responsibility for such accidents ac-cording to the negligence of boats' commanders. Baby-lonian merchants extended their business far beyond the limits of Babylonia by employing traveling salesmen, whom they called "agents." These agents often were compelled to carry considerable amounts of goods or money with them, and, in the unstable international equi-librium of the ancient world, were often waylaid and robbed. The laws took cognizance of all these dangers, de-fining the mutual responsibilities of merchants and agents according to principles which are highly just. In-deed, the underlying considerations which guided Baby-lonian legislation on all these matters more than 4000 years ago are eminently just, and were really identical with those which control modern legislation and legal de-cisions on these subjects.

In all countries and in all ages the temptation to prof-iteer is great—too great for many to resist; we are not surprised, therefore, that it existed in ancient Babylonia. It was met and checked in part, as it is met and checked in modern times, by legislation. Modern nations regulate by law railway fares and the charges of certain public utilities corporations. They often make a legal rate of interest. The Babylonians and ancient Hittites went much farther. In their legislation they regulated wages, the hire of oxen, asses, etc., the rental of land, boats, and like matters, the regulation of which we usually leave to the action of competition. Rates of interest, which we try to some extent to regulate by law, they left untouched, with the result that the money-lender exacted all he could get, charging sometimes as high as twenty per cent for the use of his money.

4. *Public morality.* The degree of sensitiveness of the public conscience of a people may be ascertained by the ideals of public service which they profess, by the efforts which they make to realize those ideals, by the care manifested for public servants, and by their attitude toward other peoples.

Ideals of public service among the Babylonians and Assyrians may be ascertained from the standards held before their monarchs. A hymn addressed to Dungi, a king of Ur, who ruled from about 2459-2392 B.C., and who was deified during his lifetime, speaks of him as "the king who brings justice, who favors the working-man."[7] Running through the hymn is the idea that justice and the prosperity of the land are closely connected. Similarly Hammurabi, two hundred years later, claims, in the preface to his laws,[8] to have subdued the bandits, to have helped his people in their need, to have established the security of their property, to have made justice prevail, and to have ruled the race with right. While these ideals prevailed in Babylonia, in Assyria kings boast of their conquests, of their piety toward the gods, and of the luxurious crops which grew during their time.[9] The As-

---

[7] See G. A. Barton, *Miscellaneous Babylonian Inscriptions*, No. 3.

[8] See R. F. Harper's *Code of Hammurabi.*

[9] See, for example, Ashurbanipal, in Schrader's *Keilinschriftliche Biblrothels,* II, 153 ff.

syrian sense of public duty, at least as represented by royalty, was less well developed than that of Babylonia.

One Babylonian king, Urkagina of Lagash, who ruled between 2900 and 2800 B.C., has left a record of his attempt to realize these ideals. His predecessors had made Lagash a military power and the resulting wealth had created a moneyed class which oppressed the poor. A kind of labor-restriction had grown up by which a man was restricted to one occupation only. A muleteer must live from his mule or donkey; a boatman, from his boat; a dyke-tender, from his little vegetable garden. To all such Urkagina, in the name of justice, gave greater freedom of occupation. Priests charged exorbitant prices for burials, marriages, and omens. This resulted not only in the oppression of the poor, but in the avoidance of marriage. Men and women lived together without marriage, to the detriment of public morals. The king reduced the prices for all these things to sums that were reasonable. Urkagina's predecessors had encroached on the property of the temples, employing both sacred domains and cattle belonging to temples for their own service and advantage. This he corrected, restoring the use of all such property to its rightful owners. Free men had been compelled to work on the royal estates like serfs; to these he restored their liberty.[10] Urkagina did not merely express in words high ideals of the ethics of public service; he endeavored to live them. Then as now, however, the moral reformer was not universally appreciated. His reforms so estranged the wealthy and military class that when, a little later, an enemy attacked his kingdom, he was left powerless to resist, and his kingdom was overthrown.

The Babylonian recognition of what was due to public servants whose duties made it impossible to care properly for their own interests or involved them in unusual

10 See L. W. King's *History of Sumer and Akkad*, pp. 177 ff.

danger, is revealed in that portion of the Code of Hammurabi[11] which deals with the interests of soldiers, levy masters, and tax gatherers. Their duties took them from home; those of the soldiers exposed them to danger and captivity. The laws allowed them privileges as to rights of property which seem a just compensation for the dangers incurred and the nature of the services performed.

In international affairs the ancient world was ethically not quite abreast of the modern world, but perhaps not very far behind it. The difference was in good part a difference of profession more than a difference of practice. Nations now profess to act upon high ethical principles, while in practice they are frankly controlled, as a rule, by self-interest. In the ancient world they made no great professions. Foreigners had no recognized rights. It was regarded as the business of a king to subdue and plunder other peoples; and most monarchs lived up to this ideal. On the whole, the kings of Babylonia would seem not to have been especially warlike. Their country was rich; their people were given to business; they were often content to protect themselves and live in peace. This their neighbors seldom permitted them to do. The rich crops of the alluvium attracted the dwellers in neighboring and less fertile lands and brought them often into Babylonia for plunder. This compelled reprisals, and some Babylonian kings, carrying the war into the enemies' countries, built up great empires.

In Assyria, on the other hand, plunder was the regular business of the monarchy. During the reigns of the prosperous Assyrian kings the army marched forth as regularly as the season came around, to prey on the weaker peoples; to rob, slay, torture, and plunder. People were impaled alive on stakes and left to die; sometimes they were skinned alive. In the barbarous and unethical busi-

[11] §§ 26-41.

ness called war, similar deeds, perhaps, have always been
perpetrated and still occur. The ethical point of view of
the Assyrians is, however, revealed by the fact that they
had pictures of these horrible deeds carved in stone and
decorated with them the walls of their palaces, so that,
as they reclined at ease, or enjoyed themselves with their
families, they could enter upon the vivid contemplation
of the horrible brutality. While modern armies are cruel,
we now hide the brutality. We have progressed in ideals,
if not in practice.

5. *The relation of morality to religion.* The influence of
the religion of Babylonia and Assyria upon morals was
both bad and good. Certain conceptions of the gods and
their relation to the world, which had been formed in prehistoric time, were never thrown off, and these, when out-
stripped by ethical development, made it difficult for ethical ideals to be universally accepted and put in practice.
On the other hand, at least one of the gods was believed
to be ethical and to demand of his worshipers all that was
upright and just, and in his worship ethical life found
both a source and a motive.

The elements in the religion which tended to retard
ethical development were two in number. The gods were
believed to be thoroughly self-centered. They had created
mankind solely that they might have servants to house
and feed themselves—to build them temples and to offer
them sacrifices. So long as this was done, it was not
thought that the gods generally cared how men acted
toward one another. To keep up the ritual was the one
necessary duty, if one would retain the favor and protection of the gods. Accordingly a Babylonian Job, who had
been overtaken by misfortune, though he was conscious
of no reason for it, does not speak of his honesty, integrity, or charity, but of his fidelity to the ritual:

But I myself thought of prayers and supplications;
Prayer was my wisdom, sacrifice, my dignity;
The day of honoring the gods was the joy of my heart,
The day of following the goddess was the acquisition of my
    wealth;
The prayer of the king—that was my delight,
And his music,—for my pleasure was its sound.
I gave direction to my land to revere the names of the god,
To honor the name of the goddess I taught my people.
Reverence for the king I greatly exalted,
And respect for the palace I taught the people;
For I knew that with the god these things are in favor.
What is innocent of itself, to the god is evil![12]

The gods were self-centered; their ways were not man's
ways. Nevertheless, they were believed to be soft-hearted
and capable of pity. The authors of the Babylonian Peni-
tential Psalms, when they appealed to the gods, did not,
therefore, like the author of the fifty-first Psalm of the
Hebrew Psalter, confess their sins and ask cleansing and
pardon; instead they begged the gods to see how unhappy
they were—how stained with tears their faces were—and
to have pity upon them. In other words, they did not appeal to the gods as to beings primarily interested in ethics, but to them as individuals that could be moved to
pity by misfortune and the signs of grief, whatever the
moral condition of the suppliant might be. Of this the
following, taken from an appeal to the goddess Ishtar, is
an example:

On account of his face which for tears is not lifted up, he raises
    to thee a wail;
On account of his feet on which fetters are laid, he raises to thee
    a wail;
On account of his hand which is powerless through oppression,
    he raises to thee a wail;

[12] See G. A. Barton, *Archaeology and the Bible,* 4th ed., p. 452.

On account of his breast, which wheezes like a bellows, he raises
    to thee a wail;
O lady, in sadness of heart I raise to thee my piteous cry, "how
    long?"
O lady, to thy servant—speak pardon to him, let thy heart be
    appeased!
To thy servant who suffers pain—favor grant him!
Turn thy gaze upon him, receive his entreaty!
To thy servant with whom thou art angry—be favorable unto
    him![13]

In such manner the gods were appealed to, not as strictly
moral beings, but as beings made in the likeness of men;
like men they held inexplicable grudges, but like men they
had hearts of pity.

Another element in the conception of deity even more
deleterious to morals was the very primitive conception
that the fertility of the earth was caused by the sexual
connection of a weather god of some sort with an earth
goddess—both the god and the goddess existed under
various names. The fertilizing waters were the semen of
the god, which was received by mother earth and caused
her to bring forth. More than one myth describes this
union in very anthropomorphic form and in terms of the
frankest kind. Gudea, a ruler of Lagash, who flourished
about 2500 B.C., and who rebuilt the temple of his god
Ningirsu, tells[14] how, when he had conducted the god and
his spouse, the goddess Bau, to the inner sanctuary, which
was fitted up with a luxurious couch for their convenience, they enjoyed such a marital union, as a result of
which, he says: "The holy bowl of the terrace of the great
dwelling was submerged, the great water-courses that
were low became like water that bowls will not hold; it
stood on their plantations; from the Tigris and Euphra-

13 See G. A. Barton, op. cit., p. 459.
14 Cylinder B, col. xvii, ll. 1-12.

tes it joyfully overflowed; whatever was needful for the city and temple it caused to grow satisfactorily.''

The effect of such beliefs upon morals came about from a belief in sympathetic magic. If fertility for the land came because of such union of the gods, such union on their part could be induced by similar unions on the part of their worshipers. Accordingly in each temple the god had a wife and a harem of concubines. The god was represented by priests. These not only practiced such unions among themselves, but with worshipers. The concubines of the gods, called by various names and consisting of different grades or classes, merged off into the common prostitute of the street. The rights of all these were recognized by law. Once in her lifetime and before marriage each woman was expected to act in this way as a temporary hierodoulos of the goddess, in order to secure abundant offspring for herself. These customs, originating in thoughts that, for a prehistoric people are comparatively innocent, when protected by religious conservatism and perpetuated far into a higher civilization, were a decided obstacle to the highest ethical development. In Babylonia, no prophets secured their abolition, as they did in Israel; they accordingly existed until Babylonian civilization perished about the beginning of the Christian era.

In spite of all this, other forces in the religion reinforced moral standards. Whatever the moral character of the gods might be, it was thought they detested lying and would punish it. The laws, therefore, provide that if, in a court, a man swears in the presence of a god, his word shall in certain cases be taken, even though it is not confirmed by other witnesses. It was not taken in all cases; in some an ordeal was demanded; but that it would be taken at all proves that religion in some degree reinforced morals.

Another powerful incentive to uprightness in life was

found in the worship of the sun-god, Utu or Shamash. As the god who sheds light upon all—light which reveals wickedness and causes the wrongdoer to slink away— Shamash was regarded as the source of right, justice, and law. It has already been pointed out how one picture of the sun became the ideogram for health, peace, and justice; another became the symbol of the god himself and of all the qualities that the god possessed as well as of many of the things he could do. The great king, Hammurabi, pictured himself as receiving from Shamash his code of laws; a hymn from the library of Ashurbanipal reveals in detail the conceptions of Shamash which powerfully reinforced ethics:

At thy rising the gods assemble;[15]
Thy terrible radiance overwhelms the land.
From all lands together resound as many tongues;
Thou knowest their designs; thou beholdest their footsteps.
Upon thee look all men together.
Thou causest the evil-doer . . . to tremble;
Out of hiding(?) thou bringest those who perverted justice.

. . . .

O Shamash, from thy net . . .
From thy snare escapes not . . .
He who contrary to his oath . . .
To him who does not fear . . .
Outspread is the wide net. . . .

. . . . . .

Whoso devisest wickedness, his horn thou destroyest.

. . . .

Thou hearest the down-trodden, as thou movest over them; thou
    discoverest their right;
Each one, every one is entrusted into thy hand;
Thou rulest their judgments; what is bound thou dost loose.

[15] Translated by Jeremias in *Hastings' Encyclopædia of Religion and Ethics*, V, 445.

The hymn contains much more of the same tenor, and makes clear to us how, in the cult of the sun-god, religion in Babylonia and Assyria came to the reinforcement of ethics.

THE HISTORY OF HINDU ETHICS

E. WASHBURN HOPKINS

IV.

ALTHOUGH Hindu as a synonym of Indian is not quite accurate, since the word properly applies only to the later periods of Indian thought, yet in view of the double meaning of Indian it is, as a matter of clarity and convenience, useful to include under the word Hindu even the earliest phenomena of India, as we use English and Greek to include all the literary products of Great Britain and Hellas.

The history of Hindu ethics before foreign influence began to be felt is from two or three thousand years in duration and is of inestimable value for the reason, apart from its intrinsic worth, that it presents an uninterrupted development of moral teaching extending for a much longer period than can be seen in any other system of ethical education untouched by alien thought. From 1500 B.C. to 1500 A.D. India's ethical growth was all her own; foreigners did not influence it to any appreciable extent till Mohammedan conquests brought with them their moral teachings and began to stress the code imported from the West. The earliest Hindu literature, which reverts at least to 1000 B.C. and may be older, is already full of ethical wisdom, and since it implies a limited criminal code which in many points is comparable to those of sister races, notably those of Persia and Germany, and this criminal code in turn is an expression of moral values, it will be no exaggeration to suppose that the Hindu ethical rules found in the earliest literature belong to the middle of the second millennium before Christ. At the other extreme, the conquest of the Ghazni invader in 1002 A.D. sets the lowest limit for Mohammedan influence, which did not really amount to much from an ethical point of view till Kabîr, about 1500 A.D., united that influence with the old stream of pure Hindu thought.

The Rig Veda, the oldest literary document of India, includes under its general polytheistic system an impulse toward monotheism and another tentative trend toward pantheism, both of which reappeared later in systematic form. But in the Rig Veda itself there is perceptible only the first beginning of an intellectual effort to bring the gods under one head, either as separate forms of one being or as morally united under one ethical leader. It is a mistake, however, to think that the one supreme guide and watcher of men is the only spiritual moral power recognized by the Rig Veda. On the contrary, many of the gods in the earliest Hindu pantheon are concerned with ethics. They punish the wrongdoer, they keep watch of his actions, they distinguish carefully between the "straight and crooked" (right and wrong), adjectives applied to both men and their actions. Even the departed Fathers, the Manes, are invoked as ethical powers. The Sun as a god watches man, and Indra, the battle-god, "slays those that sin even before they know" (that he is there to punish them). And there are other spiritual powers who also keep their "unwinking eyes" on what is done on earth. The fact that all these powers, and they include such material phenomena as water and fire (deified and moral guardians of men), are prayed to for forgiveness of sins shows that in general the whole pantheon consists of gods who are not only good to man but ethically good. There is a vague tradition that the battle-god was not always virtuous, but in the Rig Veda he is represented as having reformed; he no longer battles against the good gods, but stands on their side and with them supports the cause of virtue. In the older pre-Indic period he was probably a demon, as in the Zoroastrian system, but though his sins still hang over him in a dark background, he has become in the Rig Veda a staunch upholder of law and order.

All these gods, however, recognize that the norm and model of ethical order is to be found in the person of Varuna, the heaven-god. So strongly marked are his moral qualities that doubt has been expressed whether Varuna (Greek Ouranos) is really a god of the sky at all, that is, whether he ever represented a merely physical phenomenon. But, in any case, there is no doubt that his seat is in the sky and that from his throne above he watches and judges the actions of men. He is the "god of stern rule"; his order keeps the universe on its right way and man, in turn, must keep his own course "straight" and in accord with the straight "way of the gods." In its most literal sense this is a path of rectitude, any deviation from which is liable to bring down on the sinner the wrath and punishment of the gods.

The path of Right or Right Order is the path made by the high gods; it is not a cosmic order to which the gods unwillingly submit, but is instituted and supported by divine power and insight. Among men it is spiritualized as right worship and right behavior. Man "follows the stern law" of Varuna when he "walks the way of the gods," and this way is twofold, ritualistic and ethical. The gods must be worshiped with song and sacrifice, and what they approve must be done, for "all that the gods approve is blest." But their approval is shown by the manifestations of their good will and their disapproval is expressed by punishment embodied in sickness and misery. The logic is perfectly simple and is nowhere questioned except for one or two passages which voice despair, but even these express rather wonder that a good man should be unhappy than doubt as to the ethical standard. There is of course no notion of the unity of being or of a unifying principle of absolute good, but man can become religiously ethical without philosophy and the idea of Rita (Right, Order) is a unifying conception tending to harmonize man's ideal life with the divine life, which is manifested in the regularity of nature and the inerrant course of natural phenomena conceived as divine. The divinities do not deceive; they can be relied upon; they are "true." Hence, in imitation of divinity, straightness, uprightness, truth, undeviating loyalty to the true course, can be predicated as ethical rules for man.[1]

All this may be subsumed in the first great ethical rule, truth. From the beginning to the end of native Hindu civilization, to speak the truth, to act truly and loyally, to live in truth, so to speak, has been the never failing note in all moral teachings. Then, as an extension of this principle, comes already in the Rig Veda the admonition to live in such a way that truth shall not be violated by any overt act which impairs its validity; hence, the injunction not to gamble, not to commit adultery, not to slay the one who trusts, not to practice injurious magic upon an unsuspecting friend, not to speak maliciously, not to betray hospitality, etc. All such acts are offenses against the gods and are of demoniac nature. For it was recognized that there are spirits of evil, who do not follow the law of right, "spirits of darkness," as they are called, which brings out in the Rig Veda the antithesis between light and darkness in an ethical sense, right and light being forever after contrasted with wrong (untruth) and darkness; as the gods of light, the sun and sky and daylight (Mitra), are physically opposed to the blackness and terror of darkness and night.

The gods of light and truth are revered not only as sublime and sinless beings (the "sinless ones," as they are frequently described), but as members of the worshiper's own clan and family. This lends to the relationship between divine and human a very intimate touch, scarcely

[1] With this Rita may be compared the Stoic Ratio (compare *ratus*). From the same root, *ar* or *r*, comes the Greek *harmonia*. The radical idea is that of the fit, suitable.

paralleled elsewhere. We are familiar, in other religions, with the formal descriptions of sky and earth as Sky-Father and Earth-Mother. Zeus and Jupiter are examples of the fatherhood of the sky-god, but this conception is rather a cosmic idea suggested by the apparently marital relation between sky and earth and is little more than the utterance of a belief that the earth is the mother of all living things and that the fructifying principle is to be seen in the rains which descend from the sky and make all things grow. The Hindu idea is much more than this and it is morally of the greatest importance, because it emphasizes the personal family relationship between men and gods. When the god whose law must be obeyed is called familiarly "brother" as well as "father," when the rules laid upon men are laid by those who are real and personal relatives, possessing the right to command by virtue of their sublime power and wisdom, then there can be no question of the nature of sin. And so in the Rig Veda, in this earliest expression of religious faith preserved in literature, sin is not a magical miasma but an act of disobedience to divine will, as clearly sinful because opposed to divine will as it is possible to conceive. It is on this relationship with the gods that men call when desiring mercy for their sins. They invoke the gods to save them from the consequence of their errors because they feel that the gods really sympathize with men, that men are beloved by the gods as relatives and that their sin is punished not vindictively but regretfully.

It is naïve and general logic to argue that, if one is ill, illness is sent by a spiritual power. Only a few years ago our ancestors argued that rheumatism came from spiritual powers who inflicted pain maliciously. Let it be understood (as it was understood by the Hindus of the Rig Veda) that the gods are not malicious but naturally kind and that they have power to keep off malicious attacks of demoniac nature, then the inference is inevitable that all sickness is inflicted by the gods as punishment for wrongdoing. Hence, in Vedic thought, if one was not aware that one had sinned one nevertheless might from the sickness infer the previous wrongdoing. And this is the burden of many Vedic utterances: "If without knowing it we have offended against thy laws, forgive us our sin and remove from us this bond (of sickness)." Another conception is that the sinner has a debt to pay; hence the frequent allusion to the gods as "the true immortals, sinless, who exact the debt" (punish wrong). A prayer to "forgive us our debts" is equivalent to "free us from the bond." Salvation was sought both from sin and from death; sickness was in fact the outward expression of sin in process of punishment. Hence, the idea that sin clings like a disease "bound upon the body," approaches in a few instances the interpretation of sin as a magical, almost non-moral, pollution, which obtains among savages and is found in the magic-literature of India. Yet in the Rig Veda, though sin may be committed knowingly or unknowingly, it is never apart from morality, but is felt to be an infringement of divine law, a trespass committed against an acknowledged ethical authority, though it is not necessarily individual, since the children may suffer for the sins of the parents.

Punishment usually at this period is conceived in terms of sickness or death, which is followed by spiritual annihilation or by a wretched life of a shady sort in the underworld "abyss," probably merely a *sheol* or extension of the grave, though evil spirits as well as sinners of human birth exist there. But there is as yet no idea of a hell of punishment. The good man rejoins his fathers in heaven and lives with them a life of happiness; the very evil man simply passes away or lingers in the "abyss" as a woeful shade, for "there is no escape" from that "pit without a hold." On the other hand, the good man in heaven is "united with (the fruit of) his good actions on earth," so that the better is his life on earth the happier is his state hereafter.

The later Vedic period, after the Rig Veda, shows a marked decline in religious spirit. The magical practices of which the earlier Vedic priests were disdainful not only acquired a literary setting but the older texts, together with the ceremonies they accompanied, lost their original force and became formulas used with magic power to control spiritual powers. This phenomenon is a general one in the history of religion. The ignorant Arab carries a few words of the Koran as an amulet; the hocus-pocus of Biblical terms employed in Western magic is another example. But in India this took place on a grand scale; the sacrifice became, with its invocations, a meaningless performance except as a means of inducing or compelling the gods to give blessings. Naturally, therefore, the ancient relationship with the gods, the feeling that sin offended the gods and should be atoned for by repentance, the ethical import of sin, were all greatly modified. It became possible to obviate the disagreeable consequences of wrongdoing by a purely mechanical rite, and no sin was so great that a fixed ceremony, including sacrifice and gifts to the priests, could not annihilate it. Furthermore, at the close of the Rig Veda period and rising steadily after that to greater importance, appears the idea that by religious fervor, exhibited by ascetic practices, the spiritual power of man can be excessively heightened, so that by this means a mere man can attain to supernatural powers. By this fervor man becomes so spiritualized that he burns away sin and purifying himself thus becomes equal to a god or even more powerful than a god.

Thus instead of being dependent on the gods man was

now convinced that he could equal or surpass them and compel them to do his will. Yet the old formulas were retained and when new ones were added there was still the formal acknowledgment that man as a sinner needed forgiveness or at least needed to be freed from the evil of sin. But here another confusion of thought arose. In the early Rig Veda while man prayed to be forgiven for his sins he also prayed to be delivered from evils, and though evil in the form of sickness was regarded as a sort of incorporate sin, that is, as the material blossoming forth of sin in the form of its inevitable fruit of punishment, yet man distinguished between sin as a moral offense against the gods and purely material evil. In the later period, however, there seems to have been no distinction between moral and material evil. The common word meaning sin means in reality evil and it was felt that evil might come to a person without his own act or volition. Thus the wailing of women at a funeral was an evil influence which fastened on the hearer and had to be removed by a washing or some other ceremony. In this confusion between evil and moral stain it was the more easy to obliterate still further the need of divine forgiveness and to substitute for it the old magical cultus which removed all evil influence. The notion of sin as a miasma or pollution infecting a person and indistinguishable from physical infection and stain, undoubtedly arose first in the undeveloped moral stage where magical practices began, and was probably in itself older than the Rig Veda conception, but it was kept in the background or underground while the more intellectual and spiritual Rig Veda had influence. When that influence began to wane and the sacrifice became a mere machine, the lower magical cult with its interpretation of sin as synonymous with evil gradually attained supremacy, attainting even the old Vedic sacrifice.

One weighty reason for this was the increasing tendency toward pantheism. The figures of the old gods, that by the end of the Rig Veda period had already become blurred and more or less merged as the priests began to recognize the spiritual unity underlying different divine forms, lost their individuality and could no longer be invoked as familiar friends or awesome superior powers ready to avenge infraction of their rule. Thus, logically, there was no norm and no reason for morality in the authority of divine lawgivers. For this reason it is sometimes said that this was an utterly irreligious period, with no place for ethics any more than for a truly religious attitude. But despite all obstacles the moral sense persisted and even the old norm was invoked. Thus one is exhorted to speak the truth. Why? ''Because the gods speak the truth.'' Moreover, a form of divinity little recognized before but now becoming paramount, that of the Lord of Creation, an abstract Supreme God, now became not only supreme as divinity, but, as such (and this is significant), became a giver of laws, deciding ritualistic and ethical points by his word, which became of unquestioned authority.

Nor did the stereotyped ritual of this age entirely deprive the priest himself of moral admonitions, based for authority on the fear of what might happen to him hereafter if he did wrong, not perhaps a very lofty motive for avoiding sin, but still distinctly religious. Priests who betray their clients are deprived of hope hereafter. It is wrong for a priest to bargain for his fee; hence it is said that ''priests by bargaining will be deprived of heaven,'' *samvādenaiva ritvijo alokâs,* and there are numerous reproofs of wrongdoing, murder, adultery, theft, lying, arrogance, all of which are still treated as ethically wrong because opposed to divine law. For example, arrogance is condemned because it is a demoniac quality. From the moral side, therefore, this later age has lost indeed the warmth of religious feeling in its understanding of ethics; it no longer really cries for mercy to an offended god when wrong is done; but it has, nevertheless, retained the ethical superstructure which rested on the old foundation, though it must be confessed that it totters badly. Thus the caste system, which at this period becomes prominent in the form that it marks off as aristocrats the knights and priests from the farmers and traders, who are grouped with the common people and slaves, begins to make itself felt to the impairment of right, and a high caste man is favored by the judge in a contest with a man of lower caste, while in other regards also social position tends to interfere in an equitable adjustment of rights and wrongs. The old primitive virtues of truth and hospitality, however, are still recognized as such and the fear of hell for wrongdoing becomes more and more pronounced, though rightdoing is less and less referred to divine example. Acts are performed not for love of the gods, but for fear of inevitable punishments after death. In other words, the fear of divine retribution hereafter has now become a prominent factor in the maintenance of ethics, and this retribution is exacted not by a loving god whom one may perhaps move by pity, but by a mechanical process carried out by a god who has become simply a lord of hell and whom it is vain to attempt to placate. Something of the ritualistic inevitableness in the performance of sacrifice, which need not be performed with ardor but must be performed with meticulous exactitude to have any effect, has crept into the conception of ethical affairs. A man who does wrong is punished by rule in the next world. It is as vain to ask for pardon as it would be to expect mercy from a machine.

Although this attitude is less religious than that of the previous age, it has one advantage which scholars have apparently overlooked. It brings together in logical and inexorable combination cause and effect and prepares the way for that so-called Buddhistic discovery of causality which is the main claim to originality in the system of Gotama. But of this anon. At present, in the sub-Vedic period which we are now discussing, other ideas of moment are prominent. One of these is the doctrine of rebirth according to one's deeds, which begins to appear in antithesis to the older belief that one may be reborn on earth if he wishes, in which view rebirth may even be looked upon as a reward for virtue. Another is that virtue embraces not only moral qualities but intellectual power. If a man knows the right doctrine it is a virtue for which he is rewarded. The converse of this, that true knowledge embraces ethical conduct and that an unmoral wisdom is really ignorance, was yet to be formulated, but its germ is already visible. The reward of right knowledge is "immortality, unending, without bounds," *amritam anantam aparyantam.* The theory on which this view is established is not without interest. Fire is the god of truth and by knowing the mystery of the fire-sacrifice one's spirit becomes one with that truthful spirit of fire, which is identified with both sun and air. One's eye becomes one with the sun, etc., and being thus divine, one "becomes whatever deity one will, and is at rest." The fire-god links the human with the divine as representative of absolute truth, as even from the earliest period the fire-god was the special god of truth (as "guardian of vows" in the fire ordeal, the marriage rite, etc.). Immortality, which is no longer a boon granted by the gods, is won by good works or by knowledge. And the hope of immortality may be impaired even by wrong desires. Thus the later disputation as to whether it is right for a man to commit suicide is here anticipated dogmatically by the statement that it is wrong to desire to die before one reaches the full term of life and, being wrong, it is *alo-kyam*, "not conducive to heaven." It is recognized that immortality is impossible without death; hence the saying "in death is immortality," *anantaram mrityor amritam*.

But while one group of priests contented itself at this period with learning the minutiæ of religious ritual, there was another group that devoted itself to meditation and philosophy. In this latter group arose a series of essays on the interpretation of life, essays which, known as Upanishads, sessions in the sense of lectures, contain in an unsystematic form the seeds of the later philosophical systems. Incidentally the subject of ethics inevitably mingled with the discussions in regard to life and absolute being. But in these compositions there is no discussion of ethics and it is remarkable that this is true even in the later literature, which nowhere has any formal treatment of this subject. Like history, ethics was a matter always talked about but never separated from other objects of interest to be dealt with systematically. A chapter on good conduct in a law book merely records what good conduct is; even the scientifically arranged systems of the later philosophers treat ethics merely incidentally.

We cannot expect, therefore, to find in the Upanishads any theory of ethics. But we do find ethical teachings, and some of these touch on deep moral problems. In the first place, in these essays, some of which are only a few pages in length, it is universally assumed that the quest is to discover the way of salvation. It is not a quest of truth for itself, but an attempt to find out what knowledge is salutary; "through knowing what does one become immortal?" The great discovery is that by knowing that one's own soul is one with the universal soul one frees oneself from all the limitations of a separate existence and is one with that All-Soul. Sometimes this is ex-

pressed by saying that one merges into an All-Soul as a
river merges into the ocean, but the real thought is that
one is already one with the ocean of real being on per-
ceiving the unity. What hinders one from that perception
is ignorance. But this is not a mere intellectual ignorance; it is also a spiritual ignorance which can be done
away with only by a course of training in ethical and spiritual things. Now it is assumed, as a matter of course, by
all these teachers, that ethical conduct is the first step
toward a religious life, and that only through a devout
religious life of meditation and study can one attain to
a point where insight is practicable. For this reason, the
old discipline of the priest is not given up; he is still to
learn the mysteries of the formal cultus. But that cultus
has now been given a symbolic and higher interpretation
and much of the space in the Upanishads is allotted to
what seems like foolish interpretations of ritualistic per-
formances. The fact that these Upanishads first appeared
as appendages to ritualistic discourses explains historically this large element in their present form, but it is
also no less true that, even without that origin, some such
discussion would probably have prefaced the inculcation
of deeper truths. For the priestly authors felt that they
were rising on the stepping-stones of the lower cult to the
true appreciation of the new wisdom.

Ethical behavior then in these essays was assumed as
a preliminary to the study of higher truths. All the rules
for good conduct taught to the ordinary priest were still
valid for the would-be philosopher. But from the other
extreme, also, ethics was important. For, having found
the All-Soul to be devoid of all limitations, the philosophers assume that He or It (All-Soul or the Absolute) is
without evil of any sort. They do, in fact, go out of their
way to emphasize this point. The All-Soul may "be defined only by negations" (by *na, na*), but is still more

emphatically declared to be "devoid of all evil." In other words, as was natural, their interpretation of pure spirit was that the spirit was really pure in a moral sense as well as in the sense of mere spirit. Their use of the adjectives "clean," "bright," "pure," as applied to the Absolute, proves this as well as the whole conception of this pure soul as untainted by any stain; it is "being" in the sense of "good being," *sat,* devoid of all qualities that stain the soul through passion and ignorance. The All-Soul is devoid of evil, not devoid of good; an essence expressed by the formula "joyous intelligent being," that is, God is not a (personal) being with intelligence, but God is intelligence, existent and joyous.

The cause of ethics is here cared for by an appeal to divine example just as much as when the Vedic injunction opposes lying because the gods speak the truth, only the language is now that of philosophy. The highest being is devoid of all stain, of all evil; the soul of man should seek to rid itself of all stain and evil in order to identification with the highest being. This identification is impossible so long as the soul is still stained and polluted with evil. Clarification of the intelligence by ridding the soul of ignorance in itself implies cleansing the soul of moral stains. But, strictly speaking, one cannot say cleanse the soul, for the soul is rather enwrapped in blinding material coverings than stained; but these coverings of ignorance and passion must be removed before the soul stands clear. Passion itself, typical of all vice and evil, is a product of and part of ignorance. Hence, there can be no question of the need of purity of heart in order to salvation.

This philosophy has penetrated through all classes and is part of the Hindu philosophy of life. It is expressed in popular language by saying that one becomes immortal only through "restraint of the passions," by "destruction of passion and hate." The first step toward "becoming immortal" in the words of this popular philosophy is "purification of one's nature" (mental and emotional), *âçayaçuddhi,* for only through this can one attain to that insight which makes one a sharer of the universal intelligential soul of the world.

But as the Hebrew God says, "I make evil," so it is recognized that the all-animating soul of the world is the source of evil as well as of good. The intelligential world-soul is responsible for all that is done in the world; otherwise there would be a duality of power. One system of philosophy does indeed admit this duality and to it all that is evil is material as opposed to spiritual, so that the soul in becoming perfect shakes itself free of all contamination of matter, including the materially interpreted mental and emotional qualities. But the monistic system regards this material envelope of the soul as an illusive appearance. In either case, however, for the practical moral effect the result is the same and a strict ethical code is taught by both systems.

The philosophic soul, thus enlightened and purified, is raised above the petty restrictions of legal right and wrong, above the necessity of performing duties established by custom, that is, above the conventional habitude of an active man of affairs. The man thus enlightened knows that the rules of society are good rules, but as for him he is better off if he devotes himself to meditation and religious quietism as an ascetic. He has "risen above good and evil" only in the sense that he has ceased to concern himself with "merit and demerit." This is a phrase common to Brahman and Buddhist alike, which would be enough to prove it ethical, and means no more than this.[2] But the phrase has been misinterpreted by both Hindus

[2] Compare *Dhammapada,* 39, 412, where the Buddhist friar is extolled for this very unconcern in regard to "good and evil," *i.e.,* the reward of his meritorious acts and punishment for his sins.

and foreigners in the absurd sense that a man may sin
and yet be virtuous, if he only is ascetic enough. This
parody of philosophical truth becomes popularized in the
conception of the savage, morose, sinful ascetic, who in-
dulges his passion of lust and hate, and yet remains a
figure to be reverently adored, such as he appears in the
popular tales of the epic. Such a man is said to be one who
"cannot sin" and this is understood to mean that he can
sin with impunity, whereas the real meaning of the
phrase is that sin cannot come near him because he is incapable of doing a sinful act. The only basis for this is
an unfortunate passage in the Upanishads in which it is
said that the god Indra, on becoming aware of the highest truth as to real being, was not diminished in glory because of his sins. But the passage means only that Indra
as part of the world-soul lost his individuality, and the
sins which he had previously regarded as his own he now
saw were but the activities of the universal soul of the
world, to which all activities are necessarily referred.
But there is also a further confusion in the effort to distinguish between soul and its environment of body. In
trying to express the fact that soul is immaterial some
philosophers say that the soul stands apart as a spectator and is not really implicated in the acts of the body.
It is the passions of the body that are active, not the immortal soul within the body. Hence, it may be said that
the soul is not affected by the sins of the body. This, too,
is a dangerous doctrine in the hands of ignorance or vice.
But if one remembers that, though the psychology is different from ours, this means merely that the soul in a
vicious body is still trammeled by that body, the unethical character apparent on the surface disappears. The
soul is still tied down by what the body does till the two
are absolutely separated, but so long as the body remains
vicious its passions and desires enmesh the soul.

In any case, these speculations had no effect on the practical morality of the Upanishads, in which the way to salvation begins by being a path of morality. This is all summed up by the precept given to the student on the completion of his studies, at which time the teacher tells him as a rule for his conduct in life to "do those things which are good and avoid those things which are evil." Antinomian precepts are never inculcated. To do good means not only to follow the usual rules of social intercourse but to be good spiritually, to practice forgiveness, patience, kindness to all, to be generous, hospitable, self-controlled, above all to have a pure heart.

The ethics of philosophers is apt to be more quietistic than active and such is the case here. There is more admonition in regard to being patient and serene than appeal to help others, yet generosity and good will actively manifested are not omitted from the list of virtues and the general impression one gains from a study of the ethical side of the Upanishads is that they inculcate a blameless and virtuous life having for its goal morally the suppression of evil desires as well as the avoidance of all overt acts of an unethical nature. The old rule handed down from the Vedic period "to show affection one toward the other" (abhí haryata or "love one another") is still in force. The common man is assured that virtue will bring reward and wrongdoing will bring unhappiness. Nor is there any lack of a distinction between the act as a formal matter and the intent to do right or wrong. It is the will, we are told, which leads to the deed, and it is for this deed, as preconceived by the will and desire, for which a man suffers or is rewarded in the next world.

The system of rewards and punishments has by this time become uniform. In the past it was, as we have seen, chiefly fear of the gods' anger or of hell which was held before the common sinner. Either those one had wronged or ministers of the god of hell would punish a sinner in some appropriate way (in the former case, the *lex talionis* seems to have been expected). But by now the idea was abroad that metempsychosis had an ethical significance. According as one had acted in one's previous existence, one was reborn in a high caste or in a low caste, or in the womb of animals, etc. Instead of one of these theories overthrowing the other, they were united, so that the sinner virtually suffered twice for the same sin or was rewarded twice for the same good acts. First, on dying, one went to heaven or hell to reap the reward or punishment due to him for his conduct in life, and, when that reward or punishment was done with, one was reborn on earth according to the same rule. Philosophy tried to make a distinction here and it was urged (though never much believed) that the first system of rewards and punishments still left a "remainder," for which the next system of rebirth was put in operation. There was also a tendency to explain ritual good works as rewarded immediately after death, while works of good conduct were rewarded later by a "good birth." But these speculations never had authority, and historically it is evident that we have merely two systems awkwardly combined, but nevertheless ethically cogent in their several arrangements of rewards and punishments. And for the general mass of Hindus this combination has remained effective till this day. A man believes that heaven is his reward for good acts and that after his heavenly reward he will be born again on earth in a form answering to the same acts, in a good birth for good acts, in an evil birth, such as a bird or worm, for evil acts, after suffering in hell for the same. Different sects have a modified form of this belief; for instance, the Jains believe that when one's evil deeds counterbalance one's good deeds, one is re-

born not in any lower form, but as a man. There is, too,
a constant reversion to the old Vedic belief that punishment is sometimes *anantara,* that is, immediate, not in
the next life. A Vedic seer broke his arm just after making a liturgical change; naturally, it was the "punishment" for doing wrong. Moral teaching could scarcely be
more strongly enforced than it is by some of the ethical
writers, who hold that if a person does wrong he suffers
before death through a loss or injury and will then be
tormented after death, and after that torment will be
born to the torture of a low birth. Some say one's life on
earth will be shortened, one will incur obloquy, misery
will overtake, and finally hell will torment one who is
hînâcârâçrita, that is, "addicted to low conduct."[3]

To sum up the ethical attitude of the early philosophers: Salvation is the result of a cleansed or clarified
activity of the whole self or soul, which may be immediate but it is usually the result of a long spiritual and intellectual training, the foundation of which is moral excellence. Good and evil belong to the finite world, not to
the infinite spirit in which is no evil and which is only
good. The man who has a soul trained to perfection
"overcomes all evil"; he becomes first self-controlled,
satisfied, patient, and then "free from all evil and stain."
Thus moral training lies at the root of salvation and its
fruit is deliverance from all that is evil and sinful as well
as deliverance from the bonds of ignorance. But wisdom
alone cannot save. For it is said, "He cannot obtain God
by wisdom who has not first turned away from wickedness." All the discipline of austerity is part of the training of the soul. We may regard askance the mortification
of the flesh, but it was based on an ethical principle; it
was for the training of the soul, as in more ancient times

[3] The Brahmanic and Buddhistic views here coincide. Compare *Dhammapada,* 137, and *Vas.,* 6, 6; 20, 3, etc.

it had been practiced for the acquisition of power. Yet even in its oldest form, there was latent the thought that by overcoming the weakness of the flesh one attained to spiritual power.

At about the time when the Upanishads were composed as a new departure in literature arose the heresy called Buddhism. In this great revolt against the orthodox teaching, the idea of a Supreme Being was denied and the individual soul, which had not been questioned by the Brahmans, was resolved into a complex of thought and feeling capable of dissolution as soon as the fire of desire, which was regarded as originating the complex, was definitively extinguished. The theory of Karma, however, was held exactly as in Brahmanism, that is, the theory that man suffered or was rewarded hereafter for the deed, *karma,* done in this life, and as with the Brahmans so with the Buddhists, the reward and punishment were expressed by twofold experiences, one in heaven or hell, the other in rebirth in high or low form. This theory at the very beginning of Buddhism was already completely established, whereas in the first Upanishads it was only beginning to attract attention. It would seem, therefore, that Buddhism arose shortly after the first Upanishads were composed (*c.* 700 B.C.), or, possibly, that the Upanishads were first composed in the western part of the country and Karma was a doctrine that sprang up in the eastern part, where Buddhism originated. However that may have been, from an ethical point of view the two religions, orthodox and heterodox, were very similar. Both held out the hope of a happy future to the good man and condemned the man who was a slave of desire to an unhappy fate hereafter. Both defined the good man in almost the same terms. From the Upanishads we learn, for example, that the marks of a man not freed from his evil nature are fear, sloth, wrath, niggardliness, desire, envy, greed,

cruelty, meanness, pride, passion, deceit, etc., all of which
are equally condemned by the Buddhists. The latter, in
their rôle of protestants, objected to the Brahmans as
men made proud by a sense of caste superiority and condemned them in so far as they neglected morality for
formal ritualistic righteousness. In this reproach there
was undoubtedly much truth, for the Brahmans were in
fact an aristocratic caste, who despised other men as
lower because of their lower birth, and though the ethical
teachers among the Brahmans did not hesitate to blame
the same substitution of ritual for ethics, yet, as a caste,
the great multitude of priests probably offered a large
number of examples of individuals who based their superiority not on moral but on social preëminence.

But there were a few definite points of disagreement
between the Brahmans and Buddhists. The Brahmans
had inherited an elaborate ritual of worship, which en-
tailed the slaughter of animals. The Buddhists objected,
first, to any ritual of worship and, secondly, to all slaughter of animals. There was a pronounced feeling against
doing injury to animate beings and a horror of slaughter,
culminating, some centuries before the Christian era, in
reprobation of all those who killed other beings. The
Brahmans, too, came under the influence of this humanitarian spirit, which sought to stop the slaughter of war
and the slaying of animals (animals being regarded as
also the "children of the Lord of Creation" and thus
quasi brothers of men), but they maintained that in making bloody sacrifice they were obeying an older and
higher law; it was impiety toward the gods to refuse them
their wonted sacrifice and impiety toward the Manes not
to join in the monthly feast in their honor, which also en-
tailed eating of meat. So the Brahmans paused at this
point and declared that it was unethical to kill except
when religion commanded the death of the victim. The

Buddhists, who had no gods to worship, rejected this plea and condemned the Brahmans as cruel. Likewise in war, theoretically taboo to the Buddhist on account of its cruelty, the Brahmans held that killing was not only not wrong, but was a duty. A third difference from the ethical point of view consisted in the spiritual value placed by Brahmanism on the ritualistic good works of a man, the works to which the Buddhists assigned no value whatever. Otherwise the two systems of ethics were so much alike that the whole scheme of sinful acts tabulated by the Buddhists under the threefold head of acts of mind, speech, and body, was incorporated bodily into the Brahmanic code. Some of the Brahmanic sects, that is, sects that did not completely agree with the Brahman priests but did not split off to found unorthodox bodies, even went so far as to renounce animal sacrifices and to substitute their own body of scripture as authoritative alongside the holy (Brahmanic) Vedas. So that, despite the profound differences in creed and cult, there was yet substantial agreement between the two great religious bodies in many matters, and they were at one as to the question of personal morality, but with certain exceptions.

For example, the stricter rules of conduct which the Brahmans imposed upon young students, abstinence from luxuries, not going to shows and festivals, and the like, were also imposed upon the friars of the Buddhistic order; but to the Buddhist laic a greater liberty was permitted. No Buddhist, moreover, might drink intoxicants, while total abstinence was required in the Brahman fold only of priests. Again, the Brahman had certain carefully explained exceptions to the rule that one must always speak the truth (he might lie if a life depended upon it), whereas it was the boast of Buddhism that a Buddhist "could not tell a lie," even if his life depended upon it.

In general, the Buddhist was more of a puritan and less
apt to be shrewdly sensible, more apt to abide by the letter of the law and suffer the consequences for his often
foolish refusal to commit a venial fault. One Buddhist
friar is reported as much agitated in spirit because he
had stolen something, which was, of course, a great sin.
But careful probing of the case showed that in passing a
garden he had "stolen the perfume of a flower." The
sweet odor had been inhaled by him although the owner
of the flower and of the perfume had not given him permission to "steal" it. Such nonsense (we are glad to
learn) was regarded as "negligible" by the superior to
whom the conscience-ridden friar confided his sense of
sin.

But the Buddhists were quite wrong in their general
allegation that the Brahman did not distinguish between
moral and social worth and that they failed to emphasize
ethical purity in distinction from ritual purity. The Brahmans made, in fact, this very distinction and laid considerable weight upon it. The real moral objection to the
Brahmanic point of view is that they continued to hold,
despite this distinction, the theory that sacrifice and the
practice of austerities were in themselves saving means
of grace which could win salvation and superhuman powers for the practitioner. Even the Buddhist, as time went
on, was led to believe that the austere Yogi was, because
of his austerity, a pious worker of wonders, and that a
mere boy of seven years of age might be so magically
imbued with esoteric wisdom that he could free himself
from the bonds of mundane existence and become a great
saint, sure of his salvation. But such mysticism was of
the age and did not belong to any one religion.

The Buddhists had a regular fortnightly meeting at
which the friars were supposed to confess any sins they
had committed, "in thought, word, or deed," since the

last meeting. The Brahmans held that open confession was unnecessary, but in atoning for faults the sinner had to confess to his spiritual director and then receive from him the penance which he must perform in order to redeem himself from his fault. It was a mooted question whether such atonement then freed the sinner from the penalty for his sin in the next world. But it was generally agreed that suffering for his fault now (and some of the penances were very severe) at least mitigated the punishment hereafter. Some legislators declare that there is no use at all in performing a penance, since "the deed does not die," that is, the sinner will be confronted with his deed in the next life and pay the penalty there and then.

Buddhistic ethics may be studied in the formal canons but also in the laws of conduct laid down by the great emperor Asoka, the first king to take Buddhism under royal patronage, and in the tales of the previous births of Buddha, which, for the most part, are really adaptations of animal stories, written to inculcate Buddhistic morality under the guise of a fable. The formal canons inculcate self-control, purification of the spirit, observance of the laws not to kill, steal, commit adultery, lie, or drink intoxicants, and, in the case of friars, to be abstemious in eating, to refrain from idle amusements (dancing, singing, music, and spectacles), and from luxuries such as garlands, scents, unguents, ornaments, finery, and too comfortable beds; and to accept no gold or silver. Stress is constantly laid upon right thinking and meditation; the friar, who represents an ideal incapable of fulfillment in the laic, is urged to devote himself to the contemplation of the miseries of life and the means of escaping them in future rebirths, in order to the attainment of annihilation of self, which expires like a lamp devoid of fuel when the flame of existence is not fed with the oil of desire. The primitive Buddhist sought the happiness of

eternal freedom from rebirth. Later Buddhism sought
rather eternal peace and interpreted the extinction of desire as leading to a state of impersonal, unending repose.
But another form of Buddhism, especially prominent in
the Far East, though originating in India, revived the
idea of a heaven of happiness in the presence of a Great
Spirit, who was to the worshiper virtually a form of
Buddha as divinity. The ethics of the later cult laid more
stress on imitating Buddha than on carrying out his
teachings, and since Buddha had devoted himself to the
good of mankind this later form of Buddhism is marked
by an altruistic spirit not prominent in primitive Buddhism except in the case of those saints who devoted themselves to missionary efforts among the border tribes and
in foreign lands. Personal morality was somewhat insidi-
ously affected, as a matter of fact, by this change in
Buddhism and the later sects laid less stress on strict
ethics than did primitive Buddhism. In certain forms of
debased Buddhism, where it amalgamated with Hinduism of a low type, the ethical side was lost sight of in a
gross mysticism. But in its original form no religion has
ever placed so much weight upon the gradual ennobling
of the mind through moral and spiritual effort. The injunction is ever to be firm in well-doing, never to grow
slack in mental and moral training, to be always on one's
guard against evil thoughts and acts; to be pure-minded
and do right, to be kind to all, to hurt no living thing.

The great Emperor Asoka, in the middle of the third
century B.C., had carved on rocks and pillars the rules of
morality which he deemed most important for his people
to follow. Prominent here is the law of non-injury; no
animal should be slaughtered for sacrifice; cruelty to living creatures must cease. Next is impressed upon the
people the necessity for veneration of parents and of
spiritual teachers, whether Brahmans or Buddhists, for

Asoka was no bigot. He extols also liberality of thought and deprecates the folly of sect quarreling with sect. The king feels that it is his own duty to "toil for the public good"; this public service he regards as a debt he is bound to repay: "I toil for the public good . . . that I may discharge my debt to animate beings." This is a reflection from the noble old Hindu theory that man is born in debt. Every man is bound to discharge his debts, to the seers of old, by study of their wisdom; to the gods, by sacrifice; to his fathers, by having a son; to other men, by hospitality, etc. That the popular presentation of happiness hereafter is by no means that of the abstruse sage with his vision of extinction or senseless calm, is shown by the king's adding to the above: ("that I may discharge my debt) . . . and that while I make some happy in this world, they may gain heaven in the next world," *i.e.*, by following the ethical code he has engraved for them in durable form. Another significant remark of this great king is his admission that all the different sects should remain undisturbed "because they all desire control of the senses and purity of heart." This shows clearly that the inner cult was to all these sects as important as or more important than outward observance, a point very grudgingly admitted by many today whose zeal for their own set blinds them to the virtues of others. Another pleasing inscription of Asoka says that, though some devout people are unable to be lavishly liberal (presumably to the Buddhist friars), yet even a lowly man can do meritorious acts; for such a person, though poor, can "master his senses, be pure of heart, show gratitude, and be faithful." This is perhaps the earliest case of formal approval of "gratitude" as a virtue. Later it became a common saying that "there is expiation for every sin, but for ingratitude no expiation is known," as a matter of fact a rhetorical exaggeration, since several other sins were called "sins with no expiation," but an exaggeration indicative of a recognition of a moral principle which, as in this edict of Asoka (Rock Inscription VII), is coupled with fidelity or loyalty. "Earnestness is the way to immortality, indifference is the way to death," is the lesson the king would teach in another short edict urging "utmost exertion" upon his people in conforming to the law of piety, which law is defined as "kind treatment of slaves and servants, obedience to father and mother, charity to ascetics and Brahmans, and respect for the sanctity of life" (the doctrine of "non-injury"), and, to add to the law of piety an item from another edict otherwise similar, "truth must be spoken." But enough has been given to show how near to the heart of Buddhism was ethical conduct. To the great philosopher and to the great saint morality may be said to have been a "subordinate matter" (as Western scholars sometimes declare), but it is subordinate only as arithmetic is of subordinate interest to the mathematician who is working on the calculus; he does not spend his time explaining rules of addition and subtraction. In other words, in no religion is morality more fundamental than in primitive Buddhism. The cleansed spirit is the only spirit that can even begin to walk upon the path that leads to salvation. Lust, wrath, and pride, all such qualities must be overcome before one can even start on the course of "earnest meditation" which leads to the goal. If it is immoral to believe that life on earth is not worth living, the early Buddhist may be called an immoral pessimist, but it must be granted to him that ethically he was above reproach in all other regards, except in one. That one is, in a word, selfishness. This primitive Buddhist's only real concern was to save himself and ensure his own salvation. He was as intent on doing this as the average Christian is to save his soul. But, as we have seen, a nobler idea soon sprang up in Buddhism, which made the Buddhist eager to renounce his own immediate felicity for the good of mankind. Asoka himself says nothing of gaining his own happiness hereafter, but speaks only of toiling "for the public good." And even in the matter of "pessimism," one should try to realize what an unending vista of millions of years of rebirths lay before the Buddhist because of his belief in metempsychosis (in so far as he believed in soul at all) and in Karma, before one condemns him for thinking that an infinity of rebirths as an animal, etc., is not a desirable prospect. It is not life on earth for once but life here forever, with interludes of heavenly joys and hellish pains, only to come repeatedly back to earth. This is what he and any sensible man would say was undesirable. In reality, the Buddhist is an optimist, because he believes that "by noble living and by noble thought" one may earn the harvest of eventual felicity, whether in the form of bliss eternal or in that of unending calm existence. If this be pessimism, he might say, make the most of it!

The quite delightful tales of what Buddha did in previous lives give us an opportunity to see in informal compositions those ideals which Buddhism, by means of such stories, held up before the simple friars and common people of India, from the time of Asoka, in the middle of the third century B.C., till, we may say, the fifth century A.D. Here Buddha is represented as gladly offering his life on many occasions to save others from death or from misery; by means of these examples it is shown that one must not be arrogant, proud, contemptuous of others; that it is better to live at peace than in bickering with others; that virtue is suitably rewarded, if not here then hereafter; that kindness to animals wins their hearts and that cruelty is a horrible sin; that one must strive to follow a golden mean between selfishness and absurd ex-

travagance; that calmness, gentleness, affection, are ethical qualities; that respect for one's parents is a moral
law; that covetousness and greed destroy a man's character, as do anger and lust, etc.; innumerable homely fables offering a complete *résumé* of life as it should be led
by the "real Buddhist," that is, the Buddhist who is not
cloaking an evil nature with hypocrisy.

After the time of the early Upanishads and the beginning of Buddhism the ethics of the two great religions
was, so far as formal pronouncement goes, almost identical, as may be shown by the circumstance that the main
sins are arranged in the same categories and comprise
the same subjects. Thus, the law book of Manu incorpo-
rates the Buddhistic group of sins of thought, speech, and
deed in inverted order: "Covetousness, thinking of
wrong things, adherence to false doctrine are the three
mental sins; abuse, lying, detraction, and idle chatter are
the four vocal sins; theft, killing (injury), and adultery
are the three bodily sins." The rule given in the Buddhist
Mahâsudassana Sutta is one that would have appealed
equally to the Brahman: "Do not kill, do not steal, do not
be sensual, do not lie, do not drink intoxicants; and eat as
you have been accustomed to eat." There is, of course,
always the religious difference between the two bodies,
the Brahman believing in the sacredness of tradition, in
an immortal soul, and in a God, the Buddhistic iconoclast
trampling on tradition, denying the immortality of the
soul or self, and mocking at the notion of the Brahman's
Supreme Spirit; but in contradistinction to the antinomian philosophers of Buddha's day, who were religiously
unethical, both Buddhist and Brahman maintained the
same high standard of personal morality, though the
claims of a rigid social order affected the Brahman's legal code to the detriment of the depressed classes, so that
it appears as if there were a moral laxity where, in fact,

there is only social solidarity, the determination to keep the *kâla pûga* (black mass) in their proper place. Thus, the violation by a black man of a white woman is a much greater offense than that an Aryan (white) should misuse a black woman. Such offenses, however, were in the abstract not regarded very seriously anyway at that time; it was only when the offender was of low caste that it became serious. The Buddhist, on the other hand, whose religious body was largely recruited from the lowest castes, made the offense equally grave or unimportant in either case, so that with him it became a question of self-control, irrespective of the person or caste involved. This ignoring of caste gives to the Buddhist teaching a more universal character and helps onward the growing conviction that all men are brothers, which the Brahmans were the first to enunciate in their formula of "all men are children of One Father," but which they were not prone to apply practically to the equalization of Aryan aristocrats with the illiterate and more or less disgusting members of the lower orders. All the Aryans, those who boasted of their descent from the original conquerors, were by tradition trained in the "good conduct" of their forefathers. They had for generations been more or less instructed in morals, customs, and in literature. They stood far above the mass of the common people in discipline, education, and morality, as well as in social position. They were very conscious of this and very proud of it and it is absurd to blame them for it. They were, in fact, superior, just as much so as the F.F.V. were superior to their ante-bellum slaves. On the other hand, the Buddhists, who collected their congregation from all classes, as Christian missionaries collect their converts, were, like these, more inclined to stress the nobility of character and to depreciate the value of caste, especially when, after the political troubles which followed the in-

vasion of Alexander, a slave dynasty came into power,
which must have helped their propaganda. It is all the
more to the credit of the Brahmans that they did actually
follow the lead, though rather slowly, of the Buddhists in
teaching that a man's character was more important than
his family. But they still had and maintained the idea
that the sacrosanct character of a priest was something
that personal unworthiness did not alter to such an extent as to render invalid his consecrated work, and they
continued to play with the question whether a priest *quâ*
priest was not "worthy of reverence" and fit to perform
his priestly duties even if, personally, he were "unworthy." But the strong moral nature of the Aryan at
last prevailed, even in this delicate matter, and the Brahman position, outside of the narrower circle of priestly
teachers, eventually coincided with that of the Buddhists,
to wit, that a Brahman was "no better than a slave" and
"not a real Brahman" if he were a moral reprobate. Nor
was any great crime requisite in order to establish this
inferiority. "If a member of the Brahman caste acts in a
low manner, then he is no better than a low-born man," it
is said in the Brahmanized epic. In theory this is also the
position of even the stricter Brahmanism of the law
books, which gives us the undiluted opinion of the priestly
caste.

These law books, which date from the time when Buddhism arose to the centuries immediately following the
Christian era, and are, therefore, more or less synchro-
nous with the teachings of the epic, present a very vivid
picture of the Brahmanic ideal of life. This life, with all
its swagger as to the incontestable superiority of the aristocratic castes, is hedged about with innumerable taboos,
of which some seem to us incredibly foolish, partly because we do not understand their inner meaning;[4] some

---

[4] A good instance of this, which has been the object of scornful contempt

have no moral significance, because ritualistic purity and ethical purity are, as in all early codes, somewhat confused; but of which many are of the highest ethical importance. Let us look at some of these in detail.

Manu, one of the most authoritative lawgivers of the strict Brahmanic set, has depicted the ideal Brahman as one who "fits himself for immortality" (that is, tries to attain heaven) by a worthy character. He must "restrain his senses," a well-known formula elsewhere explained as subduing all evil desires, being patient and long-suffering, harboring no ill will, being free from wrath, pride, greed, and arrogance, etc.; he "must destroy lust and anger," and last, but by no means least, he must "refrain from doing any injury to any living creature." Another legal writer, following Manu, says that every man, and especially a Brahman seeking salvation, by leading the life of a religious mendicant, must "grow in intelligence," and in order to effect the beginning of the wisdom and knowledge necessary to salvation he must attain to a general purification of his nature, *âçayaçuddhi* (*Yâj.*, 3, 62). The idea that ritual purity can take the place of ethical purity is repudiated by the earliest of these lawgivers, Gautama, whose manual belongs to the

on the part of foreign observers, may be found in the list of those who are excluded from the deeply solemn feast held monthly in honor of the departed ancestors. The foreigner admits that he can appreciate the reason why a sinner is excluded but he jeers at the exclusion of "such men as are afflicted with disease or are bald-headed" and thinks he detects therein a complete absence of ethical standards. It is moral perhaps to exclude a thief but why a bald-headed man? This shows, he concludes triumphantly, that the Hindus had no real ethics, only a lot of trumpery rules without moral significance. But a little reflection would advise such a critic that, according to the Karma theory, any such physical disability argued an unworthy person expiating in this life the sin still clinging to him. We may ridicule the belief, but we may not justly ridicule the implications of the belief. The man who is bald-headed is one who has "broken a covenant" in a former life and is still suffering for his sin. As such it is quite consistent with morality that he should stand on the same level as any other sinful person, whose presence defiles the family rite.

time of the early Upanishads and may revert to even
older injunctions. At any rate, Gautama (to be distinguished from Gautama Buddha, whose contemporary he
may have been) says distinctly that not all the rituals together can save a man whose soul is lacking in ethical
qualities. As a later legal-religious writer says, "One is
purified by forgiveness" rather than by ritual, that is, it
is the saintly spirit that cleanses the soul, not the formal
ritual of purification.

This principle, so much ignored by those criticizing the
Brahmanic "ritualistic salvation," is emphatically inculcated and elaborated by still another legal writer, Vas-
ishtha: "Not austerities, nor [study of the] Veda, nor
sacrifices, nor lavish liberality can ever save him who de-
parts from the rules of good conduct. The Vedas do not
purify him who is deficient in good conduct." Good conduct is then explained as consisting first, in outward observance of the rules of decent behavior, in respect of
cleanliness, eating, etc., and secondly, in inner conduct,
which again is twofold, mental and ethical, so that the
person of good conduct will train his mind by concentra-
tion of thought and austere practices and at the same
time train his moral sense by subjugation of the senses
in the practice of "liberality, truth, purity, and compassion." In order to impress his meaning the author speaks
then of those qualities which a man of good conduct
should avoid, mentioning among others, "lack of patience, giving way to the passions and call of the senses,
envy, covetousness, lying, harboring grudges, harboring long wrath,[5] peevishness, backbiting, maliciousness,
ingratitude, and lack of compassion." Especially to be noticed here is the last item, *nirdayatvam*, "absence of compassion," another way of recommending "non-injury,"
the increasingly important ethical rule that one should

[5] *Vas.*, 6, 26 (Calcutta edition, *dīrgharoshaka*).

not hurt living creatures, usually expressed by repudiation of action but here, by a deeper touch, associated with
sins of the mind; one who is moral will not even wish to
injure.

After the law books and in part contemporary with
them, the great epic of India is a mine of moral jewels,
usually buried deep in some theological stratum but often
lying on the surface of a tale or appearing sporadically
in some little treatise on the question of right and wrong
which perplexes the epic heroes, who waver in the most
human manner between atrocious behavior and the desire
to be "worthy Aryans." A kind sage or reproving
teacher is often introduced to give them some necessary
information in regard to "good conduct." In general,
the admonitions here are more or less repetitive of what
has already been set forth in the law books; but it is of
great interest to see that in some particulars the epic
advocates as universally obligatory what the law books
assume as moral conduct compatible only with extreme
saintliness. Thus, the rule, "When cursed let one answer
with a blessing," is given by Manu as one for a hermit,
who through long years of discipline has reached such a
moral standard that he can not only forgive his enemies
but bless them that curse him, whereas in the epic the
same rule is given as one of general application for all
ethically-minded men. Here, too, in the epic is promul-
gated that startling doctrine which declares that a slave
is one who is a slave of his evil nature not of a human
master, and boldly lays down the rule that a Brahman
priest is no better than a slave if he be immoral, while
a slave in social position, if he be a good man, is better
than a priest who is a bad man. The epic even goes so far
as to permit slaves to study the Vedas, which is a privilege no lawgiver ever thought of granting to a member
of this despised caste. It is not unlikely that this epic

liberality may be a consequence of Buddhistic teaching, as Buddhistic stories are also received into the body of the work.

The source of evil is generally given as ignorance in Brahmanic writings and as desire ("thirst," longing for something exterior) in Buddhistic works. But there is no very clear *prius* in either case, for both systems of thought assume the effect upon the immediate individual of countless lives (rebirths), mediating between the present and the past of a million years ago. As far as the present individual is concerned, he is reaping the harvest of thoughts and deeds in a remote antiquity, and whether it was aboriginally ignorance which caused the first yielding to desire or desire which introduced the cloud of ignorance remains a question of doubt and debate. In popular presentations, such as that of Manu when he describes the "eighteen vices of a king," the general root of evil is declared to be desire, greed, covetousness, *lobha,* and in a more general discussion the same author says that all actions, both good and bad, arise from this same principle (*Manu,* 2, 2, and 7, 45 *seq.*). It is generally admitted that action is prompted by desire or by the opposite "aversion," but it is also maintained that if a man's thoughts are not confused his intelligence will keep him from having wrong desires. The "three gates of hell" which the epic mentions are desire, wrath, and greed, but the Sankhya philosophers substitute error or ignorance for desire and set up as the three origins of impulse, error, greed, and wrath. But, in the Vaiçeshika school, will is traced to desire and aversion, both of which the Naiyayika school refers back to error or ignorance (also called "mental confusion").

The ethical predisposition of the individual is logically derived from his own past experiences, as they must be on the basis of the Karma doctrine, but the Hindus could not escape the observation that the inheritance of the parents also predetermines to some extent the predisposition of the child. "Children are born wicked if their parents are wicked," is the rather crude way the epic expresses this belief.[6] From the fact that the parents are here mentioned in the plural rather the dual may be inferred that the inheritance of evil is received from a succession of ancestors. But this truth of experience was never logically worked out, and, indeed, another speaker[7] in the same passage retorts that good children are sometimes born of bad parents, so that the notion of heredity is set aside as of little value.

The epic on the whole, when it discusses the origin of an evil disposition, inclines to take the philosophical view, but expresses it metaphorically: "The tree of desire in the heart is born of ignorance (mental confusion, *moha*); ignorance is its root; wrath and pride are its trunk; its vigor of growth comes from evil past lives."[8]

The teaching of this great epic storehouse of ethical wisdom is condensed into one phrase, *satyena çîlena sukham,* "happiness is acquired only by the attainment of truth and by ethical behavior." Truth dispels ignorance. Intelligence is necessary to the appreciation of what is really good. Without intelligence, which comprises a moral attitude of mind, there is no salvation.

In the so-called New Testament of the Hindus, the Bhagavad Gîta, which is filled with ethical teaching, this point of view is brought out more fully than anywhere else. The very definition of "knowledge," by which is meant intelligent appreciation, shows that knowledge is much more than an intellectual faculty. It implies an in-

---

6 *Mbh.,* 12, 264, 9: *lubdhebhyo jâyate lubdhas* (*lubh* like Latin *lubet,* the same root as in the *lobha* above; literally, "from the greedy is born the greedy").

7 *Ibid.,* 268, 11.

8 *Ibid.,* 255, 1 *seq., purâdushkritasâravân . . . kâmadrumas.*

telligence trained morally as well as mentally: "This is saving knowledge, that one is virtuous and knows," is the gist of it; but what is most interesting and instructive is that ethical qualities really lead in the list of those factors that constitute "knowledge." The whole passage is as follows: "Salvation is the fruit of knowledge. Now knowledge is humility, simplicity, non-injury, forgiveness, uprightness, service of the teacher, purity, steadiness, self-restraint, freedom from passion and from egotism, appreciation of human ills, . . . loving devotion to God . . . and understanding of the relation between soul and God" (G., xiii). Intellectual conviction and ethical mentality are blended into one and the union of belief and moral nature is indissoluble. According to this teaching, which is here more clearly expressed but is always implicit, morality is necessarily intellectual and spiritual, and religion is necessarily moral. The word "knowledge," *jñānam*, is the same as γνῶσις; it means not only knowledge but intelligence partly expressed in character.

So it is also when the apocalyptic vision vouchsafed to great saints reveals God in the heart "as a brilliant light, like fire, like a flash of lightning";[9] for this light is that "removed from all darkness" ("truth is light") and it is only because of the darkness of lust and ignorance that one is unable to see God. God is the Supreme Energy, *atitejo'nça*, residing in the heart of every man, and this light in the heart is immaculate; it is conceived as radiant force or forceful light opposed to all darkness of lust and ignorance.

It is, then, not fair to the Hindus to say that with them salvation is the fruit of mere intellectual qualities, as we define those qualities. It is only, according to Hindu ideas, by getting rid of the strain of immoral qualities that one is capable of true knowledge. Man is a blend of

[9] *Mbh.*, 12, 307, 20.

passionate and darkening strains as well as of the pure strain of good being. Only as he frees himself from passion and darkness (confusion of mind) can a man attain to "goodness." Vice and ignorance, lingering from past lives (rebirths), reveal themselves in him as predispositions from which the man seeking absolute goodness or godhead will exert himself to escape. Life is thus a constant training-ground in virtue as well as in wisdom. Even the old Brahmanic lore expressed this by saying, "life is one long sacrifice," that is, it is, as it were, a service devoted to spirituality, to the highest, as the old ritual sacrifice was a service to God. The command to "love thy neighbor as thyself" finds its counterpart in the Brahmanic injunction to injure no living being, because every such being is in reality one's own self, that is, all individual beings are one in being one with God.

That there is an ethical danger in postulating a God without attributes, to whom right and wrong as such are meaningless, has already been explained. But it must not be forgotten that in this philosophical assumption God is merely a name for Absolute Being, and that the conception of God as a Holy Spirit synonymous with Dharma, righteousness, was not ruled out by the philosophical endeavor to find a First Cause behind the personal God. In the Bhagavad Gîta and in the qualified monism that came later, God is an ethical Supreme Being, to whose paradise none may come who is not morally purified.

As compared with other systems of ethics, the ethics of Hinduism, though hampered by the doctrine of caste and greatly influenced by the belief in Karma, approaches nearer to that of Christianity than does that of any other moral system. It recognizes to the full the importance of building up of character, though it holds that character is developed by intelligence, of which it is indeed a part. Again, though it inclines rather to a quietistic attitude, seeing in the meditative sage rather than the active man of affairs its human ideal (this is true of both Brahmanism and Buddhism), it nevertheless, even from the time of the Upanishads, recognizes the truth brought out fully in the Bhagavad Gîta, that it is not so much a question of outward activity or quietism as it is a question of inner disposition and appreciation of truth. So long as a man is bound, that is, limited, by the hope of reward for good action, he is, no matter how good, or how quietistic, in slavery to his desires. But if a man lives an active life, doing good without thought of reward, if, as the Gîta puts it, he ".does all as it were for God," then is he free of the bonds of desire and not only may but should (such is the Gîta doctrine) avoid quietism and live an active, virtuous life, doing his duty in that station to which he has been born. Here is a distinct repudiation of quietism as a mode of life; one should toil and do the work for which one is born, leaving the "reward" in the hands of God, who declares that He will receive and bless the soul that loves Him and is pure. Even the sinner may be saved through faith and love of God, for such an one "becomes righteous through love," that is, through his loving devotion he turns from sin and becomes morally pure as well as devout. For he has attained to that "knowledge" which, as we have said above, is declared by the same author to begin with ethical betterment.

It was the contention of the eminent jurist, Leist, author of *Jus Gentium*, that the Aryans entered India bearing with them the sacred Indo-European law code, which was thus formulated: Thou shalt honor the gods; Thou shalt honor thy parents; Thou shalt honor thy native country; Thou shalt honor a guest (anyone seeking shelter or refuge). To these the Hindus, he thinks, soon added five other laws: Thou shalt keep thyself pure; Thou shalt restrain thy senses (passions; includes injury through insult); Thou shalt not kill; Thou shalt not steal; Thou shalt not lie. The form in which Leist has rendered these laws or commandments, with which, as a group of nine, he compares the Ten Commandments of the Hebrews, is not historically justified, since it assumes a divinity as author of the commands. But there never was a "Thou shalt (not)" in Hindu legislation. All the laws and ethical rules are handed down as general commands, except in special cases where a god gives an individual command, as the sun-god says to the gambler of the Rig Veda, "Play not with dice." Ethical rules were not inherited as *logia* of a divine being but were made in accordance with what was thought to be the wish of the gods or fashioned after the pattern left by divine example in antithesis to demoniac ways. Thus, as we have seen, lying is an offense because it is truth which the gods honor and themselves practice, and *hybris* (arrogance and pride) is deprecated because it is a demoniac trait.

As to the order of appearance in history of the laws cited by Leist, it is probable that the ethical sense against killing, stealing, and calumniating, though not in his list of original laws, was even older than what is termed above "honor thy native country," the Hindu content of which is merely that one should honor the heroes of old. It is, in fact, hazardous to attempt to discover any historical succession in the development of moral qualities. One is justified only in saying that in the very earliest period killing, stealing, lying, inhospitable behavior, sorcery to injure friends, and other forms of disloyalty were strongly condemned; that probably even before the Aryans entered India they had rules of ritual purity and of general behavior and penances for violation of these rules, as they had an appreciation of the virtues of harmony, concord, and other gentle qualities; and that the ethical sense was highly developed at a very early period, so that by the time of the first lawgivers, six or seven centuries before the Christian era, it was recognized that the moral qualities subsumed under the caption of "self-restraint," that is, avoidance of wrath, greed, lust, impatience, and the like, were essential to an ideal character and that a man should train himself to avoid such vices of character, just as he trained himself to avoid infringement of legal prohibitions. In the latter case there were legal penalties; in the former, spiritual loss and sometimes religious penances. In one particular the Hindu soared far above other moral systems. This was in his gradually developed sense of the ethical value of the *ahinsâ* (non-injury) doctrine with its correlate, "sympathy for all living beings."

After the time of the Bhagavad Gîta the religious tendency to believe in a personal Supreme Being of a merciful character, whose grace alone was sufficient to effect salvation, strongly affected the implications of the Karma doctrine. In both Brahmanism and Buddhism the feeling that the sinner, instead of working out his own salvation from sin and suffering, as was the older tenet, might cast his sins upon the Lord and thus escape the direful penalty of wrongdoing, became a leading feature of moral religion, sometimes leading to antinomian disregard of the fundamental principles of right living. But, in general, this evil tendency was corrected by the recognition of the righteousness and holiness of God himself, so that the sinner strives through repentance to show that his passionate love for God has really resulted in an ethical improvement. In the Gîta itself the sinner must become morally worthy in order to receive divine grace and such is also the implication in the religion of those who follow the sect of Râmânuja, whose deity is a moral Supreme Power worshiped rightly only by those "who have cleansed the heart."

THE ETHICS OF ZOROASTRIANISM

A. V. WILLIAMS JACKSON

V.[1]

THE moral and ethical code which a people sets up for itself, and the way in which it lives up to this, may be taken as a sort of thermometric register by which the social, physical, and spiritual condition of the nation can be judged. The history of the ancient race of Iran affords a fair illustration of this truth; and the moral status of Persia throughout its earlier history, including the mighty empire of the Achæmenian kings and the sovereign sway of the Sasanian rulers in early Christian times, will here be briefly sketched. It is the lessons of the past that teach the wisdom of the present and the future.

In order better to understand the moral and ethical code of Zoroastrianism, however, a few words regarding the nature of the religion itself may be given by way of introduction. The devoted believers in this early faith, worshipers of fire as they are sometimes wrongly termed, paid pious homage to the great god Ormazd, or Ahura Mazda, as he was called, and by creed they were the faithful followers of Zoroaster. This was the prophet of ancient Iran, whose clarion voice of reform rang out over the land six centuries or more before the birth of the Christ,[2] or some years previous to the time when the Jews were carried up into captivity at Babylon, or the gentle Buddha preached to thirsting souls of India the doctrine of salvation from misery through renunciation.

[1] Cordial acknowledgment is made to the editorial board of the *International Journal of Ethics* (University of Chicago) for the privilege of reproducing, with additions and changes, the material which appeared in that journal, vol 7, no. 1, October, 1896, in an article by the present writer. Since that date a very comprehensive small book by M. A. Buch, *Zoroastrian Ethics*, Baroda [1921], has been published in India. References to a couple of other books which touch on the subject will be found in the footnotes below.

[2] A number of scholars believe that the era of Zoroaster should be placed several centuries earlier than the traditional date, approximately B.C. 660-583, as found in the Pahlavi Books and later sources, the date which is still adhered to by the writer of this article.

A characteristic tenet of the old Zoroastrian creed philosophically was Dualism. This dogma recognized the existence of two primeval spirits, Ormazd and Ahriman, the Good and the Evil, whose influence pervades the world. The incessant warfare and constant struggle of these primordial principles is evinced at every turn in human life. This cardinal doctrine is one of the hinges on which the entire system of Zoroastrian ethics turns. The moral and ethical law of this creed is based, indeed, upon a systematic theory of morality and is founded on philosophic principles.

A contrast may be aptly drawn between India and Iran with regard to the effect produced on each nation by the working of its respective philosophic ideas. The ancient Iranian, by influence of his creed, is characterized by action, exertion, and practical views of life; the Indian has tended rather toward inaction, introspection, and meditation. The Hindu, with his pantheistic speculations, evolved the quietism of the Upanishads; the Persian, whose sacred books ring with the call of "up and doing," like a valiant soldier girt with the armor of faith, was summoned to fight boldly the good fight in the mighty struggle between the warring powers of good and of evil.

As a prime factor in the dualistic tenet of the contending kingdoms of Ormazd and Ahriman, as taught by Zoroastrianism, we must recognize the great doctrine of the freedom of the will. This article of the religion forms the basis and foundation of the ethical and moral part of Zoroaster's religious system. Man is Ormazd's creature, and by birthright he belongs to the kingdom of good; but, created as a free agent, he has the right to choose. Upon that choice, however, his own salvation and his share in the ultimate triumph of good or of evil in the world depend. Every good deed that man does increases the power of good; every evil act he commits augments the kingdom of evil. His weight thrown in either scale turns the beam of the balance in that direction. Hence, man ought to choose the good. It was to guide him in this choice that Zoroaster believed himself to be sent. This was the great teacher's mission. How far he succeeded in fulfilling that mission must be judged from the character of the faith that this prophet of the Magi founded, and from its effect and influence in ancient days, if the kingdom of Media, of Bactria, of Persia, in fact, the whole of Iran, has stood for anything in the world's history.

As a second important element in the general ethics of the religion, we must notice the doctrine of man's responsibility to account. A strict watch over each man's actions was believed to be kept by the divinities. All good deeds were carefully recorded; all sinful acts were sternly set down. No doctrine of a recording angel could be clearer and more precise than this of the Zoroastrian creed. Whether these actions were written in an account book,[3] or whether they were heaped up to be weighed in the balance when the soul was placed on the judgment scale after death,[4] as the later development of the religion taught, it is not necessary here to decide. Allusions to such a record, account, or weighing are often found throughout the sacred books of Zoroastrianism from the earliest days to latest times.

[3] See Jackson, *JAOS.*, 13 (*Proceedings*), p. xx, October, 1888, on Av. *cinman,* and later on the survival of the life account (TPhl. *dafēdagīh*), under Zoroastrian influence, in Manichæism. So also BkPhl. *dastak,* ''account book,'' *cf.* Mod. Pers. *dastak,* in the reference to the reckoning of the soul in the well-known later Zoroastrian work, Dēnkart, 6. 112 (transl. D. D. P. Sanjana, 11, 23, Bombay and London, 1910). Numerous other references are found in Zoroastrian Pahlavi literature to such an account as kept (*e.g.*, Dāṭistān-ī Dēnīk, 31. 10, transl. West, in *SBE.*, 18, 66, and many besides).

[4] The idea of deeds, good and bad, being balanced (Av. *henkeretā*) is certainly very old in Zoroaster's system of ethics. See such Gathic passages in the Avesta as Ys. 31. 14, and *cf.* Ys. 46. 10, 15-17; Ys. 33. 1. The references in the later Pahlavi religious works are abundant; see the recent dissertation by Jal D. C. Pavry, *The Zoroastrian Doctrine of a Future Life,* pp. 80-91, New York, 1926.

To pass from the general to the particular, however, the quintessence of the moral and ethical teachings of Zoroaster may best be summed up in that doctrinal triad, so familiar to every reader of the Avesta, "good thoughts, good words, good deeds," or *humata, hūkhta, hvarshta,* as is the expression in the original text. The brief triad of this article of faith forms the pith and kernel of the ancient prophet's teaching.[5] "I practise good thoughts, good words, good deeds; I abjure all evil thoughts, evil words, evil deeds," is the watchword of the faith, the ever-recurring phrase in the sacred liturgy, the note on which constant changes are rung from the period of the Gāthās, or Zoroastrian Psalms, to the latest recorded utterances of the religion. At the judgment after death the soul of the righteous man is met by a beautiful maiden, personifying his good conscience or religion as shown in these three qualities of ethical perfection, to guide him forward to felicity; but the wicked is confronted by a hideous hag, embodying his own threefold evil characteristics, to hurry him to damnation. Moreover, the good thoughts, good words, good deeds, gathered together respectively, form the three mansions or stages through which the sanctified soul ascends into the infinite light (*anaghra raochāo*) of heaven. Evil thoughts, evil words, evil deeds, are the grades through which the spirit of the damned falls to endless darkness and perdition. In the Avesta, the man who practices this triune doctrine of the holy faith is the *Ashavan,* or "righteous"; he is the man who lives according to the Law of Righteousness, as opposed to the *Anashavan,* or "wicked man," the *Dregvant* or follower of Falsehood.

Space does not permit of cataloguing the virtues and duties that are inculcated and enjoined, or the vices and faults which are denounced as to be shunned. The virtues

---

[5] See M. N. Dhalla, *Zoroastrian Theology,* pp. 30-33, New York, 1914.

may be comprised, in general terms, as purity alike of body and soul, uprightness, charity, generosity, and benevolence; and no people are more renowned, perhaps, for their princely generosity today than are the Parsis or Modern Zoroastrians of Bombay. In addition to these good qualities, the ancient creed laid particular stress upon the faithful keeping of one's word and pledge, the avoidance of all deceit, especially of lying, and the importance of keeping out of debt, as well as of shunning theft and robbery. According to Herodotus (1. 136), the Persians taught their sons three things,—these were "to ride horseback, to use the bow, and to speak the truth." And next to the sin of lying they considered it the greatest disgrace to be in debt, because, besides incurring many other evils, this fault implied also an additional evil, the necessity of telling lies, "for a man who is in debt," says Herodotus (1. 138), "must of necessity tell lies." In the magnificent Old Persian rock inscription of the great king Darius, there is hardly a line that does not emphasize the ideals of this mighty monarch as the foe to duplicity and the lover of truth.

Connected with the spiritual side of the Persians' education was also the side of physical obligation, the duty of outdoor exercise, which played a prominent part in the theory of youthful bringing up. In the conduct of life, moreover, from the very beginning, the importance of maintaining soberness and chastity was not lost sight of, although the ideas may have been somewhat more lax than would be exemplified by the Parsis of today. Incontinence, sexual excesses, seduction, abortion, and unmentionable sins are evils that are strongly denounced in the Avesta; the outcast woman is anathematized. But it must be remembered that among the ancient Iranians polygamy and concubinage were doubtless the rule, or at least they were not uncommon. The Persians appear to have drunk wine freely; still, the vice of intemperance seems to have been severely punished, if we may judge from some classical allusions to the subject;[6] and Strabo[7] speaks of the Persians as being moderate in most of their habits. It is true that no Brahmanical asceticism was practised in ancient Iran, and, as the Avesta shows, the Zoroastrian religion allowed a wholesome and whole-souled enjoyment of life. The family was the unit in the state, and a large family of children was a virtue rewarded by the king as a bulwark to the throne.[8] But with all this, in the oldest days, temperance, discretion, restraint, and a certain self-control seem in general to have been a racial characteristic. The whole tone of the Avesta, for example, and of the Pahlavi writings is exceedingly chaste. The position of woman in ancient Iran was apparently in nowise inferior to her standing in the Vedic times of early India.[9] As among other Oriental nations, however, submission to her lord and master is taken for granted, and the woman who is "obedient" comes in for a special meed of praise in the Avesta and elsewhere;[10] but it is perfectly evident, as a rule, there was not that subjection which results in loss of personality and individuality. The Zoroastrian scriptures plainly show this fact.

Among general virtues, also, a feeling of national pride was cultivated, as we gather from the Avesta and from classical authors.[11] Submission to those in civil and religious authority was insisted upon. Contentment, indus-

[6] See Jivanji Jamshedji Modi, *Wine among the Ancient Persians*, Bombay, 1888 (Gazette Steam Press).

[7] Strabo, 15, 22 (p. 735).

[8] *Cf.* Hdt., 1. 136.

[9] See Darab D. P. Sanjana, *Position of Zoroastrian Women*, Bombay, 1892.

[10] *Cf.* Avesta, Vsp., 3. 4; Gāh, 4. 9; Pahlavi, Ardā Vīrāf, 12. 1.

[11] See Hdt., 1. 134; and *cf.* Avesta, Ys. 26. 9; Vsp. 16. 2; also Pahlavi, Dēnkart, 5. 3. 2 (transl. Sanjana, 9, p. 619).

try, courage and valor, love of wisdom and of knowledge
—all were instilled; and reverence for the divine power
and practice of religious rites and ceremonies were
strictly enjoined. In short, we may find in the Zoroastrian
moral and ethical code almost every article of our own
duty toward God and duty toward our neighbor.

Among the various special rules that were rigidly
enforced by the ancient Persian faith during its entire
history may be mentioned those that were designed for
preserving the purity of the elements, earth, fire, and
water, and for freeing these from defilement, especially
from pollution arising through contact with dead matter.[12] It was the rigid observance of this law, doubtless
originally in part a sanitary precaution, that so markedly
characterized the Zoroastrian belief in the eyes of antiquity. In carrying out these prescriptions in daily life,
however, not a few were the practical difficulties and pre-
dicaments that arose, as the Greek and Latin writers and
the Persian scriptures themselves tend to show. Equally
praiseworthy in the eyes of modern times would be the
Zoroastrian duty of preserving and fostering useful animal life, especially of giving care to the cow and to the
dog, for both these animals were of importance to an
early pastoral people.[13] But this avoidance of injury to
animal life was carried to no absurd extreme, as among
the Jains of ancient India. The Zoroastrian creed taught
that it was especially meritorious to destroy noxious animals, like serpents, toads, rats, and vermin.[14] By destroying these evil creatures, the power of Ahriman is reduced
and the kingdom of Ormazd is expanded. Expiation for

[12] The Avesta and the Zoroastrian Pahlavi books later, as well, abound in
references to this subject.
[13] *Cf.* now likewise the brochure by M. A. Buch, *Zoroastrian Ethics*, pp.
80-84, where references to the texts are included.
[14] For example, Avesta, Vd., 14. 5-6; 16. 12; 18. 73; likewise, Hdt., 1. 140;
Plutarch, Is. et Os, 46; also the Acta Pers. Martyr., p. 203; Agathias, 2. 24.

faults and atonement for sins might in this way be effected, as is indicated in the Avesta.[15]

Throughout all ages, the Persian faith upheld the practice of "the good deeds of husbandry" (Avesta), of irrigation, of agriculture, and of farming occupations, as opposed to the wild nomadic life of the marauding mountaineers.[16] The parks (or garden "paradises") of the Persian kings have been famous from time immemorial, and the few Zoroastrians that are left today in their old Iranian home are employed chiefly in gardening and in peasant life; although their Parsi kinsmen in India have been drawn principally into mercantile pursuits. Each class in the constitution of the Zoroastrian state and in the different walks of life—the priest, the warrior, the husbandman, and the craftsman—had its own moral obligations to fulfill and its own particular duties incumbent upon it to perform. The reform of Zoroaster was in part a social reform as well as a religious and ethical reaction.

The ideal picture must not, however, be overdrawn. There was a darker side as well as the bright side. This cannot be denied. Millennial days come not at once with a reformer. It cannot be gainsaid that certain practices existed, were overlooked, or recognized, which today would meet with general social ostracism. The list, moreover, of sins, vices, and faults that were prevalent was no meager one, as a glance at a passage in that Dantesque vision of hell, seen by the saint Ardā Vīrāf, will show. Some of the offenses recorded in that Pahlavi work[17]— like walking barefoot, lamenting excessively over the

15 Vd., 14. 5-6, and the references in the preceding note.

16 A chapter in the Avesta (Vd., 3. 1-6, 23-32) rings with praises of tilling the earth.

17 See Ardā Vīrāf, chs. 18-100, translated by Jamaspji-Haug-West, London and Bombay, 1882 (a section of which is reprinted in C. F. Horne, *Sacred Books and Early Literature of the East*, 7, 206-207, New York, 1917). *Cf.* also the French translation by M. A. Barthélemy, *Livre d'Ardā Vīrāf*, pp. 43-129, Paris, 1887.

dead, or the offense of a woman's performing her hair-dressing over the fire—strike us as trivial; while the enormity of other sins may appear to us to have been underrated. But in general the Zoroastrian standard was a high one; a strain of idealism flowed in Iranian veins. A certain custom, however, which was undeniably practised with religious zeal by the worshipers of Ormazd, is in our eyes incestuous. This was the practice of next-of-kin marriages.[18] Whatever may be the meaning of the much-discussed word *hvaētvadatha* in the Avesta, or of *khvētūk-das* in the Pahlavi patristic writings of Sasanian times, there can be no doubt that marriage among relatives, even between parents and children, brothers and sisters, occurred among the Iranians from the earliest ages. It doubtless originated in part from a desire of preserving the unity and perpetuating the religious strength of the faithful community. It is needless to add that such shocking marriages as those within the first degree of kinship would not be tolerated by the modern Zoroastrians, nor have they been for centuries.

It must be allowed, also, that a few grossly ignorant superstitions worked their way into the faith, which to our mind were not without unfavorable influence upon the moral and ethical stamina of the people; and certain unpleasant customs were recognized, or at least were not deemed improper, which meet with disapproval in our sight. It must likewise be acknowledged that the ancient Iranians did not shrink from cruel practices, and from inflicting horrible punishments; but in most cases these were done, it must be remembered, with a distinct purpose, to deter from national crimes or to punish great offenders. Other nations of antiquity have not acted in a manner that is much different. Mercy was a virtue incul-

[18] See L. H. Gray, ''Next-of-Kin Marriage,'' in Hastings, *Encyclopædia of Religion and Ethics*, 8, 456-459.

cated by the Avesta.[19] It cannot be denied, finally, that
with the decadence of the Achæmenian dynasty the moral
strength of Iran was weakened by the wave of luxury
and voluptuous indulgence that swept over the land between the Tigris and the Indus, carrying away the ethical
bulwarks of the people and swallowing up those sterling
traits of the hardy mountain race that had made Persia,
under Cyrus, the mistress of Asia. But to offset this, it
must be added, the faith contained within itself the sovereign remedy against dissolution; and in the opening
centuries of our era, under Sasanian rule, the pristine
ideals of Zoroastrian Iran once more returned in all their
majesty, until Persia sank before the rising power of
Islam, on the day when the Mussulman conquest wrought
a change, or rather a revolution, in the religious spirit
and national character of the Iranian folk. But in our day
the New Persia, with its national aspirations and revival
of standards that are best, its tolerance and breadth of
vision, gives every sign of promise for the future.[20]

Taken for all in all, it may be said that no better proof
of the real merit of the Zoroastrian creed as a working
hypothesis can be found than is illustrated in the character of those who profess the faith today. These are the
community of the Parsis in India, religious exiles from
Iran since the days of the Mohammedan invasion, and the
small remnant of Zoroastrians that still survives in Persia. Together they number somewhat over one hundred
and ten thousand souls, and of these about a hundred
thousand reside not in the land of their birth but in the
neighborhood of Bombay. They are the living exemplifi-

19 *Cf.* Av. Vsp., 21. 3, also Phl. Dēnkart, 5 (transl. Sanjana, vol. 9, pp.
643-644).

20 One of the signs of this, ethically, was the stand taken at the Geneva
Congress in 1924 for limiting the production and control of opium, she herself having long been among the producers of this drug which she now desires to join in confining strictly to medicinal use, if backed by other nations.

cation of the true worth of the doctrines taught by the ancient Persian sage. They piously uphold the best of the tenets of the old faith with regard to religious observances; they live in love and charity with their neighbors; their life is marked by temperance, soberness, and chastity, and their fame for acts of liberality and generosity is world-wide. Among them there is no practice of polygamy; they are strict monogamists; unfaithfulness to the marriage vow is almost unknown; and prostitution among Parsi women is hardly to be found. The horror of falsehood, duplicity, and of debt is as keenly felt by the Parsis today as it was over two thousand years ago. In Teheran, for example, a Zoroastrian has for years been entrusted by his Mohammedan colleagues with the expenditure of large public funds for municipal purposes because of his high reputation for honesty in discharging the duties of his office.

Or to conclude, if we take the Zoroastrian religion in its entirety, and view it in the light of the early period to which it belongs, we shall come to the conviction that outside of the light of biblical revelation it would be hard to find among the Gentile nations a higher standard of morality, a nobler code of ethics, than that set up by Zoroaster to be maintained by the ancient people of the Land of the Lion and the Sun.

EARLY HEBREW ETHICS

LEWIS BAYLES PATON

VI.

THE purpose of this chapter is to exhibit the Hebrew conception of the divine requirements, both religious and moral, in the period that preceded Amos, 760 B.C. From the time before the division of the monarchy in 931 B.C. only oral traditions have come down to us, and these are not sufficiently clear to permit the reconstruction of a system of Mosaic, much less of Patriarchal, ethics. Alphabetic writing first appeared in Israel about 1000 B.C., and in the course of a century was sufficiently diffused to make the writing of books a possibility. The Judean (J) documents were written in the southern kingdom between 900 and 800 B.C., and excerpts from these have been used in the composition of the present Pentateuch, Joshua, Judges, Samuel, and Kings. The Ephraimite (E) documents were written in the northern kingdom between 800 and 760 B.C., and have come down in excerpts in the same books of the Old Testament in which the J documents are found. Scattered through the Books of Kings are a number of sections containing stories of the early prophets (Pr) which disclose in the main a religious standpoint earlier than Amos. Deuteronomy (D) was not written before 650 B.C. and was the law book discovered in the temple in the eighteenth year of Josiah (619 B.C., II Kings 22-23). As a whole, its theology is later than the prophets of the Assyrian period; nevertheless, it contains many ancient laws, so that its evidence cannot be neglected. The Holiness Code in Leviticus 17-26 was written about 600 B.C.; but, like Deuteronomy, it contains ancient legislation. The Priestly Code (P), written about 500 B.C., has furnished the solid block of legislation in Exodus 35:1— Numbers 10:28 (including H), and kindred sections in the earlier and the later parts of the Pentateuch and Book of Joshua. Its theological standpoint as a whole is post-exilic, but it contains some old laws and institutions. The method by which old elements are discriminated in the later documents is comparison with other Semitic religions. Beliefs and customs which are found in these documents and also in other parts of the Semitic world must be survivals from ancient times. Beliefs and customs that are peculiar to Israel are probably late.

From our oldest sources we learn that the early religion of Israel rested upon two historical facts, the exodus from Egypt and the conquest of Canaan. Yahweh was not the ancestral god of Israel, but was the god of the Kenites who dwelt at Mount Sinai. Israel had no natural claim on him, yet he took pity upon its sufferings, delivered it from bondage, and brought it into "the land flowing with milk and honey." This showed that in moral character and in power He was superior to all other gods. On this basis rested the ethical requirements of the old Hebrew religion.[1]

A. *Allegiance to Yahweh*

Since Yahweh was both better and stronger than all other gods, it followed that He alone deserved to be worshiped.

a. Israel must be the people of Yahweh. Corresponding to the fact that Yahweh had shown Himself to be "the god of Israel," stood His demand that Israel should prove itself to be "the people of Yahweh."[2]

1. *Fear of Yahweh*. Allegiance to Yahweh showed itself in awe before His "holiness," that is, His superhuman qualities. The usual Old Testament term for this frame of mind is "the fear of Yahweh." Fear was the

[1] See K. Budde, *Religion of Israel to the Exile*, Ch. I; L. B. Paton, *The Early Religion of Israel*, Ch. III.

[2] J, Gen. 48: 15a; II Sam. 14: 13a; II Ki. 11: 17; E, Josh. 24: 15b, 16, 18, 21-23; I Sam. 12: 12b, 20b.

dominant motive of the old Hebrew religion, for Yahweh was "a jealous God, a consuming fire."[3]

2. *Submission.* Whatever Yahweh did, the pious early Hebrew exclaimed, "It is Yahweh: let Him do what seemeth Him good." This is the same attitude that prevails in Muhammadanism where *Islām,* or "Resignation," is the native name for religion.[4]

3. *Reverence.* Revolt against the authority of Yahweh, which expressed itself in reviling Him, or cursing His name, was regarded as a deadly sin that was punishable with death.[5]

4. *Obedience.* Allegiance to Yahweh required prompt and willing response to all His commandments as revealed by priest, wise man, or prophet. Yahweh said to Israel, "Observe that which I command thee this day," "Hearken unto the voice of the words of Yahweh," "Keep my commandments always"; and the proper response of the nation was, "All that Yahweh hath spoken we will do."[6]

5. *Trust.* Corresponding to obedience to Yahweh's commands was trust in His promises or predictions. "Abraham believed Yahweh, and He counted it to him for righteousness." The people in Egypt believed the word of Moses, and Yahweh rewarded their faith with deliverance. David "strengthened himself in Yahweh," and He rescued him from his peril.[7]

6. *Love.* Love for Yahweh, which is so frequently demanded by Deuteronomy, is scarcely mentioned in the

[3] J, II Sam. 6: 9; E, Gen. 20: 11; 42: 18; Ex. 1: 17, 21a; 20: 20; I Sam. 12: 14, 18b; II Ki. 17: 25a.

[4] J, II Sam. 10: 12b; 15: 25b, 26; E, I Sam. 3: 18.

[5] E, Ex. 22: 28; Pr, I Ki. 21: 10, 13.

[6] J, Gen. 24: 40a; Ex. 34: 11a; I Sam. 15: 1, 22, 23; II Ki. 22: 13c; 23: 3c; E, Gen. 31: 16b; Ex. 16: 4b; 19: 7, 8a; 24: 3; I Sam. 10: 8; 12: 14b, 24; 13: 8-13; I Ki. 20: 35, 36a; Pr, I Ki. 13: 21b, 26a.

[7] J, Gen. 15: 6; Ex. 4: 29-31a; Num. 13: 30; I Sam. 30: 6b; E, Deut. 31: 23a; Pr, I Ki. 19: 9b; II Ki. 18: 30, 32b; 19: 5b, 6, 9b, 10, 21.

ancient religion. Still the Song of Deborah in its closing verse says: "Let those that love Him be as the sun when he goeth forth in his strength."[8]

b. *No Other God Must be Worshiped*. The reverse side of allegiance to Yahweh was hostility to all other gods. In the primitive Decalogue that underlies J's recension of the Book of the Covenant in Exodus 34 and E's recension in Exodus 20-23, the first commandment, according to J, is, "Thou shalt not bow down unto another god," and according to E, "Ye shall not make (gods) with me." From the beginning Yahweh was a "jealous God," who tolerated no rivals or associates, and as early as the time of Moses the doctrine "Yahweh, the God of Israel," meant already "Yahweh, the only God of Israel." This did not mean that other gods did not exist, but only that they must not be worshiped. This was henotheism, or monolatry, rather than monotheism.

1. *Foreign Gods were Forbidden*. Toward the divinities of other nations the religious leaders of Israel always manifested extreme hostility. The early histories record how Joshua, the judges, and the early prophets warned Israel against serving other gods. Elijah devoted his life to the struggle against the Tyrian ba'al.[9] It seems, however, that foreigners were allowed to carry on the worship of their ancestral gods, even though they might reside in Israel.[10]

2. *The Gods of Canaan were Forbidden*. So long as the ba'als, or "owners," were felt to be foreign gods, their worship was strictly prohibited; but when Yahweh absorbed them and appropriated their sanctuaries, they were regarded as local manifestations of Himself. Not until later did the prophets of the eighth century realize

8 J, Jud. 5: 31b; E, Ex. 20: 6.
9 J, Ex. 34: 14; II Ki. 22: 17; E, Gen. 35: 2a, 4; Ex. 20: 3, 23a; 23: 13; Josh. 24: 2b, 14, 15, 19, 20, 23; I Sam. 12: 21; Pr, II Ki. 5: 18, 19.
10 I Ki. 11: 7f.; 15: 11-13.

that the ba'als had been conquered only in name, then the old warfare against them broke out afresh.[11]

Hostility to the gods of Canaan involved destruction of their sanctuaries,[12] holy stones, altars, images, and asherahs,[13] avoidance of their customs,[14] refraining from making treaties with them,[15] or marriages with them.[16] Some laws even went so far as to command annihilation of the Canaanites lest they should seduce Israel into worshiping their gods.[17]

3. *The Cult of the Dead was Forbidden.* Spirits of the dead were deified by the primitive Hebrews, as by all the other Semites. In I Sam. 28:13 the ghost of Samuel is called *ĕlôhîm*, "deity," and the old Hebrew rites of mourning point to a primitive cult of the dead. Consequently, the shades were included in the general prohibition, "Thou shalt have no other gods besides me."[18] Rites of mourning for the dead were still tolerated because they were not clearly recognized as acts of worship; nevertheless, it was felt that they were in some way connected with "other gods," and therefore rendered one "unclean," *i.e.*, debarred one from taking part in the worship of Yahweh.[19]

c. *Magical Arts were Forbidden.* From the point of view of hostility to "other gods" we are to explain the prohibition of divination, augury, enchantment, sorcery,

[11] J, Ex. 34: 15b; II Ki. 23: 5b; E, Jud. 2: 13; 6: 10; I Sam. 7: 3, 4; II Ki. 3: 13a, 14b; 9: 22; 10: 28; Pr, I Ki. 18: 18-22; 19: 10a, 14a; II Ki. 1: 3-6, 16.

[12] J, II Ki. 11:18a; 23: 13; E, II Ki. 10: 27.

[13] J, Ex. 34: 13; II Sam. 5: 21; I Ki. 15: 12-13; II Ki. 11: 18; E, Jud. 6: 25-30; II Ki. 10: 25-27.

[14] E, Ex. 23: 24b.

[15] J, Ex. 34: 12, 15a; Josh. 9: 7; Jud. 19: 11-12; E, Ex. 23: 32.

[16] J, Gen. 24: 3b, 37; 38: 2; Ex. 34: 16; Jud. 14: 3a.

[17] J, Num. 21: 3; Josh. 6: 17; 8: 25; I Sam. 15: 2, 3, 7-9, 13-21, 26a, 32, 33; 28: 18; II Sam. 21: 2b; E, Ex. 23: 33a; Josh. 6: 24a; 8: 26.

[18] I Sam. 28: 9; Isa. 8: 19; Deut. 26: 14; Lev. 19: 31; 20: 6, 27.

[19] Am. 6: 10; Hos. 9: 4; Deut. 26: 14.

charms, and other forms of magic. These arts were regarded as belonging to the cults of other gods, and as
rivals to the legitimate methods of inquiry, such as ark,
ephod, urim and thummim, and prophecy, which belonged
to Yahweh.[20]

d. The Distinction of "Holy, Unclean, and Clean."—
1. *Meaning of "Holy."* "Holiness" in Semitic religion
and in the early religion of Israel was not a moral but a
physical quality. It was a destructive energy, like a high-
tension electric current, that dwelt in the gods and made
them awe-inspiring. Thus, after Yahweh had smitten the
men who ventured to look into the ark, the people of Beth-
Shemesh said: "Who is able to stand before Yahweh,
this holy God? and to whom shall He go up from us?"[21]
This destructive energy could be transmitted to everything connected with the deity. Accordingly, the ancient
Hebrew spoke of holy places, holy trees, holy stones, holy
temples, holy garments, holy prophets, holy nazirites,
holy offerings, holy times, and the holy land, meaning
thereby "awe-inspiring," or "dangerous" things and
persons because they belonged to Yahweh. Even the prostitutes who were attached to sanctuaries were called
qādhēsh and *qĕdhēshā*, "holy one," because they were devoted to the service of the deity. The same idea is found
in all primitive religions, and is commonly called by the
Polynesian word *tabu*. "Holy," accordingly, in the old
Hebrew religion meant *"tabu* for Yahweh."

2. *Meaning of "Unclean."* "Unclean," on the other
hand, meant *"tabu* for some other god." A great many
old Semitic *tabus* were felt to belong to inferior spirits,
or to rival gods rather than to Yahweh; these were now
regarded as "unclean" because they excluded one from
the worship of Yahweh. They had exactly the same

[20] Deut. 18: 10; Lev. 19: 26.
[21] I Sam. 6: 20.

quality as "holy" things—they were dangerous and must be avoided—but the theory on which they were shunned differed from the theory in regard to "holy" things.

"Unclean" things included: (1) everything definitely connected with the worship of other gods;[22] (2) everything connected with foreigners, because they were worshipers of these other gods;[23] (3) all physical defects, because these were believed to be caused by the activity of evil spirits;[24] (4) all diseases, because these were caused by obsession of demons;[25] (5) everything connected with the sexual life, because this belonged to the old Semitic mother-goddess 'Ashtart, or Astarte;[26] (6) certain plants and animals, because these were the totems of ancient Hebrew clans;[27] (7) everything connected with death, because spirits of the dead were worshiped by the primitive Hebrews.[28] All these *tabus* were highly infectious, and contact with a person who was "unclean" rendered one also "unclean." The Israelites were strictly forbidden to contract "uncleanness"; and if one entered a holy place with the taint adhering to him, he was certain to be slain by Yahweh.[29]

If pollution was accidentally contracted, it must be removed by ceremonial methods. Circumcision was an initial purificatory rite that cleansed one from the taint of 'Ashtart.[30] Other sorts of "uncleanness" were removed by washing.[31] Sexual relations could not be forbidden, but

[22] Hos. 5: 3; 6: 10; Jer. 2: 7, 23; 3: 2, 9; 7: 30; Lev. 18: 24, 30; 19: 31; 20: 23; Ezek. 36: 18; 43: 7, 9.

[23] Am. 7: 17; Hos. 9: 3; Deut. 23: 2, 3, 7, 8; Lev. 22: 25.

[24] J, II Sam. 5: 8b; Deut. 23: 1.

[25] J, II Ki. 15: 5b; Pr, II Ki. 5: 27.

[26] Deut. 23: 9-11; Lev. 18: 19; 20: 18; 12: 2-5; 15: 19, 25, 33.

[27] J, Gen. 7: 2, 8, 9; 8: 20b; Deut. 14: 3-21; Lev. 11: 2-47; 19: 23-25.

[28] J, II Ki. 23: 6b, 14b; Pr, I Ki. 13: 2b; Deut. 26: 14.

[29] Lev. 21: 6a; 22: 2, 3, 9; Ex. 30: 20, 21; Lev. 7: 20, 21; 8: 35b; 10: 9, 10; 15: 31.

[30] J, Ex. 4: 24-26; Josh. 5: 2, 3, 9; E, I Sam. 17: 26b, 36.

[31] J, II Sam. 12: 20a; E, Ex. 19: 10b, 14b; I Sam. 16: 5; Josh. 3: 5; 7: 13.

they must be abstained from for a certain length of time before taking part in religious exercises.[32] Fasting also was useful for the purpose of getting "unclean" food out of one's system.

3. *Meaning of "Clean."* "Clean" denoted that which was neither *tabu* for Yahweh nor *tabu* for another god, and which, therefore, might be used freely. It was *profanus* in the original meaning of the word as the opposite of *sacer*. This was also occasionally called loosely "holy" in antithesis to "unclean," and the commandment, "Ye shall be holy," meant only, "Ye shall be free from the taint of the *tabus* of other gods."[33]

Having now considered Yahweh's fundamental demand of Israel, exclusive allegiance to Himself, we pass to His second main requirement, namely, worship.

B. *Worship of Yahweh*

a. Holy Places. Yahweh revealed His presence and His power in a multitude of places throughout the land of Canaan. In every such place, so to speak, He was at home, and there He might be worshiped. As the ancient Book of the Covenant expresses it, "In every place where I cause my name to be remembered I will come unto thee and bless thee." These places were "holy," that is, they partook of the awe-inspiring character of Yahweh Himself, so that it was dangerous to enter them without propitiatory rites. Thus when Yahweh appeared to Moses in the burning bush, He said to him: "Draw not nigh hither; put thy sandals from off thy feet, for the place whereon thou standest is holy ground." Concerning all high places Yahweh commanded, "Ye shall reverence my sanctuaries."[34]

[32] J, II Sam. 11: 6-13; E, Ex. 19: 15; I Sam. 1: 19b; 21: 4b, 5.
[33] E, Ex. 22: 31.
[34] Ex. 20: 24; Jud. 13: 19; I Sam. 14: 33, 35; Jer. 2: 20, 28; 11: 13; Ex. 3: 5; 19: 12f.; Lev. 26: 2b.

b. Holy Objects. At the holy places holy objects were found in which the sanctity of the spot focused itself. Holy trees were present at most of the high places, and were believed to have been planted by the Patriarchs. *Maṣṣēbhôth,* or standing stones, were extremely numerous. Yahweh was thought actually to inhabit these, as is shown by the fact that the one set up by Jacob was called Beth-el, "House of a god," or El-beth-el, "God of the house of a god." In Josh. 24: 27 it is said of this stone, "It hath heard all the words of Yahweh which He hath spoken unto us." Similar in character were the *ăshērîm,* or sacred posts, which both in Samaria and Jerusalem stood in the temple of Yahweh. The ark did not differ in character from these other fetishes. It was a box that was believed to be inhabited by Yahweh. When it went into battle, Yahweh went with it. When it was captured by the Philistines, it brought disaster upon them. The men of Beth-shemesh who looked into it were smitten, and so also was Uzzah who touched it. It was the chief cult-object in Solomon's temple. The ephod was another sacred object that is often mentioned in the early histories. It may have been a box similar to the ark, or a wooden image covered with plates of gold or silver. Other images were the teraphim and the golden bullocks that Jeroboam I set up at Dan and Bethel. These were images of Yahweh, since Jeroboam said of them: "Behold thy God, O Israel, that brought thee up out of the land of Egypt." The only prohibition of images that is found in the early legislation is that of "molten gods" in Ex. 20: 23; 34: 17.

c. Holy Times. The belief that Yahweh should be worshiped in certain holy places had for its counterpart the belief that He should be worshiped at certain holy times. These were His office-hours, so to speak, when He was more apt to be found than at other times. The early Hebrew feasts were partly survivals from primitive Semitic times, partly institutions of the Mosaic age, and partly acquisitions from the Canaanites. They may be grouped under the following heads:

1. *Astronomical Holy Days.* The most important of these in early times were the New Moons. These were observed with rest from field-work and from trade, and with family sacrificial meals. They were also occasions for gatherings at sanctuaries.[35] With them are constantly associated Sabbaths, in the formula "New Moons and Sabbaths." The Sabbath was probably originally a lunar holy day, as among the Babylonians, falling on the seventh, fourteenth, twenty-first, and twenty-eighth days of the lunar month. It was appropriated by Yahweh, and was made to come every seventh day irrespective of the moon's phases to cut it loose from its old associations with moon-worship.[36]

2. *Pastoral Holy Days.* Here belong the Passover, a primitive Semitic spring festival of sacrifice of first-born animals, which Moses retained on account of its coincidence with the exodus;[37] also the Feast of Sheep-Shearing;[38] and the three annual Pilgrimage Feasts, which seem to have originated in the nomadic period.[39]

3. *Agricultural Holy Days.* These arose after the conquest of Canaan, and were borrowed from the cult of the Canaanite ba'als. They were Unleavened Bread, which consisted in eating cakes of new grain baked without yeast in the month Abib;[40] Feast of Weeks, celebrated seven weeks after the sickle was first put to the early

[35] E, I Sam. 20: 5a, 18, 24, 27, 34; Pr, II Ki. 4: 23; Hos. 2: 11; Am. 8: 5; Isa. 1: 13.

[36] J, Ex. 34: 21; II Ki. 11: 5, 7; E, Ex. 20: 8-11; 23: 12; Pr, II Ki. 4: 23.

[37] J, Ex. 3: 18b; 12: 21-23, 25-27, 31, 32; 34: 25, 26b; E, Ex. 3: 12b; 5: 1, 3; 23: 18, 19b.

[38] J, I Sam. 25: 2-11, 36a; II Sam. 13: 23-25.

[39] J, Ex. 34: 23, 24; E, Ex. 23: 14, 17; I Sam. 1: 3a, 19, 21; 2: 19b, 20b.

[40] J, Ex. 12: 34, 39; 13: 3-10; 34: 18; E, Ex. 23: 15a.

harvest;[41] and Feast of Ingathering, observed in the autumn when all the crops had been gathered in.[42]

4. *Sabbatical Year*. The Sabbatical Year, in which fields were allowed to lie fallow, and the natural increase was left for the poor, was known as early as the Book of the Covenant.[43]

d. Rites on Entering a Holy Place. Before entering a sanctuary the worshiper purified himself from ceremonial "uncleanness." In earliest times he then removed his garments, because the primitive Semites went naked, and religious conservatism retained this as the proper condition for worship. Thus Saul stripped off his garments when he prophesied and lay all night naked.[44] In later times this was felt to be indecent, and the so-called "sackcloth," a primitive loin cloth, was worn as the nearest approach to nakedness.[45] Still later only sandals were removed as a conventional substitute for stripping.[46]

In singular contrast to the custom of stripping the body on entering a sanctuary was the practice of covering the head. Thus Moses hid his face before entering the holy ground at Sinai, and Elijah wrapped his face in his mantle as he stood at the door of the cave in Horeb. The reason for this act was to protect oneself from death by inadvertently gazing upon Yahweh as one entered his abode.[47]

The worshiper then danced around the standing stone or other sacred object. Thus the people danced around the golden bullock that they had made to represent Yahweh, the daughters of Shiloh danced at the annual feast of

---

[41] J, Ex. 34: 22a, 26; E, Ex. 23: 16a, 19a.

[42] J, Ex. 34: 22b; Jud. 21: 19a; I Ki. 8: 2; E, Ex. 23: 16b.

[43] E, Ex. 23: 10-11.

[44] E, I Sam. 19: 24; J, II Ki. 22: 11, 19b; Pr, I Ki. 21: 27a; II Ki. 18: 37; 19: 1a.

[45] E, II Ki. 6: 30b; Pr, I Ki. 21: 27b; II Ki. 19: 1-2a.

[46] J, Ex. 3: 5; Josh. 5:15.

[47] E, Ex. 3: 6b; Pr, I Ki. 19: 13a.

Yahweh, and David danced with all his might before the ark, girt only with a linen loin cloth. Even the Hebrew word ḥāg, "feast," meant originally "a circular dance." As civilization advanced these primitive dances became solemn and stately processionals, accompanied with music and song instead of shouting.[48]

If all went well thus far, the worshiper then drew near and ventured to stroke or kiss the sacred object. The phrase which our version generally translates "entreat the favour of Yahweh" means literally "stroke the face of Yahweh." According to Hosea, the people kissed the golden bullocks at Bethel and Dan, and the worshipers of the Tyrian ba'al kissed his image.[49]

e. Sacrifices. All the rites described thus far were only preliminary to that act which for the ancient Hebrew was the essence of worship, namely, the slaughter of an animal as a sacrifice. "None shall appear before me empty," that is, "without a victim," says the Book of the Covenant; and the Deuteronomic Decalogue paraphrases this by saying: "Thou shalt not invoke the name of Yahweh, thy God, for nothing" (authorized version: "Thou shalt not take the name of the Lord, thy God, in vain").[50] The primitive conception of sacrifice was a meal, in which the worshiper partook, and thus sealed his communion with his God. This appears from the ancient Hebrew name for sacrifice, *leḥem ĕlôhîm,* "food of deity," from the expression "smelled the sweet savour," used of God in connection with sacrifice, and from the polemic of later teachers against this conception of sacrifice.[51]

The only kinds of animals sacrificed were "clean" domestic animals, and these must be free from every

48 J, Jud. 21: 21a, 23a; II Sam. 6: 14a, 16, 20b, 21; E, Ex. 15: 20; 32: 19.

49 Pr, I Ki. 19: 18c; Hos. 13: 2.

50 J, Ex. 34: 20c; E, Ex. 23: 15b; 20: 7; Deut. 5: 11; 16: 16b-17.

51 Lev. 21: 8; Gen. 8: 21; Psa. 50: 12f.

imperfection. Originally every slaughter was at the same time a sacrifice, so that there is only one word in the Hebrew language for these two ideas. Every animal killed for food must be brought to one of the numerous local sanctuaries and there have its blood poured out ritually at the altar. Only two varieties of sacrifice were known to the ancient Hebrews, the '*ôlāh*, or "burnt offering," which was wholly consumed on the altar,[52] and the *zebaḥ* or *shelem*, the "sacrifice" or "peace offering," which was partly burned on the altar and partly eaten by the worshipers in a sacrificial meal.[53] The blood of sacrifices must not be eaten, but must be poured out as a libation to Yahweh,[54] hence the prohibition of eating animals that had died accidentally, because their blood had not been offered ritually.[55] The fat also must not be eaten, but must be burned on the altar.[56] The firstborn of all "clean" domestic animals must be sacrificed to Yahweh on the eighth day after birth, a provision which, of course, implied a multiplicity of sanctuaries.[57]

Firstborn children also were undoubtably sacrificed to Yahweh in early times.[58] Archæology shows that this custom did not disappear from the Hebrews until after the Exile. Melek (Molech), "King," was one of the titles of Yahweh, and child-sacrifice to Him under this name is still forbidden by the latest codes.[59] Nevertheless, in prophetic circles opposition to this practice arose at an early

[52] J. Gen. 8: 20b; 15: 9-11, etc.; E, Gen. 22: 2, 3, 6-8, 13; Ex. 18: 12; 20: 24; 24: 5; 32: 6, etc.

[53] J, Ex. 10: 25; 34: 25, etc.; E, Gen. 31: 54; 46: 1; Ex. 18: 12; 20: 24, etc.

[54] J, I Sam. 14: 31b-33a.

[55] E, Ex. 22: 31.

[56] E, I Sam. 2: 15-17.

[57] J, Gen. 4: 4, 7; Ex. 13: 12b, 13a, 15b; 34: 19b, 20a; Jud. 5: 2a; E, Ex. 22: 30.

[58] J, Ex. 34: 19a; E, Ex. 22: 29b.

[59] II Ki. 16: 3; II Chr. 28: 3; Mic. 6: 7; Jer. 7: 31; 19: 5; 32: 35; Ezek. 20: 24-26, 31; Lev. 18: 21; 20: 2-5; II Ki. 23: 10.

date.[60] Sacrifice of adults in times of special need was also known. Jephthah offered up his daughter in fulfilment of a vow; and Hiel the Bethelite devoted his oldest son when he laid the foundations of Jericho, and his youngest son when he set up the gates.[61] The *herem,* or "ban," in accordance with which the Hebrews vowed utterly to destroy the people of a city if Yahweh gave them victory, did not differ essentially from human sacrifice.[62]

The vegetable offerings that Yahweh required were appropriated from the agricultural ritual of the Canaanites. They consisted of first-fruits,[63] loaves of bread,[64] meal,[65] libations of wine and oil.[66] Since these were borrowed from the ba'als of Canaan, they were regarded as less acceptable to Yahweh than the original bloody sacrifices of the desert.[67]

f. Prayer. Our modern conception of the laws of nature was unknown to the ancient Israelite. In every phenomenon he saw the direct activity of Yahweh, and he believed that whatever Yahweh chose to do He could accomplish. "Is anything too hard for Yahweh?" he said; or, "There is no restraint to Yahweh to save by many or by few";[68] accordingly, he felt no hesitation in asking Yahweh for anything that he desired. Thought and conversation habitually cast themselves into the form of prayer. As in the modern Orient, ejaculations such as "God forbid," "God bless thee," "As Yahweh liveth," "Peace be unto thee," and attestations of statements by oaths were constantly upon the lips of the ancient Hebrews.

[60] E, Gen. 22: 1-13.
[61] J, Jud. 11: 31, 39; E, I Ki. 16: 34.
[62] J, Num. 21: 1-3; I Sam. 15: 33; II Sam. 21: 6b, 9b, 14b.
[63] J, Gen. 4: 3, 5; E, Ex. 22: 29a.
[64] J, II Ki. 23: 9b; E, I Sam. 21: 3, 4a, 6.
[65] J, Jud. 6: 18-21; 13: 19, 23.
[66] J, Gen. 35: 14; E, Gen. 28: 18b.
[67] J, Gen. 4: 4-5.
[68] J, Gen. 18: 14; Num. 11: 23; I Sam. 14: 6.

Prayer was offered to Yahweh whenever there was need of His help;[69] nevertheless, the feeling was strong that it was more likely to be answered if it were offered at a sanctuary, at one of the appointed times of worship.[70] In prayer the palms of the hands were extended upward. This is the origin of the gesture frequently mentioned in the Old Testament "spread out the hands." It was the same gesture that we see in the Babylonian and Egyptian monuments, and was a conventional substitute for "stroking the face" of the primitive fetish or idol.[71] In early times prayer was always uttered in a loud voice, from the naïve feeling that it would be better heard by Yahweh. Silent prayer was so unusual that Eli thought Hannah was drunk when he saw her lips move and heard no sound.[72]

The prayers of this period may be divided into seven main classes:

1. *Invocations.* On entering the sanctuary it was customary to cry out the name of Yahweh to give warning of one's approach, lest, coming upon Him unexpectedly, one might be slain for one's temerity. Accordingly, the technical expression for worship is "call out [not call upon] the name of Yahweh."[73]

2. *Declarations.* These consisted either in profession of one's righteousness that entitled one to the divine favour,[74] or else in confession of one's sin.[75]

[69] E, Gen. 21: 16; 32:11; J, Gen. 24: 12; 48: 15f.; Ex. 3: 7; II Sam. 15: 8; II Ki. 5: 17.

[70] J, Ex. 8: 29a, 30; 9: 29, 33; 10: 18a; II Sam. 15: 7; Jud. 11: 11; E, I Sam. 1: 10, 26; 7: 5-9; 10: 17-22; Ex. 33: 7.

[71] J, Ex. 9: 29b, 33b.

[72] E, I Sam. 1: 12, 13, 15, 16.

[73] J, Gen. 4: 26; 12: 8c; 13: 4b; 21: 33b; 26: 25b; Ex. 34: 5b; I Ki. 8: 12, 13; E, Ex. 20: 7; Pr, II Ki. 19: 15.

[74] J, Gen. 4: 9b; Num. 16: 15b; E, Gen. 20: 4, 5; I Sam. 3: 4, 10; Pr, II Ki. 20: 3a.

[75] J, Ex. 9: 27; 10: 16; I Sam. 15: 24, 30a; II Sam. 12: 13a; 24: 10a, 17b; E, Num. 21: 7; I Sam. 7: 6b; 12: 10a.

3. *Petitions for One's Self.* Among these were petitions for forgiveness,[76] for deliverance from distress,[77] for guidance,[78] for blessings,[79] and for the gift of children.[80] Oaths were petitions that evil might befall one's self if one did not speak the truth.[81]

4. *Petitions Concerning Others.* These included prayers that others might be delivered from distress,[82] or that particular blessings might be bestowed upon them.[83] Prayers for the defeat of enemies were frequent,[84] and curses were prayers that evil might fall upon others.[85]

5. *Promissory Prayers.* Vows were prayers accompanied with promises to do something, if one's petition were granted.[86] The ban was a vow to slay the people in a city, if Yahweh granted victory to Israel.[87]

6. *Argumentative Prayers.* In the supplications of this period we find no trace of submission of one's will to God. Instead of the Christian attitude, "not my will but thine be done," we find rather the heathen determination to

76 J, I Sam. 15: 25; II Sam. 24: 10b.
77 J, Gen. 4: 13, 14; 19: 18-20; Ex. 3: 7, 9a; 4: 1, 10; Num. 11: 11-13, 15; Jud. 15: 18; I Sam. 26: 24; E, Ex. 3: 11; 14: 10b; Num. 11: 14; I Sam. 16: 2a; II Ki. 13: 4a.
78 J, Gen. 24: 12-14, 42-44; Ex. 33: 12b, 13; Jud. 6: 15, 17, 18; 13: 8; E, Ex. 3: 13; Jud. 6: 36, 37, 39.
79 J, Gen. 32: 26; I Ki. 3: 11b; E, I Sam. 12: 18a; Pr, I Ki. 18: 36, 37; II Ki. 20: 11.
80 J, Gen. 15: 3; 25: 21a; 29: 31-33; 30: 6, 24; E, Gen. 15: 2; 30: 17b, 22b; I Sam. 1: 11, 17, 20b; II Sam. 7: 25-29.
81 J, Gen. 24: 2-4, 8a, 9, 37, 39, 41; 47: 29b, 31; 50: 5, 6, etc.; E, Gen. 25: 33; 50: 25, etc.
82 J, Gen. 18: 23-25, 27-32; Ex. 5: 22, 23; 33: 15, 16; 34: 9, etc.; E, Gen. 20: 7b, 17; 43: 14; Ex. 32: 31; Num. 12: 13; 21: 7b, etc.
83 J, Gen. 9: 26, 27; 24: 60, etc.; E, Gen. 27: 7b, 10b, 23, 28, 29b, 35b-38, 39b, 40; 31: 55; 48: 15-20, etc.
84 J, Num. 16: 15a; Jud. 5: 31a; 16: 28; II Sam. 15: 31; I Ki. 3: 11c; Pr, II Ki. 1: 10, 12; 6: 18a.
85 J, Gen. 9: 24, 25; 12: 3; 27: 29c, etc.; E, Gen. 27: 12, 13; Ex. 21: 17; 22: 28; Num. 22: 12; 23: 7, 8, 11, 13, 25; 24: 9b, etc.
86 J, Jud. 11: 11b, 30, 31; II Sam. 15: 7, 8a; E, Gen. 28: 20, 21a, 22b; 31: 13c; Jud. 17: 2a, 3b; I Sam. 1: 11; 12: 10b.
87 J, Num. 21: 1, 2.

force, or to wheedle God into granting one's request, *fatigare deos,* as the Romans called it. All sorts of arguments were addressed to Yahweh to convince Him that His justice or His reputation would be jeopardized if He did not do a particular thing. The expression commonly translated by our version "entreat the Lord" means literally "hammer away at Yahweh."[88]

7. *Thanksgivings.* Thanks for mercies received were not so common as petitions in the early period, still they were not wholly lacking. There were thanks for personal blessings, such as guidance and the gift of children, and thanks for national victories over enemies.[89]

C. *Yahweh's Moral Requirements*

As we have just seen, Yahweh's demands of His people in the early period were mainly ceremonial, still morality also was a part of His service. Everything that was customary was right, and was protected by a divine sanction. The result was that many social usages that we should consider ethically indifferent were regarded as religious duties, while other matters that seem to us of the highest importance were ignored.

I. *Universal Human Rights*

The doctrine of the Declaration of Independence "That all men are created equal; that they are endowed by their Creator with certain unalienable rights; that among these are life, liberty, and the pursuit of happiness," is a modern conception that rests upon the teaching of Jesus, that God is the Father of all men, and that all men are brothers. Of this broad conception no trace is found in the Old Testament. "Brother" and "neighbour" meant

88 J, Gen. 18: 23-33; 19: 19; Josh. 7: 9; E, Gen. 20: 4b.
89 J, Gen. 16: 13; 19: 19; 24: 26, 27, 48, 52; 29: 35; Ex. 15: 1-18; 18: 10; I Sam. 25: 32, 39a; I Ki. 1: 47b, 48; 3: 6a, 7a; E, II Sam. 7: 18-21.

always "fellow-Israelite." Non-Israelites stood outside
of the pale of moral obligation.

Yahweh commanded Israel to exterminate the inhabitants of Canaan, and on capturing cities they executed
this order with grim thoroughness.[90] Moses commanded
to "blot out the remembrance of Amalek from under
heaven," and Samuel brought Saul the message: "Go
and smite Amalek, and utterly destroy all that they have,
and spare them not, but slay both man and woman, infant
and suckling."[91] David attempted to slay every male of
the Edomites.[92] "He put the prisoners of the Ammonites
at work with saws, and harrows of iron, and axes of iron,
and made them toil in the brickkiln."[93] The Moabites "he
made to lie down on the ground, and measured two lines
to put to death, and one full line to keep alive."[94] By the
time of Elisha, however, a humaner treatment of prisoners seems to have become usual. Elisha said to Jehoram,
"Wouldst thou smite those whom thou hast taken captive
with thy sword and with thy bow?"[95] In the land of conquered enemies they razed every city, felled every fruit
tree, stopped every spring, and covered every good field
with stones.[96]

The only foreigners who were treated with kindness
were the Kenites. These were the original worshipers of
Yahweh at Sinai, who had accompanied Israel into the
land of Canaan. They were united in the bond of a common religion; and, therefore, were treated as "brothers."[97]

Aliens residing in the land of Israel had no legal rights.

[90] See note 17.
[91] J, I Sam. 15: 1-5, 13-19; E, Ex. 17: 14, 16; Deut. 25: 17-19.
[92] J, II Sam. 8: 13, 14a; I Ki. 11: 15, 16.
[93] J, II Sam. 12: 31.
[94] J, II Sam. 8: 2.
[95] Pr, II Ki. 6: 21-23.
[96] E, II Ki. 3: 19, 25.
[97] J, Num. 10: 29-32; I Sam. 15: 6; E, II Ki. 10: 15, 16.

Even as late a code as Deuteronomy enacts that carrion, which may not be eaten by an Israelite, may be sold to an alien; debts, which may not be exacted of an Israelite, may be exacted of an alien; and interest, which may not be taken of an Israelite, may be taken of an alien.[98] Still, the Book of the Covenant says: "An alien shalt thou not wrong, neither shalt thou oppress him, for ye were aliens in the land of Egypt."[99]

Hebrew slaves were denied civil privileges, although they were guarded from gross injustice. Women and children also did not possess status as citizens. In general we may say that full rights of life, liberty, and the pursuit of happiness belonged only to free-born male Israelites.

II. *Rights of All Israelites*

a. Rights of Life. The postulate of early Hebrew legislation is: "Whoso sheddeth man's blood, by man shall his blood be shed." Accordingly, the Book of the Covenant enacts: "He that smiteth a man so that he dieth shall surely be put to death."[100] In accordance with the primitive Semitic principle of blood revenge, the duty of executing sentence upon the man-slayer rested upon the next of kin.[101] In case of accidental homicide, the slayer might flee to the nearest altar, and there be safe from the avenger of blood.[102] If, however, it could be shown that the murder was deliberate, the law prescribed, "Thou shalt take him from my altar that he may die."[103] If man did not inflict the penalty, the blood cried from the earth

98 J, Gen. 19: 9a; Deut. 14:21a; 15: 3; 23: 20.
99 E, Ex. 22: 21; 23: 9.
100 E, Ex. 21: 12, 23.
101 J, Jud. 8: 18-21; II Sam. 2: 18-23; 3: 22-27, 30; 14: 7a, 11; 21: 4, 5; Deut. 19: 6, 12; Num. 35: 12; Josh. 20: 5, 9.
102 J, I Ki. 1: 50, 51; 2: 28b, 29, 30b, 31; II Ki. 11: 15; E, Ex. 21: 13, 14.
103 J, 34: 26, 30; 49: 5-7; II Sam. 3: 28, 37-39; 4: 5-12; E, Ex. 20: 13; 21: 14.

to Yahweh, and he avenged it.[104] If a slave was killed by his master, the master was punished, but not with death. Even this did not happen if the slave lingered a day or two after he was injured.[105] Infanticide, and the sacrifice of children to Yahweh, were not punishable.[106] If one man's ox gored another man, the owner was not punished, unless it could be shown that he had known that the ox was dangerous and had failed to keep it in. If an ox gored a slave, the owner of the ox paid thirty shekels to the owner of the slave.[107]

Permanent bodily injuries were punished by the *lex talionis,* or tit-for-tat rule, "eye for eye, tooth for tooth, hand for hand, foot for foot, burning for burning, wound for wound, stripe for stripe."[108] Temporary bodily injuries were made good by paying the loss of time and the doctor's bill of the victim.[109] Permanent bodily injuries to a slave were compensated by giving him freedom.[110]

b. Rights of Liberty. Slavery was an established institution, and no moral objections were raised against it. Slaves were either foreign captives of war, foreigners acquired by purchase, Hebrews born in slavery, or Hebrews enslaved for debt. These, of course, enjoyed no rights of liberty. Free-born Israelites, however, were protected in their freedom. Kidnapping a freeman to sell him as a slave was punishable with death.[111]

c. Rights of Property.—1. *Theft of Real Estate.* Among the Bedawy Arabs there is no private ownership of land. A spring with the adjacent territory is the prop-

104 J, Gen. 4: 8-11.
105 E, Ex. 21:20-21.
106 E, Ex. 1: 17; Ezek. 16: 4, 5; see notes 58-61.
107 E, Ex. 21: 28-32.
108 J, Jud. 1: 6-7; 15: 11b; E, Ex. 21: 24, 25; Deut. 19: 21; Lev. 24: 19-20.
109 E, Ex. 21: 18, 19, 22.
110 E, Ex. 21: 26-27.
111 J, Gen. 37: 27a, 28b; E, Ex. 21: 16; Deut. 24: 7.

erty of a clan, and all members of the clan have rights of
water and of grazing in common. This was doubtless the
custom also among the nomadic Hebrews. After the conquest of Canaan this method was continued by many
clans. There was private ownership only of houses in villages, which corresponded to the primitive tents, while
the fields that lay about the village were the common
property of the inhabitants. At stated intervals lots were
drawn to determine which fields individuals should cultivate for a certain period. Gradually, however, this system
gave way in most places to private ownership of land.
Only landowners enjoyed full citizenship, so that the re-
tention of land in the family was a matter of the highest
importance. "Yahweh forbid it to me," said Naboth to
Ahab, "that I should give the inheritance of my fathers
unto thee."[112] Rights of real estate, accordingly, were sa-
credly guarded. Ahab's seizure of Naboth's vineyard was
denounced by Elijah; and Deuteronomy, doubtless following older legislation, enacts: "Thou shalt not remove
thy neighbour's landmark, which they of old time have
set"; "Cursed be he that removeth his neighbour's landmark."[113]

Theft of crops was forbidden, but one was permitted to
eat fruit or grain while passing through an orchard or
field.[114] Damage to crops by letting animals loose must be
compensated with an equal amount from one's own
crops.[115] Damage through starting fire must be made good
in a similar manner.[116]

2. *Theft of Personal Property.* The general commandment, "Thou shalt not steal," first appears in the Deuteronomic Decalogue, still there is abundant evidence that

112 Pr, I Ki. 21: 3.
113 Deut. 19:14; 27: 17; Pr, I Ki. 21: 17-19.
114 Deut. 23: 24-25.
115 E, Ex. 22: 5.
116 E, Ex. 22: 6.

theft of all sorts was condemned by the early Hebrew religion.[117] A special law in regard to burglary provided that a man breaking into a house might be killed in the nighttime, but not in the daytime.[118] If a man stole another's animal, and killed it or sold it, he must pay five oxen for an ox and four sheep for a sheep. If the animal was found alive in his hand, he must restore it, and give another animal in addition.[119]

3. *Injuries to Personal Property.* If one killed another's animal, either intentionally or accidentally, one must give an equally good animal in its place. If one injured an animal, one must make good the damage.[120] If one left a pit open, and an animal fell into it, one must pay the owner the value of the animal, and keep it for one's self. If one man's ox gored another man's ox, they must sell both the living and the dead ox, and divide the proceeds.[121]

4. *Buyer and Seller.* Deuteronomy and the Holiness Code, both in dependence upon ancient custom, enact: "Thou shalt not have in thy bag diverse weights, a great and a small. Thou shalt not have in thy house diverse measures, a great and a small. A perfect and a just weight shalt thou have, a perfect and a just measure shalt thou have.''[122]

5. *Employer and Employee.* Deuteronomy and the Holiness Code, again in dependence upon ancient custom, both prescribe that the wages of a hired man must not be withheld, but must be paid at the end of each day's work.[123]

6. *Principal and Agent.* If one man entrusted another with money, goods, or animals, and these were stolen, or

117 J, Gen. 44: 8b, 9; E, Gen. 31: 19b, 30b, 32; Ex. 22: 7b, 9b.
118 E, Ex. 22: 2-3.
119 E, Ex. 22: 1, 4.
120 Lev. 24: 18.
121 E, Ex. 21: 33-36.
122 Deut. 25: 13-16; Lev. 19: 35, 36.
123 Deut. 24: 14, 15; Lev. 19:13b.

strayed away and could not be found, the agent was required to "come before God," that is, go to a sanctuary, and there take oath that he had not stolen the principal's property. If he could do this, he was freed from responsibility; if he could not do it, he was regarded as the thief, and must pay double. If the animal entrusted to a keeper was killed by a wild beast, the agent might show the remains of the animal, and was cleared from accountability.[124]

7. *Lender and Borrower.* If a man borrowed anything from another, and it was lost or injured, he was required to make it good; but if the owner was present at the time of the loss, he was not required to make restitution. If the thing was hired, the owner was required to take the risk.[125]

8. *Creditor and Debtor.* In general it was assumed that money borrowed must be repaid, because failure to do so would be a form of theft. The Hebrew legislation, however, contained a number of humane provisions designed to protect the poor debtor from unnecessary rapacity on the part of the creditor. The Book of the Covenant says that, if the outer garment is taken as a pledge, it must be returned at nightfall, in order that the debtor may have something warm to sleep in. Deuteronomy adds that the mill or the millstone must not be taken in pledge, and that the creditor must not go into the house to select his own pledge, but must take what the debtor brings out to him.[126] The taking of interest from a fellow Hebrew was also forbidden, but there is no evidence that this law was ever obeyed.[127] Outlawing of debts at the end of seven years is an institution that probably did not exist before Deuteronomy.[128]

124 E, Ex. 22: 7-13.
125 E, Ex. 22: 14-15.
126 E, Ex. 22: 26-27; Deut. 24: 6, 10-13.
127 E, Ex. 22: 25; Deut. 23: 19-20a; Lev. 25: 35-37.
128 Deut. 15: 1-3.

These meager provisions were inadequate to protect the poor from great hardships. In times of war or of famine the peasants were compelled to borrow to escape starvation. The loans were secured by mortgages on communal or private lands as the case might be. The interest, which was taken from agricultural produce, was exorbitant, and borrowers were seldom able to repay the principal. They kept on borrowing until their security was exhausted, then the money-lenders foreclosed the mortgages and seized the farms.[129] People who had no land and were compelled to borrow mortgaged first their children, and then themselves; and if they failed to pay, they were sold to recover trifling sums of money.[130] Against such abuses the command is aimed: "Ye shall not afflict any widow or fatherless child.[131]

d. Rights of Truth.—1. *Rights of Reputation.* False witness was forbidden, and was punished by inflicting upon the offender the same penalty that he had tried to fix upon his neighbor. In order to guard against perjury it was prescribed that a man should not be convicted of a crime except on the testimony of two witnesses.[132] Slander and gossip also were forbidden.[133]

2. *Rights of Contract.* When a man pledged himself to do a particular thing, he was required to keep his promise. Agreements of every sort were confirmed with an oath, that is, a prayer to Yahweh to punish the one who did not keep his promise. Accordingly, breach of contract was a religious as well as a civil offense.[134]

129 Am. 2: 7-8; 5: 11; Hos. 5: 10; Isa. 5: 8; Mic. 2: 1-2, 8.
130 Am. 2: 6-8; 8: 6; Deut. 15: 12; II Ki. 4: 1.
131 E, Ex. 22: 22-24; Deut. 24: 17; 27: 19.
132 E, Ex. 23: 1b; 20: 16; Deut. 5: 20; Lev. 19: 16b; Deut. 17: 6-7; 19:15; I Ki. 21: 9b-10.
133 E, Ex. 23: 1a; Lev. 19: 16a.
134 J, Gen. 26: 28b-31; 31: 44, 46b, 49; Josh. 9: 6, 7, 11b, 14, 15; I Sam. 11: 1; I Ki. 5: 12b; II Ki. 11: 4b; E, Gen. 21: 23-32; 31: 53, 54; I Sam. 18: 3, 20: 8a, 14-17, 23, 42; 23: 18; I Ki. 20: 34. See also note 81.

3. *Rights of Knowledge.* Apart from reputation and contracts, rights of truth were scarcely recognized among the ancient Hebrews. They lied on all occasions, unless they were put on oath; and the early literature narrates instances of deceit without condemnation, and with delight in the cleverness of the successful liar.[135]

e. Rights of Kindness.—1. *Good Will.* Not merely was one required to abstain from injuring a fellow Israelite, one was also required to show positive virtues of friendliness and helpfulness. These duties, which the primitive Semite had recognized only in relation to the clan, the religion of Yahweh extended to the entire nation. All Israelites were to be regarded as "brothers" and "neighbours," and the proper attitude toward them was summed up in the phrase "kindness and fidelity." It was called "the kindness of God," or "of Yahweh," because it was divinely required.[136]

2. *Peaceableness.* "And Abram said unto Lot, Let there be no strife, I pray thee, between me and thee, and between my herdmen and thy herdmen, for we be brethren."[137]

3. *Forgiveness of Injuries.* It was considered magnanimous to pardon a wrong done to one's self, and the taking of revenge upon an enemy was condemned as a sin against Yahweh. Thus Joseph forgave the crime committed against him by his brothers, and David rejoiced that he had been withheld from slaying Naboth for his insult. He also spared Saul's life when he had the opportunity to kill him, and thus elicited from Saul the comment, "Thou art more righteous than I, for thou hast

[135] J, Gen. 12: 11-16; 26: 7, 9; 27: 18b-20, 24; 38: 14; Josh. 2: 4b; I Sam. 27: 10-12; 28: 2; 29: 8; II Sam. 15: 33, 34; 16: 16-19; 17: 18-20; 19: 25-27a, 29; E, Gen. 20: 2a, 5, 12, 13; 27: 7b-18a; 29: 25; 31: 35; 37: 31, 32; I Sam. 16: 2, 5; 20: 6a, 28; 21: 1b, 2.

[136] J, Gen. 24: 49; 47: 29.

[137] J, Gen. 13: 8.

rendered unto me good, whereas I have rendered unto thee evil.'' David also refused to kill Shimei when he cursed him, and spared his life after he was restored to power.[138] The Book of the Covenant enacts: ''If thou meet thine enemy's ox or his ass going astray, thou shalt surely bring it back to him again. If thou see the ass of him that hateth thee lying under his burden, thou shalt forbear to leave him, thou shalt surely release it with him.''[139] It is needless to say that this ideal treatment of enemies was not realized in the majority of cases.

4. *Friendship.* Love and loyalty toward friends were greatly admired. The friendship between David and Jonathan is held up in the Book of Samuel as a model. Jonathan loved David, in spite of the fact that he knew that David would deprive him of the throne. He shielded David from the anger of Saul at the risk of his own life. David's appreciation of this friendship was shown in his lament over Jonathan, where he said: ''I am distressed for thee, my brother Jonathan; very pleasant hast thou been unto me; thy love to me was wonderful, passing the love of women.[140]

5. *Gratitude.* Gratitude for favours received was highly commended, and ingratitude was condemned as the basest sort of conduct. David showed his gratitude to Jonathan by befriending his son, and his gratitude toward Barzillai the Gileadite who had helped him in his flight from Absalom in a similar way. Jotham scored the people of Shechem for their ingratitude to Gideon, and Joab blamed David for ingratitude to his followers in mourning for Absalom.[141]

6. *Fidelity.* Faithfulness in friends toward one an-

138 J, Gen. 50: 21; II Sam. 2: 24-28; 18: 16; 19: 16-23a; I Ki. 1: 52-53; E, Gen. 50:17b, 19.
139 E, Ex. 23: 4-5.
140 I Sam. 18-20; II Sam. 1: 26.
141 J, II Sam. 19: 5-8, 28-33, 37-40; I Ki. 2: 7; E, Jud. 9: 16-20.

other, and in servants toward their masters, were regarded as high virtues.[142]

7. *Hospitality.* Entertaining strangers was a duty inherited from the nomadic period. The patriarchs are represented as always eager to receive guests. The obligation of the host went so far that Lot was constrained to give up his two daughters to save his guests from assault.[143]

8. *Generosity.* Liberality on the part of the rich toward the poor was a primitive Bedawy virtue that was cherished by the later Hebrews; in fact, most of the words for "prince," or "noble," mean primarily "generous." When the wealthy Nabal made a feast at the time of his sheep-shearing and refused to give anything to David and his men, this was considered most churlish behavior. Solomon showed a truly royal disposition by giving the Queen of Sheba "all her desire, whatsoever she asked, besides that which Solomon gave her of his royal bounty." Generosity toward the poor was considered a religious duty, but the only specific provision for relief of poverty in the early legislation is the demand in the Book of the Covenant that the natural produce of land lying fallow every seventh year shall be left for the poor. Deuteronomy and the Holiness Code both enact that the gleanings of fields and of orchards are to be left for the poor, so that it is probable that here also we have ancient legislation.[144]

III. *Rights Derived from Family Relations*

a. Degrees of Kinship in Marriage. Marriage with

[142] See note 136.

[143] J, Gen. 18: 3-8, 16; 19: 1b-3, 8; 24: 25, 31; Ex. 2: 20; Jud. 13: 15; 19: 15b, 17-24; I Sam. 28: 22-24; II Sam. 16: 1, 2; 17: 27-29; Pr, I Ki. 13: 11-14, 19, 23.

[144] J, I Sam. 25: 2-13; I Ki. 10: 13; E, Ex. 23: 10f.; Deut. 24: 19-22; Lev. 19: 9-10; 23: 22.

mother, stepmother, own sister, daughter, granddaughter, and daughter-in-law, was forbidden by early legislation.[145] Marriage with a half-sister on the father's side was permitted, as among the other Semites and the Egyptians; but not with a half-sister on the mother's side—a survival from primitive matriarchal times.[146] Marriage with a sister-in-law was not forbidden, and was required in case that a brother died childless.[147] Marriage with two sisters was also permitted.[148] Marriage with a step-sister, aunt, aunt by marriage, mother-in-law, step-daughter, and step-granddaughter is prohibited by the Holiness Code; but it is uncertain whether these restrictions existed in ancient times.[149] Except for the limitations just mentioned, it was considered desirable to marry the nearest kin possible in order to keep property in the family. A cousin on the father's side was regarded as the most desirable of all relations.[150]

b. Rights of the Husband.—1. *Polygamy.* Polygamy was permitted, and was in existence as late as the time of Deuteronomy; still, it was the exception, and declined in frequency during the whole period of the monarchy.[151]

2. *Concubinage.* Female slaves were habitually taken as concubines without gaining the status of wives. The slave-maid of Sarah was taken by Abraham, and the slave-maids of Leah and Rachel by Jacob, and the children of these concubines were counted as the children of the mistresses of the slaves. Yahweh rewarded Leah for

[145] J, Gen. 35: 22a; 49: 4; II Sam. 16: 21-22; 20: 3; Gen. 19: 31-36; H, Lev. 18: 6-11, 15.

[146] J, Gen. 11: 29; 12: 13; II Sam. 13: 1-22.

[147] J, Gen. 38: 8-10, 14b, 25, 26; Deut. 25: 5-10; H, Lev. 18: 16; 20: 21a.

[148] E, Gen. 29: 23, 28b; H, Lev. 18: 18.

[149] Lev. 18: 12-17.

[150] J, Gen. 24: 4, 7a, 38, 40b; E, Gen. 29: 19.

[151] J, Gen. 31: 50b; I Sam. 25: 39b-43; 27: 3b; II Sam. 2: 2; 3: 2-5; 5: 13-16; E, Gen. 29: 27, 28; I Sam. 1: 2a; Deut. 21: 15.

giving her maid cheerfully to Jacob. Free women also were taken as concubines by kings.[152]

3. *Prostitution*. Chastity before marriage, or fidelity in the marriage relation, was not required of the husband. Prostitution was a recognized institution that brought no disgrace to the women that followed it, or to the men who associated with them. Prostitutes were of two sorts, the *zônāh*, or ordinary harlot, and the *qĕdēshāh*, or "holy woman," consecrated to the service of a sanctuary.[153]

4. *The Husband's Relation to the Wife*. The regular Hebrew word for "husband" is *ba'al*, "owner." The wife was the chattel of her husband, like all the rest of his personal property. "Thou shalt not covet thy neighbour's house, thou shalt not covet thy neighbour's wife, nor his male slave, nor his female slave, nor his ox, nor his ass, nor anything that is thy neighbour's," says the Decalogue. All duties of the wife, accordingly, were regarded from the point of view of property rights.[154]

5. *Chastity in the Wife*. Absolute chastity in a betrothed girl and in a wife was required by the old Hebrew legislation. A betrothed girl that consented to seduction was stoned to death. If she was raped, she was unpunished. The man who seduced or raped the girl was punished with stoning, for violating the property rights of the man to whom the girl was betrothed.[155] Adultery in the wife was punished with death. An ancient ordeal preserved by P prescribes that, if a man suspect his wife of infidelity, he may compel her to drink the "water of bitterness" to prove or disprove her chastity.[156] The man who seduced the wife was also punished with death, for

152 J, Gen. 16: 2b-6; 30: 3b, 4, 9; II Sam. 15:16; I Ki. 1: 1-4; E, Gen. 21: 9-14; 30: 3a; Ex. 21: 7-10.
153 J, Gen. 34: 31; 38:12, 15-23; Jud. 16: 1; I Ki. 3: 16; E, Josh. 2: 1.
154 J, Gen. 3: 16b; E, Ex. 20: 17.
155 Deut. 22: 23-27.
156 J, Gen. 38: 24; 39: 7-12; Deut. 22: 22; Lev. 20: 10; Num. 5: 11-31.

destroying the property rights of the husband.[157] Rape of a married woman was punished with death, and attempted rape also was severely punished.[158]

6. *The Wife's Duty to Bear Children.* Children were intensely desired, both to continue the family, and to make offerings of food and drink for the spirits of ancestors. Childlessness was regarded as the greatest possible misfortune, and the proper blessing for a bride was, ''Be thou the mother of thousands of ten thousands.''[159] The desire for children was the chief reason for polygamy. If a wife was barren, she was regarded as failing in her duty, and the husband took a second wife, or his wife gave him her female slaves as concubines. If these means failed, a slave, or some person outside of the family, was adopted as a son, and was given the inheritance on condition that he kept up the ancestral rites.[160] If this device also failed, the nearest male relative of the deceased was required to take his widow and raise up seed for him.[161]

7. *Divorce.* A man might divorce his wife for barrenness, or for any other cause, as was customary among all the Semites. If the divorced wife married again and were redivorced, or the second husband died, the first husband was not allowed to marry her again.[162]

c. *Rights of the* Wife. In comparison with the rights of the husband the rights of the wife were very limited. She might not practice polyandry or concubinage, or ''play the harlot'' with other men. She could not demand chastity in her husband, and adultery in him was not an offense against her, but only a violation of the property rights of some other man in his daughter or his wife. She

---

157 Deut. 22: 22; Lev. 20: 10.
158 J, Gen. 39: 7-20; Jud. 19: 25-30; 20: 3b-8.
159 J, Jud. 11: 38; II Sam. 6: 22-23; E, I Sam. 1: 6-8; Pr, II Ki. 4: 14; see also note 80.
160 J, Gen. 48: 16b; E, Gen. 48: 10b, 12a.
161 See note 147.
162 Deut. 24: 1-4.

might not divorce her husband, even for adultery or extreme cruelty. The only rights that she could demand were life, food, clothing, and cohabitation.[163] Still, although the wife had few legal rights, she was usually safe in the love of her husband; and old Hebrew family life was quite as happy as modern family life. "Am I not better to thee than ten sons?" says Elkanah to Hannah, and there are many other beautiful instances of happy wedlock. In the ancient J document the wife is "a help meet for the man, bone of his bones, and flesh of his flesh. Therefore shall a man leave his father and his mother and shall cleave unto his wife."[164]

If a man divorced his wife, he was compelled to give her a bill of divorcement to protect her legal status, and she was free to marry again. If a man grew tired of his slave concubine, he could not sell her as a slave; he must either continue to treat her as a wife, or give her freedom. If a man falsely accused his wife of not being a virgin when he married her, he was beaten and fined, and not allowed ever to divorce her.[165]

d. *Rights of Parents.*—1. *Right to Kill Children.* The father had the legal right to put his child to death, if he saw fit; but naturally this right was not often exercised on account of parental love and the craving for children. Infanticide of male children was never practised, but exposure of female infants was an ancient Semitic custom that lasted among the Hebrews as late as the time of Ezekiel, and that still exists among the peasants of modern Palestine.[166] A father also had the undisputed right to offer up his child as a sacrifice to Yahweh, and an ancient law prescribed the sacrifice of the firstborn son.[167]

[163] Ex. 21: 10-11.
[164] E, I Sam. 1: 8; J, Gen. 2: 18, 23-24.
[165] E, Ex. 21: 7-8; Deut. 22: 13-19.
[166] E, Ex. 1: 17; Ezek. 16: 4-5.
[167] See notes 58-61.

2. *Right to Dispose of Children's Lives.* A father had the right to sell his children into slavery. A daughter was sold as a wife, if she were fair enough to bring the requisite price, otherwise she was sold as a concubine slave. Lot proposed to give his two daughters up to the lust of the men of Sodom to save his guests, and the old man of Gibeah made the same proposal in the case of his daughter. A father could also dedicate his daughter to be a "holy woman" in a temple, or could make a harlot of her. Samson and Samuel were dedicated to Yahweh as Nazirites before they were born. In no particular did the position of children differ from that of slaves so long as they remained under the paternal roof.[168]

If a man seduced an unbetrothed girl, his only punishment was that he must pay her father the dowry that she would have brought if she had been sold as a wife. In other words, seduction was regarded as merely an invasion of the property rights of a father in his daughter. If a daughter at the time of marriage was found not to be a virgin, she was stoned to death for having destroyed her market value for her father, and for having let herself be sold as damaged goods to her husband.[169]

3. *Rights of Reverence and Obedience.* Children were required to honor father and mother, and striking or cursing them was punishable with death. A rebellious son was to be reported to the elders of the city, and they were to stone him to death.[170]

e. *Rights of Children.* The only specified rights of children in the old Hebrew legislation were those of inheritance. In this all sons shared alike, regardless of the sta-

168 J, Gen. 19: 8; Jud. 19: 24; Jud. 13: 5, 12-14; E, I Sam. 1: 11; Deut. 23: 17-18; Lev. 19: 29.
169 J, Gen. 34: 2b, 7, 11, 19, 26, 29b, 31a; E, Ex. 22: 16-17; Deut. 22: 28-29.
170 E, Ex. 20: 12a; 21: 15, 17; Deut. 5: 16; 21: 18-21; 27: 16; Lev. 19: 3a; 20: 9.

tus of the mother. Sons of concubines and of slaves were just as legitimate children as those of wives. The sons of Jacob by the slave-maids Bilhah and Zilpah had as good standing among the tribes of Israel as the sons of Leah and Rachel. This was much more humane than the Roman law, *proles sequitur ventrem,* or the law in our own southern states, according to which the children of a slave-woman were also slaves, even though their father was the master of the slave. When a man left no sons, his daughters inherited his property, with the proviso that they should marry men of their own tribe, to prevent the possibility of property being alienated from the tribe.[171] The firstborn son received a double portion of the estate to compensate him for his obligation to keep up the ancestral cult, and with this went a special blessing of his father. It was specified also that a man might not give the birthright to a favorite son, but must give it to the firstborn, regardless of his personal preferences.[172]

f. Rights of Masters over Slaves. Slaves stood in much the same relation as children to the head of the household. They were personal property, and injury to them must be compensated to their master. They were required to be respectful and to render prompt obedience. Fidelity in slaves was commended as highly virtuous. Eliezer, the slave of Abraham, Joseph, the slave of Potiphar, Ittai, the Philistine of David's bodyguard, and many other slaves are held up by the early histories for our admiration on account of their perfect loyalty. Slaves were considered members of the household; and since they were no worse off than children, they did not feel hardship in their position.[173]

171 Pr, I Ki. 21: 1-4; P, Num. 27: 1-11; 36: 1-2; Josh. 17: 3-5.

172 J, Gen. 25: 5, 6; 27: 2, 4b, 19, 24, 25a, 31b-34; 29: 26; 43: 33a; 48: 10a, 13, 14, 17-19; 49: 3; E, Gen. 21: 10; 25: 31-34; 27: 7b, 10b, 23, 35-37; 48: 22; Deut. 21: 15-17.

173 J, Gen. 15: 2-3; 24: 1-66; E, Gen. 39: 21-23.

g. Rights of Slaves from their Masters. A Hebrew who
was enslaved for debt was to be set free in the seventh
year. If he was married when enslaved, his wife was freed
with him. If his master gave him a wife, she remained
with the master when he went out. If he preferred to remain with his master in the seventh year, he was brought
to a sanctuary, and his ear was pierced with an awl; then
he remained in permanent servitude. Hebrew women who
were enslaved were not set free in the seventh year.[174] A
master who killed his slave was punished, but not with
death. If a master injured his male or his female slave
permanently, he was obliged to set him or her free. A
runaway slave was not to be returned to his master.[175]

IV. *Rights Derived from Governmental Relations*

a. Rights of Rulers.—1. *Rulers are Ordained by God.*
According to the E document of the Hexateuch, judges
and officers were appointed by Moses at the command of
Yahweh.[176] According to both J and E, the "judges," or
"dictators," were raised up by Yahweh and inspired by
His Spirit to deliver Israel.[177] The first kings were chosen
and anointed by prophets, and one of their standing titles
was "Yahweh's Anointed."[178]

2. *Functions of Rulers.* The early elders and judges had
no legislative functions, but only judicial and executive.
They decided cases on the basis of the consuetudinary
rights and duties that have been described in the preceding sections, and they executed judgment upon the offender; but they made no new law, except, as in English

174 E, Ex. 21: 2-11.
175 E, Ex. 21: 20, 21, 26, 27; Deut. 23: 15-16.
176 E, Ex. 18: 21-26; 24: 14b; Num. 11: 16-17.
177 J, Jud. 5: 12b; 6: 14-16; 10: 1-3; 12: 8-13; 13: 5c.
178 J, I Sam. 9: 15-17, 20-21; 10: 1; 28: 17; II Sam. 6: 21b; E, I Sam.
8: 4, 5, 19-22; 16: 1-13; 25: 30; Pr, I Ki. 12: 21-24; 14: 2b; 19: 15-16; II
Ki. 8: 13.

common law, that their decisions constituted precedents. They also had the right to call out their clansmen to war, and were the commanders of their respective contingents. The only lawmaking power possessed by the king was that of imposing taxes, and in this apparently he had to gain the consent of the elders. In other matters he was bound to conform to the custom of the nation. He was the supreme judge, and his decision was the court of last appeal. He had also the rights of declaring war, and of calling out both the standing army and the militia, and he was the commander-in-chief of the monarchy. At first the prerogatives of the kings were carefully guarded. Saul had little more authority than one of the "judges."[179] The early kings, before they ascended the throne, were compelled to make a covenant with the elders of the tribes to respect the common law; and violation of this agreement was regarded as just cause for revolt.[180] The old communal government at first remained unchanged. and the elders themselves often served as lower officials of the king. Custom and public opinion put a wholesome restraint upon royal despotism. Prophets could rebuke and oppose the king without fear of violence;[181] and Ahab's hesitation to take the coveted field of Naboth called forth from his Sidonian queen the amazed remark, "Dost thou now govern the kingdom of Israel?"[182] The old Hebrew kingdom, accordingly, may properly be described as a constitutional monarchy.

3. *Obedience to Rulers.* Since rulers were ordained by God, it was the duty of their subjects to render them respect and obedience. "Thou shalt not revile God [*i.e.,* the oracular decision of the priests], nor curse a ruler of thy people," says the Book of the Covenant. David would not

179 E, I Sam. 22: 6-8.
180 J, II Sam. 5: 3; I Ki. 12: 4.
181 I Sam. 12: 1-15; II Sam. 7: 1-17; 24: 11-14.
182 I Ki. 21: 7.

lift his hand against Saul because he was "Yahweh's Anointed."[183] Prompt obedience to the call to arms was the duty of every citizen, but exemption from military service was granted to the newly wed and in other special cases.[184]

b. *Rights of the Ruled.*—1. *No Abuse of Legislative Functions.* No edicts could be issued that were contrary to the common law, and taxation must not exceed a reasonable limit. As time went on, however, the kings imposed ever heavier burdens. No sooner had David thrown off the Philistine yoke than he undertook aggressive wars against the neighboring nations.[185] These demanded an increased revenue, which he proposed to meet by a new system of taxation. The taking of a census preparatory to levying the tax was denounced by the prophet Gad as displeasing to Yahweh, and a pestilence that followed was interpreted as a divine punishment of the offense.[186] When David proposed to build a costly temple, the prophet Nathan forbade it on account of the oppression of Israel that it would involve.[187] In spite of this prohibition, however, Solomon undertook the building of a magnificent temple and palace, and he lived on a scale of luxury far beyond the resources of a little kingdom like Israel.[188] To meet these expenses he was compelled to resort to trade monopolies and to excessive taxation.[189] For this the prophet Ahijah stirred up Jeroboam to revolt.[190] So burdensome were Solomon's exactions that the elders

---

[183] E, Ex. 22: 28; J, I Sam. 26: 8-9, 11a, 15, 16, 23b; II Sam. 1: 10, 13-16; 18: 2a-4; 21: 15-17; E, I Sam. 24: 4-8, 10-13.

[184] J, Jud. 5: 9, 11c, 13, 14b-18, 23b; I Sam. 11: 7; II Sam. 2: 12-16; E, Ex. 17: 8-9.

[185] II Sam. 8: 10; 12: 26-31.

[186] II Sam. 24: 1-19.

[187] II Sam. 7: 1-17.

[188] I Ki. 4: 22-23; chaps. 5-7; 11: 3.

[189] I Ki. 5: 1-12; 9: 26-28; 10: 1-29; 4: 7-19.

[190] I Ki. 11: 26-31.

of Israel demanded their abolition from Rehoboam. He replied: "My father made your yoke heavy, but I will add to your yoke; my father chastised you with whips, but I will chastise you with scorpions." On hearing this, the northern tribes revolted, and made Jeroboam king;[191] and in this action they were endorsed by the prophet She-maiah.[192]

2. *No Abuse of Judicial Functions.* The early codes sternly condemn injustice in judges which shows itself in acquittal of the guilty and condemnation of the innocent. "Keep thee far from a false matter, and the innocent and the righteous slay thou not, and thou shalt not justify the wicked," says the Book of the Covenant.[193] When Ahab executed Naboth on a false charge of blasphemy, he was denounced by Elijah; and this was one of the main reasons why the dynasty of Omri was overthrown by Jehu at the instigation of Elisha.[194] The old laws demand fearlessness in judges, so that they will not be forced to an unjust verdict by the opinion of the majority;[195] they also demand a strict impartiality that favours neither the rich nor the poor;[196] and they prohibit the taking of bribes.[197]

3. *No Abuse of Executive Functions.* The monarchy steadily undermined the ancient tribal organization of the nation. Saul created a standing army in the place of the old tribal militia. David increased this force, and added to it Cretans, Philistines, and other foreign mercenaries.[198] In the place of the tribal elders there now grew up the body of the "princes," that is, the bureau-

191 I Ki. 12.
192 I Ki. 12: 22-24.
193 Ex. 23: 6-7.
194 I Ki. 21; II Ki. 9.
195 E, Ex. 23: 2; Deut. 1: 17b.
196 E, Ex. 23: 3, 6; Deut. 1: 17a; 16: 19b; Lev. 19: 15b.
197 E, Ex. 23: 8; I Sam. 8: 3; 12: 3-4; Deut. 16: 19c; 27: 25.
198 J, I Sam. 14: 52; II Sam. 8: 18; 23: 8-39.

cracy of favourites appointed by the king. Thus the monarchy in Israel gradually began to assume the character of a typical Oriental despotism. Saul's persecution of David and his slaughter of the priests at Nob were lawless acts of tyranny.[199] David slew Uriah the Hittite, and took his wife for himself; and for this deed was condemned by the prophet Nathan.[200] The Canaanites that were left in the land Solomon reduced to servitude, and compelled them to work upon his buildings. When these did not suffice, he raised a levy of 30,000 Israelites, who were sent in relays of a thousand each to hew lumber in Lebanon. Thus the bondage of Egypt was reëstablished by a Hebrew king. This was another reason for the protests of the prophets Ahijah and Shemaiah and for the revolt of the ten tribes. The E document puts into the mouth of Samuel a graphic description of the exactions of the kings of the northern kingdom, and his protest voices the spirit of the early prophets.[201]

V. *Rights of Animals*

A few early Hebrew laws require kindness to animals. The stray animal was to be returned, and the fallen animal was to be helped up.[202] It was forbidden to plow with an ox and an ass together.[203] The ox that threshed grain was not to be muzzled.[204] A mother-bird was not to be caught when she was sitting upon eggs, or upon her young.[205] The crossing of animals with a different species was also forbidden.[206]

[199] I Sam. chaps. 18-26.
[200] II Sam. 11: 1-12: 15.
[201] I Ki. 5: 13-15; 9: 20-21; I Sam. 8: 8-18.
[202] Ex. 23: 4-5; Deut. 22: 1-4.
[203] Deut. 22: 10.
[204] Deut. 25: 4.
[205] Deut. 22: 6-7.
[206] Lev. 19: 19a.

VI. *Duties to One's Self*

Of self-culture, as the Greek philosophers understood it, or of the Christian ideal of realizing the possibilities of one's nature as a child of God, the ancient Hebrew had no conception. Modesty was regarded as a virtue,[207] and such gross sexual vices as sodomy,[208] bestiality,[209] and masturbation were forbidden;[210] but in general there was no restraint upon sexual excess on the part of the man, though the woman was carefully guarded.[211] Moderation in eating was unknown,[212] and drunkenness was no disgrace.[213] Industry was commended,[214] and skill and wisdom were admired.[215] In a military age courage was naturally a highly appreciated virtue.[216] Suicide was not condemned, but was regarded as a brave act on the part of a wounded warrior or disgraced courtier.[217] This practically exhausts the list of personal virtues. When we consider the complete subordination of the individual to the group in early times, and the lack of any conception of individual immortality, it is not surprising that the ethics of the individual had a small development in ancient Israel.

From the foregoing sketch it appears that the conception of God and his requirements in ancient Israel, in

207 J, Gen. 2: 25; 3: 7, 21; 9: 20-23; II Sam. 10: 4b-5; E, Ex. 20: 26; Deut. 22: 5; 25: 11.
208 J, Gen. 19: 4-7; Jud. 19: 22, 23a; Deut. 23: 18; Lev. 18: 22; 20: 13.
209 E, Ex. 22: 19; Deut. 27: 21; Lev. 18: 23; 20: 15-16.
210 J, Gen. 38: 8-10; Lev. 18: 21(?).
211 See notes 151-158.
212 J, Gen. 19: 3; 26: 30; Jud. 14: 10, 12, 17; I Sam. 25:36; 30: 16; II Sam. 3: 20; I Ki. 3: 15; E, Gen. 21: 8; 29: 22; 40: 20.
213 J, Gen. 9: 20-24; 19: 32-36; I Sam. 25: 36; II Sam. 11: 13; E, I Sam. 1: 13, 14; I Ki. 16: 9b; 20: 16.
214 J, Gen. 2: 5b, 15; 3: 17-19, 23; I Ki. 11: 28.
215 J, Gen. 3: 6; 10: 9; I Sam. 16: 16, 18; 25: 3; E, Gen. 25: 27; 41: 8, 33, 38.
216 J, II Sam. 21: 18-22; 23: 8-15, 17b-39.
217 J, I Sam. 31: 4-5; II Sam. 1: 9; 17: 23a; E, Jud. 9: 53-54; I Ki. 16: 18.

spite of its defects, had many noble elements that made it a real preparation for the teaching of the prophets and of Jesus Christ. Yahweh's chief requirements were ritual; nevertheless, all the fundamental forms of morality were obligations to Him. Even in its preprophetic form this religion was ethically superior to all the other religions of antiquity.

ETHICS OF THE HEBREW PROPHETS

LEWIS BAYLES PATON

VII.

I. FROM AMOS TO THE DEUTERONOMIC REFORMATION

THE period of the literary prophets is naturally subdivided into two main epochs: first, from Amos to the Deuteronomic reformation; and second, from the Deuteronomic reformation to the cessation of prophecy. Our sources for the first period in chronological order are: Amos (760 B.C.), Hosea (750), the genuine prophecies of Isaiah, which are found in three main groups of the book that bears his name, 1: 1-11: 10; 14: 24-23: 18; 28: 1-33: 24 (740-700), Micah (724-680), Zephaniah (624), and Jeremiah 1-10 (424-619). These prophets all belonged to one school of thought, and taught in the main one system of theology and ethics.

As we saw in the previous chapter,[1] early Israel learned through the events of the exodus and conquest two fundamental truths: that Yahweh was better, and that He was stronger than all other gods. The religion of the prophets advanced beyond the early religion in a clearer apprehension of these two truths. All the prophets had inaugural visions, analogous to the Christian experience of conversion, through which they gained a new and overwhelming conception of Yahweh's perfect righteousness and His almighty power.[2] Through these experiences they learned (1) that Yahweh was loving in all His dealings with Israel,[3] (2) that He was absolutely just in His rule of the world,[4] (3) that He was patient and merciful

[1] See page 160.

[2] Am. 7: 1-9; 8: 1-9: 4; Hos. 1-3; Isa. 6; Mic. 3: 8; Jer. 1.

[3] Am. 3: 1-2; 2: 9, 11; Hos. 2: 15; 9: 10; 11: 1, 3; Isa. 5: 4; Mic. 6: 1-4; Jer. 2: 5.

[4] Am. 2: 6f.; cf. 3: 2, 10-12; 4: 1-3; 5: 10-12; Isa. 5: 16; cf. 6: 3, 5, 7; 10: 22; 28: 17; Mic. 6: 5; 7: 9; Zeph. 3: 5a; Jer. 9: 24b.

toward the sinner,[5] (4) that His power was absolute,[6] (5) that He was the only God,[7] (6) that He was not the God of Israel merely, but the God of the whole earth.[8]

Thus it appears that Amos and his successors for the first time in history attained ethical monotheism. Judaism, Christianity, and Muhammadanism, the three universal religions, which now number among their adherents a majority of the human race, are all descendants of the religion of the prophets.

We must now consider how the new conception of Yahweh gained by the prophets affected their idea of the divine requirements.

A. *Allegiance to Yahweh*

a. Devotion to Yahweh. The prophets agreed with the old religion that Yahweh ought to be served with wholehearted loyalty. This was all the more imperative because now He was not merely the greatest of the gods, but the only living and true God. Israel was to be His people, not in the sense that it was his favorite, but by leading the world in devotion to Him.[9] It should fear Him,[10] know Him, in the sense of acknowledging His authority,[11] obey Him,[12] trust Him,[13] and love Him.[14]

[5] Am. 3: 12; 4: 6-11; 7: 15; Hos. 3: 5; 11: 8-9; Isa. 4: 2-3; 6: 13; 7: 3; 9:8-10: 4; 17: 6; 37: 31; Mic. 2: 12; 4: 6-7; 5: 7-8.

[6] Am. 1: 3-2: 6; 4: 2; 5: 27; 6: 14; 7: 9, 11; 9: 2-7; Hos. 3: 4; 9: 3, 6; 10: 5-8, 14-15; 11: 6-7; 13: 15-16; Isa. 5: 26-30; 6: 1-3, 11-12; 7: 11; 8: 5-10; 10: 5-18; 14: 24-26; 29: 1-8; Mic. 3: 12; 5: 5-6.

[7] Isa. 2: 8, 18, 20; 10: 10f.; 19: 1, 3; 31: 7; Jer. 2: 5; 8: 19; 10: 3, 8, 11, 15; 14: 22; 16: 19-20.

[8] Am. 3: 1-2; 9: 7.

[9] Am. 3: 1-2; Hos. 1: 9-10; 2: 19-20, 23; Jer. 7: 22-23; 11: 4; 13: 11; 24: 7; Ezek. 11: 19-20, etc.

[10] Am. 3: 8; Hos. 3: 5; Isa. 8: 13; Zeph. 3: 7; Jer. 5: 22, 24; 10: 7.

[11] Hos. 2: 20; 4: 1, 6, 14b; 5: 4; 6: 3, 6; 8: 2; Isa. 1: 2-3; 5: 13; Jer. 8: 7; 9: 3, 24.

[12] Hos. 9: 17; Isa. 1: 19; 5: 24; 6: 9-10; Jer. 3: 13, 25; 7: 13, 23-26; 9: 13-14.

[13] Isa. 7: 4-9; 8: 5f.; 30: 15; Mic. 4: 9; 7: 7-9; Jer. 17: 5-8.

[14] Hos. 6: 6; 12: 6.

b. No Other God Must be Worshiped. 1. Since the gods of the heathen were not merely inferior to Yahweh but were non-existent, it was both wicked and foolish to worship them. Against all foreign gods the prophets kept up an unceasing polemic.[15]

2. They also recognized that in the popular religion Yahweh had been identified with the local ba'als of Canaan, so that He had lost His moral qualities, and had become only an agricultural divinity, who gave grain, new wine, and oil, and multiplied gold and silver. The local Yahwehs of the numerous sanctuaries of Israel they denounced as only the thinly disguised ba'als of Canaan, and they called upon the people to forsake these and return to the real Yahweh, the God of righteousness. "They that swear by the sin of Samaria, and say as thy god, O Dan, liveth, and as the way of Beersheba liveth, they shall fall and never rise up again." "Seek ye me, and ye shall live; but seek not Bethel, nor enter into Gilgal, and pass not to Beersheba. . . . Seek Yahweh, and ye shall live."[16] Hosea says expressly that Yahweh has been confused with the ba'als by receiving the title ba'al, "owner," and that He must no longer be called by this name. The feasts, new moons, sabbaths, and set times, which are nominally celebrated in honor of Yahweh, are really only "days of the ba'als."[17] This religious syncretism, which was a consequence of the conquest of Canaan and the mingling with its inhabitants, Hosea denounced as the chief sin of the nation.[18] The prophets, accordingly, were the Protestant reformers of ancient Israel, who perceived that the religion of Yahweh had been corrupted with all sorts of

[15] Am. 2: 4; 5: 26; Hos. 3: 1; 13: 4; Isa. 8: 11-12; 17: 10-11; Jer. 1: 16; 2: 10-11, 28; 5: 7, 19; 7: 6, 9, 18; see also note 7.

[16] Am. 8: 14; 5: 4-5.

[17] Hos. 2: 11, 13, 16-17.

[18] Hos. 2: 2-17; 3: 1; 4: 12-13; 5: 3-4; 6: 10; 9: 1, 10; 11: 2; 13: 1; *cf.* Zeph. 1: 4; Jer. 2: 8, 23; 7: 9; 9: 14.

heathen admixtures, and who sought to free primitive Yahwism from the taint of Canaan.

3. Foreign alliances were condemned by the prophets, because these involved recognition of the gods of other nations.[19] Foreign customs also were forbidden, because they led to intercourse with aliens and thus to adoption of their religion.[20] Horses and chariots were viewed with disfavor, because these were procured from Egypt or Assyria at the price of a commercial treaty.[21]

4. The cult of the dead was forbidden, because this came under the general prohibition of the worship of other gods. In the same way in which the gods were degraded from *ĕlôhîm*, "powers," to *ĕlîlîm*, "non-existences," spirits of the dead were degraded from *ĕlôhîm* to *rĕphāîm*, "feeble ones." In the prophetic period they were stripped of their energy so completely that they became mere shadows, unable to help or to hurt, to whom it was futile either to pray or to sacrifice.[22]

c. Magic was Forbidden. Magical arts were forbidden by the prophets, as by the older religion, because these were felt to be connected either with the cult of other gods, or with the cult of the dead.[23]

d. The Distinction of "holy, unclean, and clean." The prophets of the Assyrian period used "holy" only in an ethical, never in a ceremonial, sense. They knew the popular usage of "unclean" as equivalent to *tabu*,[24] but they themselves used it only of moral defilement.[25] The word "clean" they never used. It is evident that they attached

[19] Hos. 5: 13; 7: 8-13; 8: 7-9; 12: 1; Isa. 7: 7-9; 8: 5, 12; 20: 4-6; 28: 15; 30: 1-7; 31: 1-3; Jer. 2: 18, 36-37.
[20] Isa. 2: 6; Zeph. 1: 8-9.
[21] Am. 2: 15; 4: 10; Hos. 1: 7; 14: 3; Isa. 2: 7; 30: 16; 31: 1-3.
[22] Isa. 8: 19; Ezek. 13: 17-23; see L. B. Paton, *Spiritism and the Cult of the Dead in Antiquity,* pp. 269-271.
[23] Isa. 2: 6; Mic. 5: 12; Ezek. 21: 21.
[24] Am. 7: 17; Hos. 9: 3-4.
[25] Hos. 5: 3; 6: 10; Isa. 6: 5; Jer. 2: 23.

no importance to the elaborate system of ceremonial *tabus* that was so characteristic of the old Hebrew religion. The only circumcision that they ever mentioned was that of the heart in Jer. 4: 4.

B. *Worship of Yahweh*

a. Holy Places. The recognition that Yahweh was the living and true God, the supreme ruler of the universe, was inconsistent with the ancient belief that He dwelt at particular sanctuaries, consequently the prophets took a hostile attitude toward the old Hebrew high places. "I will visit the altars of Bethel, and the horns of the altar shall be cut off." "Come to Bethel and transgress, to Gilgal and multiply transgressions." "Seek not Bethel, nor enter into Gilgal, and pass not to Beersheba." "The high places of Isaac shall be desolate, and the sanctuaries of Israel shall be laid waste."[26] There is no hint that these places are condemned because they are rivals to the legitimate sanctuary at Jerusalem—that idea first appears in Deuteronomy—and the temple worship at Jerusalem is condemned along with the rest.[27] The few passages that speak of Yahweh as "dwelling in Zion" are probably post-deuteronomic glosses.[28] Micah declared expressly that the temple should become like the high places of a forest, and Jeremiah predicted that Yahweh would destroy it as He had destroyed Shiloh.[29]

b. Holy Objects. The lofty conception of Yahweh held by the prophets was incompatible with the ancient belief that He inhabited stones, posts, images, or other sacred objects. The early religion never objected to the asherahs and standing stones, but the prophets condemned them.[30]

[26] Am. 3: 14; 4: 4; 5: 5-6; 7: 9; Hos. 4: 13, 15; 5: 1; 6: 7-10; 8: 11; 9: 15; 10: 1-2, 8-9; 12: 11.
[27] Isa. 1: 12; Mic. 1: 5; Jer. 7: 4.
[28] Am. 1: 2; Isa. 8: 18.
[29] Mic. 3: 12; Jer. 7: 12, 14; 22: 5; 26: 6.
[30] Hos. 3: 4; 4: 12; 10: 1-2; Isa. 17: 8; Mic. 5: 13-14; Jer. 17: 2.

Molten images of the Canaanite type were forbidden by early legislation, but images of other sorts were permitted, provided that they belonged to Yahweh. Jeroboam I set up the image of a bullock in Bethel, and said: "This is thy God, O Israel, that brought thee up out of the land of Egypt";[31] and there is no reliable evidence of opposition to this cult even as late as the times of Elijah and Elisha. Hosea, however, denounced it;[32] and it is probable, on account of his frequent condemnation of Bethel, that Amos also disapproved of it, although he did not expressly mention it. All images, even those of Yahweh, were rejected by the prophets.[33]

The ark is never mentioned by the prophets before Jeremiah; the probability is, therefore, that they esteemed it no more highly than any other fetish. Jeremiah declared: "In those days, saith Yahweh, they shall say no more, The ark of the covenant of Yahweh, neither shall it come to mind, neither shall they remember it, neither shall they miss it, neither shall it be made any more," which shows how little he shared in the popular idea of its value.[34]

c. Holy Times. The ancient idea that Yahweh was limited to particular times, just as He was limited to particular places, was abhorrent to the prophets' consciousness of His omnipresence; accordingly, they condemned holy days as worthless. In most of their utterances they combined holy days with sacrifices, so that we may postpone enumeration of the passages until we consider sacrifices.

d. Rites on Entering a Holy Place. Since the prophets rejected holy places they naturally had nothing to say on

31 See p. 167.
32 Hos. 8: 5-6; 10: 5-6; 13: 2; *cf.* note 26.
33 Hos. 3: 4; 4: 17; 8: 4; 13: 2; 14: 8; Isa. 2: 8, 20; 10: 10-11; 17: 8; 30: 22; 31: 7; Mic. 1: 7; 5: 13; Jer. 1: 16; 2: 27; 8: 19; 10: 3-5, 8-9.
34 Jer. 3: 16; *cf.* Am. 5: 26(?).

this topic, which occupied such an important place in the older religion.[35]

e. Sacrifices. The prophets saw clearly that sacrifices sprang from unethical conceptions of the deity. They originated in the cult of the dead. The blood, in which the life of the animal resided, was shed in order that the shades might drink of it and renew their vigor. The primitive association with the dead is shown by the fact that the blood of the victim was always poured upon the earth, so that it might sink down into the Underworld. Offerings of food and drink also were originally made to the dead. When Yahweh forbade worship of the dead, He appropriated to His own service the sacrifices that had originally belonged to them, and they were called "food of deity."[36] Such conceptions were repugnant to the ethical monotheism of the prophets. They saw that the one thing that a righteous God required of men was righteousness like His own, and that bloody sacrifices belonged to an unworthy and outgrown conception of the divine. Consequently, they one and all declared in the most unequivocal manner that sacrifices were worthless in the sight of Yahweh.

Thus Amos says: "Go ye to Bethel and transgress, in Gilgal and increase transgression; and bring every morning your sacrifices, every third day your tithes; and burn of leavened bread a thank-offering, and proclaim freewill offerings, make them known, for so it pleased you to do, children of Israel."[37] "I hate, I despise your feasts, and I will smell no sweet savour in your festivals; for though you offer me your burnt-offerings and your meal-offerings, I will not accept them; and the peace-offerings of your fatlings I will not regard. Take away from me

[35] See p. 169.
[36] See p. 170.
[37] Am. 4: 4-5.

the din of thy songs, and the melody of thy lyres I will not hear; but let justice roll down as waters, and righteousness as an ever-flowing stream. Did ye bring me sacrifices and offerings in the desert during forty years, O house of Israel?''[38]

Similarly Hosea represents Yahweh as saying: ''It is love that I delight in and not sacrifice, yea the knowledge of God instead of burnt-offerings.''[39] ''They sacrifice flesh and they eat it, but Yahweh has no pleasure in their sacrifices.''[40]

Isaiah also declares: ''Of what use to me is the multitude of your sacrifices? saith Yahweh. I am sated with burnt-offerings of rams, and fat of fed beasts; and in the blood of bullocks, and lambs, and he-goats I take no delight. When ye come to see my face—who hath required this at your hand? Vain is the bringing of an oblation, the smoke of sacrifice is an abomination unto me. New moon and sabbath, calling of assemblies I cannot (endure). Sin is the solemn assembly. Your new moons and your set feasts my soul hateth, they are a burden unto me, I am tired of bearing it. . . . Wash you, make you clean, put away the evil of your doings from before my eyes, learn to do good, seek justice, relieve the oppressed, right the orphan, plead for the widow.''[41]

At the time of Sennacherib's advance upon Jerusalem in 701 B.C. the people fled from the country into the city bringing their cattle with them. These they sacrificed in profusion, hoping thus to avert the calamity; and since every sacrifice was accompanied with a meal, the city was turned into a huge banquet hall. Isaiah's comment on this was: ''The Lord, Yahweh of hosts, called to weeping and mourning, to baldness and girding with sackcloth; but

[38] Am. 5: 21-25.
[39] Hos. 6: 6.
[40] Hos. 8:13.
[41] Isa. 1: 11-17.

behold, joy and gladness, slaying oxen and killing sheep, eating flesh and drinking wine, (saying) Let us eat and drink, for to-morrow we shall die. But Yahweh of hosts has revealed himself in my ears: Never shall this sin be expiated until you die.''[42]

One of the finest of all the prophetic utterances concerning the worthlessness of sacrifice is that of Micah, spoken in the degenerate days of Manasseh, when the king was trying to revive every form of ancient ritual in hope of averting the impending downfall of the nation: ''Wherewith shall I come before Yahweh, and bow myself before the high God? shall I come before Him with burnt-offerings, with calves a year old? Will Yahweh be pleased with thousands of rams, or with ten thousands of rivers of oil? shall I give my first-born for my transgression, the fruit of my body for the sin of my soul? He hath showed thee, O man, what is good; and what doth Yahweh require of thee, but to do justly, and to love kindness, and to walk humbly with thy God?''[43]

Jeremiah in his earliest period, before the Deuteronomic reformation, took the same attitude toward sacrifices. ''To what purpose cometh there to me frankincense from Sheba and calamus from a far country? your burnt-offerings are not acceptable, nor your sacrifices pleasing unto me.'' ''Add your burnt-offerings unto your sacrifices, ye but eat flesh; for I spake not unto your fathers, nor commanded them in the day that I brought them out of the land of Egypt, concerning burnt-offerings or sacrifices.''[44]

f. Prayer. The only sort of worship that the prophets sanctioned was prayer. Their inaugural visions were times of communion with God, and their writings are full

42 Isa. 22: 1-14.
43 Mic. 6: 6-8.
44 Jer. 6: 20; 7: 21-22.

of questions, expostulations, petitions, and thanksgivings addressed to God.[45] They never condemned the prayers of the people as they condemned holy days and sacrifices, they only said that the prayers of wicked men should not be answered.[46] In the contents of the prayers of the prophets the chief difference from those of the earlier period lies in the fact that they are mainly petitions for spiritual blessings, such as forgiveness, grace, guidance, and strength, rather than petitions for material blessings.

C. *Yahweh's Moral Requirements*

The elimination of ritual threw the whole stress of the prophetic religion upon righteousness. The early religion said, Yahweh demands chiefly holy days and sacrifices, and secondarily right dealing with one's fellow-men; but the prophets said, "What doth Yahweh require of thee but to do justly and to love kindness?" "Seek good, and not evil, that ye may live; and so Yahweh, the God of hosts, will be with you, as ye say that He is. Hate the evil, and love the good, and establish justice in the gate." "Sow to yourselves in righteousness, reap according to kindness."[47] Every denunciation of ritual is accompanied with a corresponding exhortation to righteousness.

I. *Universal Human Rights*

The recognition that Yahweh was the universal God, rather than merely the God of Israel, led the prophets to a broader humanity in their teaching concerning the treatment of foreigners. If Yahweh had brought up the Philistines from Caphtor and the Syrians from Kir, He must care for these races, and wrong to them must be

45 Am. 7: 2, 5; Hos. 7: 14; 9: 14; 12: 4; 14: 1-3; Isa. 6: 5, 8, 11; 7: 11; Jer. 1: 6, 11, 13; 3: 4; 4: 10; 7: 16; 10: 6-9; 11: 14, 20; 12: 1-4; 14: 7-9; 15: 15-18; 16: 19-20; 17: 13-18; 18: 19-23; 20: 7-13, etc.
46 Isa. 1: 15; 29: 13; Jer. 2: 27-29; 7: 9-10; 14: 11-12.
47 Mic. 6: 8; Am. 5: 14-15; Hos. 10:12.

painful to Him. Amos denounced the people of Gaza, because they carried off the inhabitants of a whole district (apparently not Hebrew) to sell them to the Edomites; and the Moabites, because they burned the bones of the king of Edom to lime.[48] Such cruelties in war as threshing prisoners with sharp-toothed sledges, and ripping up pregnant women, which were constantly practiced by the early Hebrews were sternly condemned by the prophets.

II. *Rights of All Israelites*

As to the content of social morality the prophets did not differ greatly from the earlier religion. They did not go into detail in their ethical teaching, because they assumed that the common law of Israel and the legislation of the Book of the Covenant were well known to their contemporaries. They condemned murder,[49] robbery,[50] false weights and measures,[51] corners in grain and profiteering,[52] selling inferior goods at the full price,[53] and all other crooked practices in trade.

They were specially vehement in their denunciation of the oppression of poor debtors by rich creditors. They condemned the taking of garments as security for loans,[54] the taking of interest,[55] and the foreclosing of mortgages by which the poor were turned out of their farms. This last was a crying evil in the age of the prophets. Whole villages were being evicted, and all the arable land was rapidly being absorbed into the estates of a few rich proprietors, while the formerly free peasants were reduced

[48] Am. 1: 6; 2: 1.
[49] Hos. 1: 4; 4: 2; 6: 8-9; 12: 14; Isa. 1: 15, 21; 4: 4; Mic. 3: 10; 7: 2; Jer. 2: 34; 7: 6, 9.
[50] Hos. 4: 2; 7: 1; Isa. 1: 23; Jer. 2: 26; 7: 9, 11.
[51] Am. 8: 5; Hos. 12: 7; Mic. 6: 10-11.
[52] Am. 8: 5.
[53] Am. 8: 6.
[54] Am. 2: 8; Mic. 2: 8; Ezek. 18: 7, 12, 16; 33: 15.
[55] Jer. 15: 10; Ezek. 18: 8, 13, 17; 22: 12.

practically to the position of serfs who worked for the great landowners in return for sufficient food to keep body and soul together. Against this land-grabbing some of the most fearful woes of the prophets were directed: "The princes of Judah are like those that remove the landmark; I will pour out my wrath upon them like water. Ephraim is an oppressor, a crusher of justice, because he has determined to go after wrong." "Woe unto them that join house to house, that add field to field, till there is no room left, and they dwell alone in the midst of the land! It is in my ears saith Yahweh of hosts." "Woe unto them that devise iniquity, and plan evil upon their beds! When the morning is light, they carry it out, because it is in the power of their hand to do so; thus they oppress a brave fellow and his household, a man and his heritage." "The women of my people ye cast out from their happy homes, from their young children ye take away my glory forever."[56]

The enslaving of debtors was also condemned by the prophets. "Thus saith Yahweh: For three transgressions of Israel, yea for four, I will not turn away its doom; because they have sold the righteous for silver, and the needy for the price of a pair of sandals."[57]

The ancient legislation in regard to rights of truth was reiterated by the prophets. They condemned false swearing,[58] and breaking of contracts.[59] Lying, which was regarded as a venial offense by the early religion, was rebuked by them,[60] and their teaching was summed up by the Holiness Code in the words, "Ye shall not lie one to another."[61]

56 Hos. 5: 10; Isa. 5: 8-9; Mic. 2: 1-2, 9.
57 Am. 2: 6; 8: 6.
58 Hos. 4: 2; 10: 4; Jer. 4: 2; 5: 2, 7, 9.
59 Am. 1: 9; Hos. 10: 4; Jer. 34: 8, 10, 15, 18, 19; Ezek. 17: 11-21.
60 Hos. 4: 1; 7: 1, 3; 11: 12; 12: 1; Mic. 2: 11; 6: 12.
61 Lev. 19: 11.

All the duties of kindness to fellow-Israelites that were recognized by the early religion were retained and reinforced by the prophets. The word *hesedh,* which the A.V. usually renders "mercy," and the R.V. "kindness," or "lovingkindness," and which means "love that expresses itself in kind acts," is a favorite word of the prophets; and Micah and Hosea sum up righteousness in the two words "justice and love."[62] Kindness and generosity to the poor are specially commended. Ezekiel in his epitome of prophetic ethics in chapter eighteen adds: "Hath given his bread to the hungry, and hath covered the naked with a garment";[63] and Trito-Isaiah declares: "Is not this the fast that I have chosen: to loose the bonds of wickedness, to undo the bands of the yoke, and to let the oppressed go free, and that ye break every yoke? Is it not to deal thy bread to the hungry, and that thou bring the poor that are cast out to thy house? when thou seest the naked that thou clothe him; and that thou hide not thyself from thine own flesh?"[64]

III. *Rights Derived from Family Relations*

The prophets regarded the family as the corner-stone of society, and condemned everything that tended to impair its integrity. They did not expressly reject polygamy, but they assumed that monogamy was the natural and the normal relationship. None of the prophets is recorded to have had more than one wife.[65] By all the marriage relation was regarded as so sacred that it was the worthiest figure for Yahweh's relation to His people.[66] Through his love for his wife Hosea learned the re-

---

62 Hos. 4: 1; 6: 4, 6; 10: 12; 12: 6 (7); Mic. 6: 8.
63 Ezek. 18: 7; *cf.* 16: 49.
64 Isa. 58: 6-7.
65 Hos. 1: 1-3; Isa. 8: 3; Jer. 16: 2; Ezek. 24: 16-18.
66 Hos. 2: 2-20; 4: 11-5: 4; Isa. 1: 21; Jer. 2: 1-7, 20-25; 3: 1-20; Ezek. 16: 15-29.

deeming love of Yahweh for Israel.[67] Isaiah identified his wife so completely with his ministry that she was called "the prophetess."[68] Ezekiel made his wife a type of Judah in its relation to Yahweh; and when she, "the desire of his eyes," was taken from him, he used this to represent the destruction of the holy city.[69]

Prostitution, which was not only tolerated, but even taken under the protection of the ancient religion, was abhorred by the prophets.[70] Adultery, both in men and women, was of course condemned, as in the older religion.[71] Divorce was not expressly repudiated, but Hosea refused to put away his wife, even after repeated acts of infidelity on her part; and the prophets' frequent declaration that Yahweh refuses to put away Israel, His unfaithful bride, shows that they regarded abstention from divorce as the nobler moral conduct.[72] In general it may be said that prophetism raised the social standing of women above the level of the pre-prophetic period. The superior quality of Jewish family life above that of the entire ancient world was mainly due to their teaching.

The sacrifice of children, which was demanded by the ancient religion, was denounced by the prophets; not merely because they regarded all sacrifice as worthless, but also because they denied the right of a father to take the life of his child.[73] Reverence and obedience to parents they inculcated, as did the early religion.[74]

Slavery was accepted by the prophets as an established

[67] Hos. 3: 1-5.
[68] Isa. 8: 3.
[69] Ezek. 24: 15-18.
[70] Am. 7: 17; Hos. 1: 2; 3: 3; 4: 11-14; 6: 10; Isa. 1: 21; Mic. 1: 7; Jer. 5: 7; see p. 187.
[71] Hos. 3: 1; 4: 2; 7: 4; Jer. 5: 8; 7: 9; 9: 2; 23: 10, 14; 29: 23; Ezek. 18: 6, 11, 15; 23: 37; 33: 26.
[72] Hos. 3: 1-3; 11: 8-9; Jer. 3: 1.
[73] Mic. 6: 7; Jer. 3: 24; 7: 31; 19: 5; 32: 35; Ezek. 16: 20, 36; 20: 25-26, 31; 23: 37, 39.
[74] Hos. 11: 1-4; Jer. 35: 18-19; Ezek. 22: 7; Isa. 45: 10; Mal. 1: 6.

institution, which they did not attempt to attack. Jeremiah, however, regarded the freeing of slaves as peculiarly acceptable to Yahweh, and the reënslaving of those who had been liberated as a most heinous offense.[75] It was a fruit of the prophetic teaching when the Holiness Code forbade the enslaving of Hebrews, and allowed only slaves of foreign blood.[76] It was also a fruit of the prophetic teaching when Deuteronomy placed female slaves on the same footing as male slaves in the matter of release in the seventh year.[77]

IV. *Rights Derived from Governmental Relations*

The prophets uniformly denounced the kings and officials who bore rule in their day. Amos represented Yahweh as saying: "I will rise against the house of Jeroboam with the sword. Then Amaziah, the priest of Bethel, sent to Jeroboam, king of Israel, saying: Amos hath conspired against thee in the house of Israel; the land is not able to bear all his words."[78] Hosea declared: "The children of Israel shall remain many days without king and without prince." "They have set up kings, but not by me; they have made princes, and I knew it not." "I have given thee a king in my anger, and taken him away in my wrath."[79] Isaiah announced: "Behold the Lord, Yahweh of hosts, doth take away from Jerusalem and Judah stay and staff . . . the mighty man, and the man of war, the judge, and the prophet, and the diviner, and the elder, the captain of fifty, and the honourable man, and the counsellor, and the expert artificer, and the skillful enchanter."[80]

[75] Jer. 34: 8-19.
[76] Lev. 25: 45-46.
[77] Deut. 15: 12-18.
[78] Am. 7: 9-13.
[79] Hos. 3: 4; 8: 4; 13: 10-11.
[80] Isa. 3: 1-3; *cf.* 7: 13, 17; 22: 15-19.

Such utterances have been interpreted as indicating that the prophets were anarchists who were bent on over-throwing all civil authority; but when we examine their words more closely in the light of their historical setting, it becomes apparent that they were not attacking kings and officials in general, but only the particular men who administered these offices unworthily. They condemned revolutions against bad kings, such as the earlier proph-ets had instigated. Hosea regarded the overthrow of the house of Omri by Jehu at the suggestion of Elisha as a bloody deed that still cried for vengeance.[81] In their pic-tures of the good time coming the prophets assumed the continuance of the monarchy, only, in that day, the kings should be wise and just.[82]

A large part of the teaching of the prophets is taken up with denunciation of the injustice and oppression of the ruling class in their day. The old tribal elders, who had sympathized with the peasants, and who had represented the moral sense of the village communities, had disap-peared; and in their place had come the "princes" ap-pointed by the king, who knew no tribal bonds, and whose sole ambition was to get rich quickly. They were the chief exploiters of the poor, and they were at the same time the lawmakers and the judges who decided cases in which the poor were involved. Class prejudice led them always to take the side of the rich, so that it was impossible for the poor to get their rights.

Their unjust legislation is described by Isaiah: "Woe to them that decree unrighteous decrees, and to the writ-ers that write perverseness; to turn aside the needy from justice, and to rob the poor of my people of their right, that widows may be their spoil, and that they may make

81 Hos. 1: 4; 7; 6-7; Isa. 9: 18-21.
82 Am. 9: 11; Hos. 1: 11; 3: 5; Isa. 9: 6-7; 11: 1-9; 22: 20-25; 28: 16-17; 29: 18-21; 32:1-8; Mic. 4: 8; 5: 2-6; Jer. 3: 15; 23: 4-5.

the fatherless their prey!"[83] Similarly Jeremiah says: "How do ye say, We are wise, and the law of Yahweh is with us? But, behold, the false pen of the scribes hath wrought falsely."[84] Their oppressive taxes and their fines are mentioned by Amos.[85]

In regard to their perversion of justice the prophets declare: "They turn justice to wormwood, and cast down righteousness to the earth." "Thy princes are rebellious and companions of thieves. . . . They judge not the fatherless, neither doth the cause of the widow come before them." "They abhor justice and pervert all equity. They build up Zion with blood, and Jerusalem with iniquity." "Ephraim is an oppressor, a crusher of justice." "I will get me unto the great men, and will speak unto them, for they know the way of Yahweh, and the justice of their God; but these with one accord have broken the yoke and burst the bonds." "They plead not the cause, the cause of the fatherless, that they may prosper; and the right of the needy they do not judge."[86] In regard to their corruptibility the prophets say: "They take a bribe, and turn aside the needy in the gate." "They acquit the wicked for a bribe, and take away the vindication of the righteous from him." "Every one loveth bribes and followeth after rewards." "The heads thereof judge for reward, and the priests thereof teach for hire, and the prophets thereof divine for money; yet they lean upon Yahweh, and say, Is not Yahweh in the midst of us?"[87]

The abuse of executive powers by the ruling class the prophets describe as follows: "They know not how to do right, who store up the fruit of violence and robbery in

83 Isa. 10: 1-2.
84 Jer. 8: 8.
85 Am. 2: 8; 5: 11.
86 Am. 5: 7, 15; 6: 12; Hos. 5: 11; 9: 15; Isa. 1: 22f.; Mic. 3: 9-10; Jer. 5: 4, 5, 28; 7: 5.
87 Am. 5: 12; Isa. 1: 23; 5: 23; Mic. 3: 11; 7: 3; Ezek. 22: 12.

their palaces." "They oppress the poor and crush the needy." "They swallow up the needy, and cause the poor of the land to fail." "Ye have eaten up the vineyard, the spoil of the poor is in your houses. What mean ye that ye crush my people, and grind the face of the poor? saith the Lord, Yahweh of hosts." "Hear ye heads of Jacob, and rulers of the house of Israel: Is it not for you to know justice? ye who hate the good, and love the evil; who pluck off their skin from off them, and their flesh from off their bones; who also eat the flesh of my people, and flay their skin from off them, and break their bones, and chop them in pieces, as for the pot, and as flesh within the cauldron." "Her princes in the midst of her are roaring lions, her judges are evening wolves, they leave nothing until the morrow." "The shepherds of Israel have fed themselves and not the sheep; they have eaten the fat, and clothed themselves with the wool, and killed the fatlings; with force and with rigor they have ruled over them."[88]

The prophets found it peculiarly atrocious that the rich lived in luxury obtained by oppression of the poor. Amos represents Yahweh as saying: "I will smite the winter-house with the summer-house; and the houses of ivory shall perish, and the great houses shall have an end, saith Yahweh." "Ye have built houses of hewn stone, but ye shall not dwell in them; ye have planted pleasant vineyards, but ye shall not drink the wine thereof." "Woe to them that are at ease in Zion, and to them that are secure in the mountain of Samaria . . . that put far away the day of calamity, and cause the seat of violence to come near; that lie upon beds of ivory, and stretch themselves upon their couches; that eat lambs picked out of the flock,

[88] Am. 2: 7; 3: 9-10; 4: 1; 5: 11; 6: 3; 8: 4; Isa. 3: 14-15; Mic. 3: 1-3; 6: 10, 12, 16; 7: 3-4; Zeph. 3: 3; Jer. 5: 26-28; 6: 6, 7, 13; 8: 10; Ezek. 34: 1-10.

and calves selected from the midst of the stall; that twitter to the sound of the harp; like David, they devise for themselves instruments of music; that drink wine in bowls, and anoint themselves with the finest oils; but they are not grieved for the affliction of Joseph!" "The Lord Yahweh hath sworn by himself: I abhor the glory of Jacob, and his palaces I hate." Amos describes the fine ladies of Samaria, who "sit in the corner of a couch, in the damask of a divan," and he contemptuously calls them "fat cows of Bashan, that are in the mountain of Samaria, that oppress the poor, that crush the needy, that say unto their husbands, Bring, and let us drink." Hosea denounces their palaces, their mirth, their feasts, and the treasure of their goodly vessels; and Isaiah declares that their great and fair houses, the harp, the lute, the tabret, and the pipe in their feasts, their glory, their pomp, and their costly chariots, shall all go down in ruin before the onmarch of the Assyrians. Isaiah also condemns the luxury of the wives of the aristocrats, which was the cause of much of the oppression of the poor by their husbands. He calls them "women that are at ease, careless daughters"; and he gives in derision a long list of the latest fashions from Nineveh that were necessary to complete their toilets.[89]

Because of these sins of the aristocracy, more than for any other cause, the prophets declared that Yahweh was sending the Assyrian catastrophe upon the nation: "Therefore I will cause you to go into captivity beyond Damascus." "Therefore shall Zion for your sake be plowed as a field, and Jerusalem shall become heaps, and the mountain of the house as the high places of a forest."[90] For this reason they called upon the rulers to re-

[89] Am. 3: 12, 15; 4: 1; 5: 11; 6: 1-8, 11; Hos. 2: 11, 13; 7: 14; 8: 14; 9: 6; 13: 15; Isa. 2: 12-17; 3: 16-24; 5: 11-15; 32: 9-14; Ezek. 16: 49-50.
[90] Am. 5: 27; Mic. 3: 12.

pent, and mend their ways before it was too late: "Hate the evil, and love the good, and establish justice in the gate; it may be that Yahweh, the God of hosts, will be gracious unto the remnant of Joseph." "Seek justice, relieve the oppressed, judge the fatherless, plead for the widow. Come now and let us reason together, saith Yahweh; though your sins be as scarlet, they may become white as snow; though they be red like crimson, they may become as wool."[91]

The social ideals of the prophets are shown not merely by their direct teaching, but also by their pictures of the good time coming. After the blow has fallen, the remnant that is left shall repent; then the nation shall be restored under the rule of a righteous king. "Unto us a child shall surely be born, unto us a son shall surely be given, and the government shall be upon his shoulder; and his name shall be called, wonderful counsellor, god-like hero, enduring father, peaceful prince. Of the increase of his government and of peace there shall be no end, upon the throne of David, and upon his kingdom, to establish it, and to uphold it with justice and righteousness from this time forward." "He shall not judge after the sight of his eyes, neither decide after the hearing of his ears; but with righteousness shall he judge the poor, and decide with equity for the lowly of the land; and he shall smite the violent with the rod of his mouth, and with the breath of his lips shall he slay the wicked; and righteousness shall be the girdle of his waist, and faithfulness the girdle of his loins." "Behold a king will reign righteously, and officials rule justly. Each will be like a hiding-place from the wind, like a covert from the tempest, like streams of water in a dry place, like the shade of a great rock in a thirsty land." "Behold the days come, saith Yahweh, that I will raise up unto David a righteous branch, and he shall

91 Am. 5: 14-15; Isa. 1: 16-20.

reign as king and deal wisely, and shall execute justice and righteousness in the land. In his days Judah shall be saved, and Israel shall dwell safely; and this is his name whereby he shall be called: Yahweh is our righteousness."[92]

It appears, accordingly, that the teaching of the prophets in regard to social justice is one of the noblest elements of their ethics, a teaching that still has the greatest value for the solution of the social problems of our own age.

V. *Duties to One's Self*

In the period of the prophets a new sense of the worth of the individual grew up in Israel. As a result of the monarchy the old tribal organization began to break up, and men no longer felt that the clan was everything and the individual nothing. The religious experience of the prophets also fostered individualism. Each of them had a personal experience of God that did not depend upon the fact that they were members of the commonwealth of Israel. The nation was against them, yet they were confident that they had stood in the council of the Most High. This conviction was exemplified most perfectly in Jeremiah, whose confidence in God's individual care triumphed amid persecution and the downfall of the nation.[93] The individualism of the prophets has left its mark in the legislation of Deuteronomy and the Holiness Code, which recognize new rights of wives, children, and slaves over against the head of the house, and which prohibit the punishment of children for the crimes of fathers, or of fathers for the crimes of children.[94] This new consciousness of the dignity of the individual human being

92 Isa. 9: 6-7; 11: 4-5; 32: 1-2; Jer. 23: 5-6.

93 Jer. 1: 17-19; 17: 5-18; 20: 7-11.

94 Deut. 12: 31; 15: 12; 18: 10; 20: 5-8; 23: 15f.; 24: 16; Lev. 18: 21; 25: 42.

found noble expression in the words of Yahweh proclaimed by Ezekiel, "Behold, all souls are mine; as the soul of the father, so also the soul of the son is mine," and in the prediction of Jeremiah that in the Messianic age Yahweh would write His instruction in the heart of each individual, so that all should know Him from the least unto the greatest.[95]

This new sense of the worth of the individual led to a higher idea of responsibility for one's self. The virtues of chastity were more highly esteemed by the prophets than by their predecessors.[96] Drunkenness in particular was frequently condemned by the prophets as one of the crying sins of the age. Amos represents the fine ladies of Samaria as saying to their husbands: "Bring and let us drink." The nobles, he says, at their feasts "Drink wine in bowls," and one of his threats against them is, that "they shall plant pleasant vineyards, and shall not drink the wine thereof."[97] Hosea declares: "Whoredom and wine and new wine take away the understanding." He describes the rulers as "a band of topers devoted to harlotry," and says, "On the day of our king the princes made themselves sick with the heat of wine."[98] Isaiah proclaims: "Woe unto them that rise up early in the morning, that they may follow strong drink; that tarry late into the night, till wine inflames them!" "Woe unto them that are mighty men—at drinking wine; and heroes—at mixing strong drink." "Woe to the crown of pride of the drunkards of Ephraim . . . of them that are overcome with wine!" "These also reel with wine, and stagger with strong drink; the priest and the prophet reel with strong drink, they are swallowed up of wine, they stagger with strong drink; they err in vision, they stumble in judg-

95 Ezek. 18: 4; Jer. 31: 31-34.
96 See notes 70-72.
97 Am. 4: 1; 6: 6; 5: 11.
98 Hos. 4: 11, 18; 7: 5.

ment. All tables are full of vomit, filth is everywhere."[99] Micah satirically observes: "If a man walking in a spirit of falsehood and lies should say: I will prophecy unto thee of wine and strong drink, he might be the prophet of this people."[100]

Summing up now our survey of the ethics of the prophets of the Assyrian period, we conclude, that, in their repudiation of ritual and emphasis upon justice and love toward other men as the essence of true religion, these prophets marked the greatest ethical advance in the history of the world. Jesus correctly summarized their teaching when he said: "Thou shalt love the Lord thy God with all thy heart, and with all thy soul, and with all thy mind, and with all thy strength. This is the first and great commandment, and the second is like unto it: Thou shalt love thy neighbor as thyself. On these two commandments hang all the Law and the prophets."[101]

II. FROM THE DEUTERONOMIC REFORMATION TO MALACHI

THE second main epoch of the history of prophecy extends from the adoption of Deuteronomy as the law of the nation to the cessation of prophecy in the days of Nehemiah and Ezra. Our sources for this period are Jeremiah, chapters 11-49 (619-586 B.C.), Nahum (612), Habakkuk (605-600), Ezekiel (592-570), Obadiah (after 586), Isaiah 11:11-14:23, chapters 34-35, and chapters 40-55 (545), Haggai (520), Zechariah, chapters 1-8 (520), Isaiah, chapters 56-66 (*ca.* 500), Malachi (*ca.* 500).

The long reign of Manasseh, son of Hezekiah (691-637), was a period of intense reaction against the reform movement instituted by the prophets from Amos to Micah.

[99] Isa. 5: 11, 12, 22; 28: 1, 7-8.
[100] Mic. 2: 11.
[101] Mark 12: 30-31; Matt. 22: 37-40.

Manasseh restored all the old Canaanite heathenism that his father had tried to abolish, and introduced besides the Assyro-Babylonian astral religion.[102] When the prophetic party opposed him, he resorted to persecution; and according to Jeremiah and Kings, "He shed innocent blood very much, till he had filled Jerusalem from one end to the other."[103] This martyr period of the prophetic dispensation is graphically described by Micah in 7:1-6.

The effect of Manasseh's persecution was seriously to thin the ranks of the prophetic party. The leaders, such as Isaiah, and possibly also Micah, fell victims to the king's wrath; and the survivors were men of less clearness of vision and intensity of faith. They began to feel that the ideals of their great masters, Amos, Hosea, Isaiah, and Micah, had been set too high, and that it was necessary to yield somewhat to the prejudices of the common people, if they were to be won over to the program of reform. In this sentiment they were met half-way by the princes and the priests, who were disgusted with the extreme heathen reaction of Manasseh, and were touched with pity for the sufferings of the prophets. The moderate men on both sides felt that the need of the hour was a compromise, by which the prophetic ideals of loyalty to Yahweh and righteousness of life should be maintained, and at the same time the less objectionable elements of the old national ritual should be preserved. The fruit of the movement was the Book of Deuteronomy.

This book bears internal evidence of having been composed during the reign of Manasseh, and it proposes a compromise between the religion of the prophets and the popular religion. On the one side, Deuteronomy is a compendium of prophetic theology. It declares that Yahweh is the only true God, and that no other god must be

102 II Ki. 21: 2-9.
103 II Ki. 21: 16; Jer. 2: 34; 15: 4; 19: 4.

served. It is opposed to all foreign cults and foreign alliances as likely to lead to religious syncretism. It antagonizes the high places because of their connection with Canaanite ba'al-worship. It condemns standing stones, asherahs, images, and all other visible representations of the deity. It teaches that the supreme characteristic of Yahweh is His righteousness, and that He demands righteousness of men. In 6:4-5 it gives a summary of prophetic theology in the words: "Hear, O Israel, Yahweh our God, Yahweh is one; and thou shalt love Yahweh thy God with all thy heart, and with all thy soul, and with all thy might." This utterance was singled out by later Judaism as its confession of faith, and Jesus declared that it was the great commandment of the law.[104]

On the other side, Deuteronomy is a compendium of the religion of ancient Israel. It rejects the high places in general, but it keeps Jerusalem, "the place that Yahweh has chosen out of all the tribes to cause his name to dwell there," as the only legitimate place of worship.[105] It rejects holy objects in general; but it keeps the ark, the ancient fetish of the Jerusalem temple.[106] It keeps all the holy times of the pre-prophetic religion, but makes these commemorations of historic deliverances.[107] It also keeps all the sacrifices known to the earlier codes of J and E, but seeks to give these a symbolic meaning, so as to make them an expression of the prophetic religion; and it insists that the poor, the widow, and the orphan, shall be invited to the sacrificial meal.[108]

Thus it appears that Deuteronomy was a compromise between the religion of the prophets and the older religion of Israel, just as the older religion was a compromise

[104] Mark 12: 29-30; Matt. 22: 37-38.
[105] Deut. 12: 2-18, etc.
[106] Deut. 12: 3-4; 16: 21-22; 10: 1-5.
[107] Deut. 16: 1-17.
[108] Deut. 12: 6-18; 16: 11, 14, etc.

between Mosaism and the religion of Canaan, and the old Catholic Church was a compromise between primitive Christianity and Græco-Roman heathenism. Deuteronomy was the charter of Judaism, which was neither the religion of the prophets, nor the ancient religion of Israel, but a hybrid between the two.

At the time when Deuteronomy was written it was impossible to publish it on account of the fierceness of Manasseh's persecution. For safe keeping it was deposited in the temple in Jerusalem, unknown probably to everyone except the author and the priest who secreted it. Manasseh reigned for fifty-five years, and was succeeded by Amon, who was as bad as his father. When at last the book was discovered in the eighteenth year of Josiah (619 B.C.), all who knew about it had died, and it had to be judged solely on its own merits. The prophets of the day endorsed it as a welcome program of reform. The prophetess Huldah, when she was consulted by Hezekiah, declared that it was a word of Yahweh, and thus put the first book into the Canon of Scripture.[109] Jeremiah tells us how he went about the cities of Judah, reading the book to the people, and urging them to obey it.[110] Thus the prophets succeeded in winning the support of the nobles and of the priests so that an assembly was called by King Josiah, in which Deuteronomy was adopted as the law of the nation, and a reformation was carried out on the basis of its provisions.[111]

Through the Deuteronomic compromise the prophets won a partial victory, but they paid a heavy price for it. The adoption of Deuteronomy was speedily followed by an ethical deterioration of prophecy. Little by little the prophets abandoned the position of Amos, "righteous-

[109] II Ki. 22: 8-20.
[110] Jer. 11: 1-8.
[111] II Ki. 23: 1-25.

ness not ritual,'' and took up the Deuteronomic position, ''righteousness and ritual.'' This soon declined into the old Hebrew position, ''ritual and righteousness,'' and ended in the Pharisaic position, ''ritual not righteousness.'' When the ethical message was gone, prophecy had nothing more to live for, and soon died a natural death.

In Jeremiah the deterioration from the ethical standard of Amos, Hosea, Isaiah, and Micah, and of himself before the Deuteronomic reformation in 619, was still slight. He continued to denounce immorality and social injustice, and to threaten the nation with the Babylonian exile, down to the fall of Jerusalem in 586 B.C.; but he also exhorted to keep the Sabbath and to bring sacrifices in a manner quite contradictory to the teaching of his predecessors.[112]

The Holiness Code in Leviticus 17-26, which was written about 600 B.C., is like Deuteronomy in emphasizing morality in chapters 18-20, and in chapter 26 it announces the impending exile in genuine prophetic style; but in chapters 17 and 21-25 it develops a ritual program considerably in advance of Deuteronomy.

Ezekiel, before the destruction of Jerusalem in 586 B.C., preached righteousness, repentance, and the judgment to come, like the earlier prophets. In chapter 18 of his book he gives a summary of moral obligations that would have been entirely acceptable to the school of Amos, but mingled with these are the purely ceremonial requirements, not to sacrifice in the high places, and not to approach a woman in her ''uncleanness.'' Ezekiel also attached a high value to the temple, even though he expected it to be destroyed; and he found one of the reasons for its destruction in the fact that the people had ''defiled'' it.[113] He also regarded the distinction between ceremonially

112 Jer. 17: 19-27.
113 Ezek. 5: 11; 8: 3-18; 10: 1-4, 18-19; 20: 40; 37: 26f.

"clean" and "unclean" as very important, and protested: "Ah Lord Yahweh! behold, my soul hath not been polluted; for from my youth up even until now have I not eaten that which dieth of itself, or is torn of beasts; neither came there abominable flesh into my mouth.'"[114] He laid a new and peculiar emphasis upon the Sabbath as the sign of the covenant between Yahweh and Israel, and as an institution that could be observed away from Jerusalem,[115] and he regarded sacrifice as obligatory.[116]

After the fall of Jerusalem the character of his preaching changed fundamentally. He assumed that with this event the predictions of doom of the older prophets had found a complete fulfillment; accordingly, he no longer preached righteousness, sin, repentance, and judgment; but began to preach the restoration of Judah from the exile, and the coming glory of the nation. In chapters 40-48 he gave a plan for the new temple that was to be built after the restoration, and elaborate directions as to how its ritual was to be kept up. This code developed the ceremonial far beyond Deuteronomy and the Holiness Code, and prepared the way for the legislation of the Priestly Code in Leviticus and kindred portions of the Pentateuch. Can one imagine Amos or Isaiah devoting eight chapters of his book to material of this sort!

In Deutero-Isaiah the fundamental conception of Yahweh is not His righteousness, as in the earlier prophets, but His transcendence and almighty power. The prophet speaks of the sins of the forefathers that brought upon them the destruction of the nation, but he does not speak of the sins of his contemporaries,[117] nor does he call the nation to repentance. There is no threatening of doom, as in the preëxilic prophets, but only the joyous announce-

114 Ezek. 4: 12-15.
115 Ezek. 20: 12-24; 22: 8, 26; 23: 38; cf. 44: 24; 45: 17; 46: 1-4, 12.
116 Ezek. 20: 40.
117 Isa. 40: 1; 42: 24f.; 43: 22-28; 44: 22; 47: 6; 50: 1; 53: 5-6.

ment of the speedy return from exile. The opening verse of the prophecy strikes the keynote of its message: "Comfort ye, comfort ye my people, saith your God. Speak ye tenderly to Jerusalem, and proclaim to her that her hard service is accomplished, her debt of guilt is discharged, that she has received from Yahweh's hand double for all her sins."[118] Here the exile is regarded as having paid twice over for the sins of the nation, so that now there are no arrears of guilt, and only glory and blessedness are to be expected in the future.

Haggai and Zechariah have no other message than build the temple and look for the coming glory of Israel.[119] Zechariah says that the fathers sinned, and that Yahweh was angry with them,[120] but he finds nothing to criticize in the community of his own day.[121] Upon Judah Yahweh looks with favor only;[122] consequently, Zechariah utters no call to repentance. Not against Judah, but against the heathen, is Yahweh angry, because they have united to afflict His chosen people. "I am very sore displeased with the nations that are at ease, for I was angry but a little, but they helped for evil."[123] This is characteristic of Zechariah. Yahweh was angry with the fathers only, and then only "a little," and the nations exceeded their commission in destroying Jerusalem.[124]

Trito-Isaiah has still several echoes of the earlier ethical prophecy,[125] but with these are combined a mass of ritual requirements derived from Deuteronomy. The temple of Zerubbabel had just been completed in 516 B.C. It was a poor affair, compared with the magnificent struc-

118 Isa. 40: 1-2.
119 Hag. 1: 2-9; 2: 6-9, 15-23; Zech. 1: 16; 3: 7; 4: 9; 6:12-15; 8: 9-13.
120 Zech. 1: 4-5; 8: 14-17.
121 Zech. 3: 1-5.
122 Zech. 1: 14, 16-17; 2: 10-13; 8: 1-8.
123 Zech. 1: 15.
124 Zech. 1: 21; 5: 10f.; 6: 8.
125 Isa. 56: 1-2, 10-12; 58: 1, 6, 7, 9b, 10; 59: 2-8, 12-15; 61: 8.

ture of Solomon, and the restored community was much discouraged at its insignificance,[126] but this prophet declares that the time is soon coming when the exiles in all lands shall return, bringing the wealth of the nations with them. Then the temple shall be adorned with silver and gold, and with the glory of Lebanon, the fir tree, the pine, and the box tree together, then multitudes of flocks and clouds of frankincense shall smoke upon its altar.[127] This temple at Jerusalem is the only legitimate place of worship, and the rival sanctuary of the Samaritans on Mount Gerizim is denounced as no better than heathenism.[128] The author is puzzled with the question, whether eunuchs and foreigners should be allowed to enter the temple, and decides that they should be permitted, if they will keep the Sabbath and obey the law of Deuteronomy.[129] The Sabbath has a peculiar importance for him, as for all the post-exilic prophets, and with this he couples the new moons.[130] Sacrifice he regards as highly important: "Their burnt-offerings and their sacrifices shall come up with acceptance on my altar." "All the flocks of Kedar shall be gathered together unto thee, the rams of Nebaioth shall minister unto thee, they shall come up with acceptance on my altar, and I will glorify the house of my glory." "The children of Israel shall bring their oblation in a clean vessel into the house of Yahweh; and of them also will I take for Levitical priests, saith Yahweh . . . and it shall come to pass, that from one new moon to another, and from one sabbath to another, shall all flesh come to worship before me, saith Yahweh.'"[131] Contrast this with the utterances of the prophets of the Assyrian

126 Ezr. 3: 12-13; Hag. 2: 7-9; Zech. 4: 6-10a; 6: 15.
127 Isa. 60: 4-9, 13.
128 Isa. 56: 5-7; 64: 11; 66: 20; 57: 7-8; 65: 11; 66: 1, 3, 6.
129 Isa. 56: 3-8.
130 Isa. 56: 2, 4, 6; 58: 13-14; 66: 23.
131 Isa. 56: 7; 60: 7; 66: 20, 23.

period!¹³² Like Deutero-Isaiah, Trito-Isaiah has no call to repentance, and announces no impending judgment. His book is taken up chiefly with a prediction of the glorious time that is coming, when the Jews shall triumph over all their enemies, when those who have ruled over them shall become their slaves, and when they shall gather in the riches of the nations.¹³³

Malachi has a single reminiscence of the ethical message of the older prophecy,¹³⁴ but the three main points of his message are: do not sacrifice defective animals,¹³⁵ divorce foreign wives,¹³⁶ and "bring the whole tithe into the storehouse, that there may be food in my house, and prove me now herewith, saith Yahweh of hosts, if I will not open you the windows of heaven, and pour you out a blessing, that there shall not be room enough to receive it.'"¹³⁷ What a pathetic anticlimax of prophecy! For Malachi, as for all his predecessors since Ezekiel, the sole requirement of Yahweh was obedience to the law of Deuteronomy.¹³⁸

About 500 B.c. the Priestly Code of the Pentateuch was composed in Babylonia on the basis of priestly tradition concerning the usage of Solomon's temple. It did not contain a single moral precept, except the material taken up with the included Holiness Code in Lev. 18-20. It was brought up by Ezra out of Babylonia, and was adopted as canon law in addition to Deuteronomy in the assembly convened by Ezra in Jerusalem.¹³⁹ This event marked the death of prophecy. In its place there now arose a school of apocalyptic, which bore the same relation to prophecy

132 See notes 37-44.
133 Isa. 56: 8; 57: 14-19; 58: 8-12; 59: 15b-64: 12; 66: 7-16.
134 Mal. 3: 5.
135 Mal. 1: 6-2: 9.
136 Mal. 2: 10-16.
137 Mal. 3: 7-12.
138 Mal. 2: 6-9; 4: 4; *cf.* Hag. 2: 11-12; Zech. 7: 12; Isa. 58: 2.
139 Ezr. 7: 6, 10, 12, 14, 21, 25, 26; Neh. 8-10.

that mishna did to law, and midrash to history. It cared little for the prophetic message of righteousness, which was the high-water mark of the religion of Israel, but busied itself in constructing out of the early prophets by means of allegorical exegesis a picture of the coming Jewish world-monarchy. The ethical message of Amos and his successors still lingered in the hearts of the faithful few, and came to expression in some of the psalms; but no more prophets arose until John the Baptist and Jesus of Nazareth appeared, preaching the ancient message, "Repent ye, for the kingdom of God is at hand."[140]

[140] Matt. 3: 1-2; Mark 1: 4; Luke 3: 1-3; Matt. 4: 17; Mark 1: 14-15.

For further literature on this subject see W. S. Bruce, *The Ethics of the Old Testament*, 1895; A. Duff, *Theology and Ethics of the Hebrews*, 1902; H. G. Mitchell, *The Ethics of the Old Testament*, 1912; J. M. P. Smith, *The Moral Life of the Hebrews*, 1923; with full bibliography.

ETHICS OF THE GREEK RELIGION

PAUL SHOREY

VIII.

OF the four or five topics naturally comprised in an essay on Greek ethics the space at my disposal permits me to discuss only one. I discard without regret the conjectural reconstruction of the psychology of primitive man and the supposed prehistoric and pre-Homeric evolution of ethical ideas. Whatever their *a priori* and theoretical justification, the curiosities represented by Westermarck's *Origin of the Moral Ideas* in practice contribute little to modern culture beyond the unsettlement of moral principles and the confusion of thought that threatens to break down the administration of justice. To the interpretation of Greek life and literature these studies bring little but the systematic misapprehension of the texts in the quest for survivals. It is better to ignore them altogether and to begin with Homer.

A comparison of the practical morality of the Greeks with our own would be of the greatest interest, but it would be both too difficult and too long a task for our present limits, and would involve too much negative criticism of current misconceptions. Even L. Schmidt[1] evades it. I do not know how to determine whether the average Greek was more or less truthful, more or less observant of property rights, more or less generous than the average European. Seymour says that in Homer human life is held in light esteem. But daily reading of both Homer and the newspapers may leave a doubt whether it was held in less esteem than in Chicago or New York. I do not know whether the Greek was more or less restrained in the indulgence of his animal and sexual appetites. The best and most widely read book on the Greek view of life, now in its seventh edition, cites as "the most curious illustration we possess of the distinction between Greek civilization

---

[1] *Ethik der Griechen*, 1. 4.

and our own" the fact that the orator Demosthenes made
the statement, as a matter of course, in open court that
"every man requires beside his wife at least two mistresses." Well, it is not true. Demosthenes did not say it.
And Plato in his *Laws*[2] expresses essentially the most
scrupulous modern sentiment on the whole question. I do
not even know whether the ideals of the normal Greek in
this matter were lower than those apparently avowed by
Anatole France, Rémy de Gourmont, and their American
admirers.[3] For the rest, no generalization on these matters would be of any value that did not distinguish the
different periods of Greek life through the fifteen hundred years of ancient civilization, and even if we were
competent to judge the evidence, its collection would require a volume.

The omission of Greek philosophies of ethics may seem
a paradox. Yet in our space it would be impossible to discuss the ethical philosophies of Plato and Aristotle, not
to speak of the Stoics and Epicureans and the other later
schools. It must suffice to say, what will not be believed,
that with perhaps one exception there is no problem of
modern ethics that, with allowance for the difference of
terminology, is not adequately examined by either Plato
or Aristotle. The obvious exception is the moral aspect of
the modern conflict between capital and labor in all its
ramifications.[4] That grows out of conditions unknown to
the Greeks and outside the range of their imaginative experience. But all other problems of modern ethics are as
clearly formulated and as nearly solved by the Greek
philosophers as they are in any modern speculations. The
pre-Socratic nature philosophy and the disintegrating
criticism of the sophists, the political experiences of the

[2] 636 C, 837.
[3] *Cf.* W. H. S. Jones, *Greek Morality*, p. 119.
[4] Lowes Dickinson, *Greek View of Life* (7), p. 102.

Peloponnesian War and the restless questionings of Euripides presented to the Greek mind in Plato's youth every form of ethical nihilism, unrestrained individualism and affirmation of the right to indulge instinct and lead one's own life that baffles the modern moralist. Then, as now, all the old sanctions had broken down or at any rate been challenged in a way that necessitated a reconsideration of their defense or the discovery of new principles of social and ethical control. The evidence for this is easily accessible in the *Gorgias* and *Republic* of Plato, the *History* of Thucydides[5] in fragments of the Greek sophists and in many passages of Euripides. The ethics of Plato is in the main like the various ethical systems of today, an attempt to meet this challenge,[6] and the ethics of Aristotle is a systematization on the lower plane of common sense and ordinary Greek experience of the more absolute and ideal Platonic ethics. The two together, as we have said, leave few points in modern ethical philosophies untouched.[7] This may be denied by readers who have not taken time to acquaint themselves with what Plato and Aristotle actually said, or who feel an *a priori* certainty that the ethical and political ideas of these early thinkers must have been as far inferior to ours as we know their acquaintance with the laws of nature to have been. It is plainly beyond our scope to discuss so large a question, and there would be no profit in adding one more to the hundreds of misleading abstracts of Greek philosophy already in print. Translations of the ethical works of Plato and Aristotle abound and there is no lack of volumes of extracts which will give a sufficient idea of their

[5] *Cf.* my paper on "The Implicit Ethics and Psychology of Thucydides," *Transactions of the American Philological Association*, 1893, p. 66.

[6] *Cf.* my paper on "The Interpretation of the Timæus," *American Journal of Philology*, 1888, IX, 395.

[7] For the ethical philosophy of Plato, *cf.* my *Unity of Plato's Thought*, pp. 9-27.

ethical temper, though not, of course, of their ethical philosophy.[8]

With these omissions our subject is reduced to the ethics of the Greek writers, mainly the poets, from Homer to Euripides. We wish to learn something of the growth of ethical ideas and ideals through these centuries, of the problems debated, of the extent and discrimination of the terminologies and classifications that were worked out, and, most significant of all, the highest point reached in comparison with absolute and ideal Platonic or Christian ethics.

The first thing to note about Homeric ethics is the general character of the background. The Homeric world is, in the main, a wholesome and bracing moral atmosphere. Some inhibitions of theoretic and ideal modern ethics are unknown or unobserved. Soldiers on campaign are not faithful to their wives, as modern soldiers invariably are, and the Homeric language about those who have "killed a man" and "left town" recalls the "wild West" of fiction.

But the personages of Homer and their conduct as a whole command our respect and sympathy rather more than those of the ordinary modern novel. There is perhaps little conscious morality as there is not much explicit consciousness of duty or sin. There is little mention of crime and hardly any reference to lying and stealing. There is no allusion to unnatural vices and no drunkenness or gluttony. These and similar traits of the Homeric epic are sometimes explained as due to an expurgating revision of the poems by a later age. But that is an arbi-

8 Mr. Lowes Dickinson's *Greek View of Life* is mainly based on Plato and Aristotle; Miss Hilda Oakeley's *Greek Ethical Thought* in the Library of Greek Thought Series, edited by Principal Ernest Barker, gives a hundred and thirty-seven pages out of two hundred and twenty-one to Plato and Aristotle, and Mr. F. M. Cornford's *Greek Religious Thought*, in the same series, forty-seven out of two hundred and forty-eight.

trary hypothesis for which there is neither proof nor probability. We may attribute it if we please to the taste of Homer or to that of his aristocratic audiences. Equally without support in evidence or probability is the notion of Hegel that before Socrates there was no morality, the generalization that in the apparently ethical language of Homer the expressions of approval and disapproval have not yet developed the moral meanings which the later usage of the same words would read into them. Because "good" is sometimes equivalent to "brave in battle" or used as we speak of "good society," or older French usage spoke of "l'honnête homme," and the word for justice δίκη sometimes means merely the customary way of doing things, we may not infer that these words never are charged with ethical meaning in Homer.[9] On the contrary, there are many passages in which Homeric approval or disapproval of the good and just, the bad and unjust, action or man, is as distinctly moral as the judgments of simple and unsophisticated minds can be in any age. Homer had no philosophy of ethics and no ideal Platonic or Golden Rule as an absolute standard by which to measure all human shortcomings, and his personages did not always, and perhaps could not, distinguish moral from prudential wisdom any more than the majority of mankind do to-day. But unless we deny ethical language and ethical consciousness to all except moral philosophers and pure idealists, we must often take ethical terms in Homer in their ethical meaning.

Similarly, though the Homeric divinities are often unmoral mythological figures, magnified men, Mycenæan lords at their ease reclined, and unhampered by mortal limitations, it is idle to deny that they are also sometimes thought of as guardians of the moral law. The contradic-

[9] *Cf.* my article "Greek Religion and Ethics," in Hastings' *Encyclopædia*, and article on Homer in *New International Encyclopædia*, 1904.

tion was felt by pious ancients and is the basis of the censure of the mythology in Plato and the Christian Fathers. It differs, perhaps, only in degree from that latent in all anthropomorphic theologies. In any case, the fact remains; the gods love not evil deeds. A doer of evil is a sinner in the sight of the gods. *Theoudes,* "god-revering," is contrasted with insolence and injustice, and bracketed with hospitality in *Odyssey,* IX, 175-176, and it is associated with the righteous judgment of a good king in *Odyssey,* XIX, 109. *Opis* is the moral or avenging oversight of the gods, which the wicked and the reckless heed not— *Iliad,* XVI, 388, *Odyssey,* XXI, 28, and *Odyssey,* XIV, 82, where the suitors are also heedless of pity. The wrath of Zeus descends on those who deliver unjust judgments as his blessings are bestowed on those whose judgments are straight.[10] And Homer nearly anticipates the saying attributed in various forms to Emerson, John Knox, and pro-Boer orators, that God and one are a majority.[11]

The two chief natural sanctions of conduct in Homer are: *aidôs* and *nemesis,* both of which tempt to dissertations that I must postpone to another occasion. *Aidôs* is not, as a fascinating writer has told the social settlements of the world, pity or social compunction. It is more nearly respect for the opinion of the respectable—fear of their disapproval. Two lines of Tennyson define it better than pages of pedantry:

> (Shall) he for whose applause I strove
> I had such reverence for his blame?

It is *aidôs* that holds the soldier in his place, that makes the youth modest in the presence of his elders and abashes

---

[10] *Cf. Odyssey,* XIX, 110 ff.; *Iliad,* XVI, 386; Hesiod, *Works and Days,* 225 ff. Plato satirizes this as a utilitarian view of the profits of religion (*Republic,* 363b), and Frazer in his *Psyche* (p. 16) emphasizes the note of superstition in it—both to suit their purpose, but unfairly.

[11] *Odyssey,* XVI, 260.

all men in the presence of the Parthenos aidoie, which
does not mean "blushful" or "blushing" maid. *Nemesis*
is righteous indignation, justified disapproval at the violation of *Themis* and *Dike,* which, whatever survivals of
primitive ideas may attach to them, are in the main perfectly natural expressions for the entirety of the social,
moral, or legal code. Always to translate *Themistes,*
Dooms, with a capital letter, and *Dike,* Way, is to invite
misunderstanding. Right, lawful, just, are often much
truer to the tone of the Greek words in their context.
Other words in Homer's ethical vocabulary which contain
more than the germ of later ideas are: *agathos*—good,
and its virtual synonym—*esthlos; arete,* virtue, excellence, bravery; *saophron,* sober, chaste, discreet, prudent,
the uncontracted spelling of which misleads Jebb into the
statement that *sôphron* does not occur in Homer; *dikaios,*
just; *noêmon,* sensible, intelligent, considerate, which is
bracketed with *dikaios* and so may be pressed to yield the
fourth cardinal virtue, wisdom;[12] *sebas,* awe, reverence,
shrinking, allied to, but not to be confounded with, *aidôs;*
hosie, holiness, found only in the *Odyssey; hybris,* outrage, insolence; *kakos,* coward, bad; *ate,* infatuation, judicial blindness; *atasthalie,* wanton wickedness, presump-
tuous sin.

From the material thus sufficiently indicated, systematic books have been compiled on Homeric religion and
ethics. They contain little that the English reader cannot
find in more convenient and trustworthy summary in Seymour's *Life in the Homeric Age.* The German historian
of Greek ethics tells us that the *Iliad* and *Odyssey* throw
a clear light upon the goods to which the heart of the
Greek clung and for which he would risk everything—
the Fatherland, glory, friendship, the happiness of the

12 *Cf. Seymour,* p. 447.

home. The optimist could say as much of any great people.

Hesiod's *Works and Days* is sometimes plausibly said to represent a reaction toward realism and a criticism of life from the point of view of the common man, and the occupations of peace as opposed to the idealism, the aristocratic temper, and the martial spirit of Homer. As the beginning of cosmological and theological speculation has been found in the systematic genealogies and abstract personifications of the *Theogony,* so we may detect in the *Works and Days* the germs of ethical philosophy in the attempted explanation of the origin of evil by the myths of Prometheus and Pandora, and of the four (five) ages of man. The problem of evil, if it be one, is still open to debate. And we have as yet found no better evasion than Plato's remark in the *Lysis* that good would be meaningless without evil, or his argument in the *Theætetus* that good connotes evil as its logical opposite. Rudimentary ethical reflection may also be found in the fable of the hawk and the nightingale (202 ff.), embodying the "good old rule" of Wordsworth's "Grave of Rob Roy"; in the four (five) ages of man with its pessimistic conclusion that in the present age of iron all moral restraints have broken down and Aidôs and Nemesis have fled from earth (200); in the distinction between the good and bad Eris, corresponding to that between emulation and envy (11-25); and in the allegory of the broad and easy way to evil and the hill of Virtue before which the gods have set sweat, but which becomes easy when once the heights are gained (287 ff.). Hesiod's *arete* is not precisely our virtue[13] but no sharp line can be drawn between his expression of the thought and the succession which runs through Simonides, *The Table* of Cebes, Dante, and Spenser's

[13] *Cf.* Lowes Dickinson, *The Greek View of Life* (7), p. 137.

Faerie Queene, to Tennyson's "Ode on the Death of the Duke of Wellington" and Watson's:

> There is toil on the steeps;
> On the summit repose.

And in the present fashion of thought we are more likely to err by denying than by attributing ethical meaning to *arete.* One of the noblest passages in Pindar is spoiled by a historian of Greek ethics, who insists on translating *arete, ruhm,* i.e., fame.[14]

The most prominent ethical idea in Hesiod is justice. She is personified as the daughter of Zeus, who reports crooked judgments to him.[15] Justice is distinctly associated with courts of law and with the poet's protest against the unjust decree of the corrupt judges in the division of his father's estate between him and his brother Perses. The admonition to practice justice is confirmed by the warning that the gods inflict punishment[16] on the sinner. It is for beasts to wrangle and fight, for there is no justice among them.[17] *Hybris* is opposed to justice, as in Homer, but the farmer-poet naturally deprecates it more earnestly. Inability to refrain from *hybris* was the destruction of the second race (134) and of the third (146-147). The iron race honored *hybris* above the oath-keeping, the just, the good man (191). Perses is warned to eschew it, for justice prevails over *hybris* in the end.[18]

Other ethical precepts hardly admit of classification. Many of them, as the recommendation of industry, are especially addressed to the erring brother Perses.[19] In

14 *Pyth.,* 4, 18.
15 *Works and Days,* 256 ff.; *cf.* 220.
16 Dike, *Works and Days,* 245, 280 ff.; Opis, *Theogony,* 220. *Cf. supra.*
17 *Works and Days,* 275 ff.
18 218. *Cf.* Plato, *Republic,* 613c.
19 303, 397.

many, as often happens in this stage of ethical reflection, prudential counsels are indistinguishable from pure ethics. Industry brings wealth, and excellence (*arete*) and honor attend upon wealth. Duly worship the gods "in order that you may buy the other man's lot and not he yours" (341) is as naïve as Tennyson's northern farmer. "When you borrow, return good measure so that in case of need you may borrow again" (351) anticipates the cynical psychology of La Rochefoucauld. Some of the sayings, whether so intended or not, may be taken as symbols of higher spiritual meanings, as Plato takes "Fools, they know not how much more the half is than the whole."[20] Such are "The eye of Zeus sees all things," which anticipates the faith of Socrates in Xenophon's *Memorabilia,* I, 1. 19, and "a man who devises evil for another devises evil for himself" (265). Cambell[21] remarks that in the saying "To give is nobler than to receive" prudential morality seems to pass out of itself, but I do not know to what in Hesiod's text he refers. Other sayings, especially in the catalogue of lucky and unlucky days, belong to folklore, survivals, and the superstitions of the populace, and do not concern us here.

All Hesiodic sayings were familiar to literate Greeks, who learned them at school and met them in the allusions and paraphrases of the tragedians and philosophers. Among these familiar quotations were "The hill of Virtue" and "The two kinds of Eris" already mentioned; the remark that some men know of themselves what is best, some can learn it from others,[22] but the man who can

---

[20] *Cf.* Plato, *Republic,* 466c.

[21] *Religion in Greek Literature,* p. 110.

[22] Endlessly quoted and paraphrased from Sophocles, *Antigone,* 720, Aristotle, *Ethics,* 1095b, 10, Cicero, Livy, St. Basil, and Ascham's schoolmaster to Watson's:

> 'Tis human fortune's happiest height to be
> A spirit melodious, lucid, poised and whole;
> Second in order of felicity
> I hold it, to have walk'd with such a soul.

do neither is of little use (292); the observation that experience is the teacher of fools;[23] and reflections on the power of hope (317, 500), of Rumor (reputation, fame), who is also a goddess (763), and the recommendation of measure and season in all things (694).

Herodotus, the younger contemporary of Pindar and Æschylus, says that Hesiod lived "some four hundred years before my time."[24] Much happened in these three or four centuries, but the literary record is slight and this sketch has no place for the conjectures with which modern philological ingenuity fills the gap and essays to fix the chronology. It is easy to enumerate such topics as the growth and expansion of Greek civilization, the progress of exploration, trade, and colonization, the evolution of hereditary monarchy and aristocracy through tyranny to democracy, and the effect of these conflicts and of the increase of wealth and the extension of knowledge on the consciousness of personality and its expression in new forms of literature, the development or the emergence of religious ideas and practices unmentioned by Homer, as the ritualistic purification of blood-guiltiness, hero-worship, and the idea of a judgment of the dead. But such generalizations mean little without explicit documentation. And all we have, apart from the retrospective gossip of Herodotus, is the few Homeric hymns, the fragments of the lyrists, and the gnomic poetry of a Solon, a Phocylides, and a Theognis.

Something more is known of the beginnings of Greek philosophy and of the development of mysticism in the sixth century associated with such names as Orpheus, Musæus, Pythagoras.[25] The omission of this latter as-

[23] 218, also found in Homer, *Iliad*, XVII, 32.

[24] II, 53.

[25] *Cf.* Gomperz, *Greek Thinkers*, I, 80 ff.; Clifford Moore, *Religious Thought of the Greeks*, chap. 2; Rohde's *Psyche*, now accessible in the English translation of W. B. Hillis.

pect of our subject will seem inexcusable to those who do not understand that the language of mysticism in Plato is always literary ornament and conscious symbolism. Without detailed philological scrutiny of the evidence there is nothing profitable to be said about the religion of Greek mysticism and the mysteries, unless it be to quote again, after Matthew Arnold, Pindar's "Blessed is the man who hath beheld these things before he goeth under the earth. He knoweth the end of man's life and he knoweth its God-given beginning," qualifying Arnold's idealization with the observation of Aristotle that the mysteries taught little that was definite, but showed things that put the neophyte into a certain state of mind.

To return to the literature—the English reader will most conveniently study the so-called "Homeric Hymns" in the introduction to Andrew Lang's beautiful translation. They contain some material for the comparison of Greek religion with universal folklore, and some further illustration of the commonplace of Homeric criticism that the Greek gods as anthropomorphic figures of mythology are unmoral. For religion and ethics proper they offer little beyond one or two texts for a cynical essay on the profits of religion and a passage on the mysteries of Demeter, which is often bracketed with that of Pindar above cited: "Happy is he among deathly men who hath beheld these things! and he that is uninitiate, and hath no lot in them, hath never equal lot in death beneath the murky gloom."

The fragments of the lyrists present few ideas that cannot be equally well illustrated from Homer, Pindar, Simonides, and the tragedians. The martial elegists, Callinus and Tyrtæus, exalt the brave man whose "virtue redounds to the good of all." The passionate Archilochus reveals his entire personality, tells of his loves and hates, knows one big thing, to requite his enemy with evil,[26] warns us that anything may happen and that all comes from God, and preaches the Homeric lesson, "Endure, my heart, endure!" In an animal fable, his eagle, wronged by the fox, appeals to Zeus, who knows the *hybris* and the justice (*dike*) of beasts.[27] Mimnermus, and after him Anacreon, sings of love and of the sensualist view of life as a worthless thing when Love and swift Youth have fled. Semonides satirizes the various types of women under animal forms. And other lyrists tell of their loves and passions and occasionally moralize on the transience of human happiness, the good of the passing hour, the lure of hope, the supremacy of God. All Greek poets, in violation of the latest modern precepts, moralize— even Sappho tells us that handsome will be that handsome does, and that wealth without virtue is a dangerous companion. The Athenian statesman and reformer Solon has much to say of justice and the square deal, and expounds his own resultant philosophy of life in ripe, rambling reflections on the late punishment of the wicked, the various pursuits and ambitions of men, the uncertainty of success, and the dependence of all on God.

The collection of thirteen or fourteen hundred elegiac lines, attributed to Theognis of Megara, is a repertory of ordinary pre-Æschylean Greek ethical terms and ideas. His sayings were familiar to every educated Greek, were taken as texts by the philosophers, and are sometimes paraphrased in the choruses of Greek tragedy. Theognis is the *locus classicus* for the use of "good" in the political or social sense. He advises association with the "good" and warns against the evil communications which Æschylus, Menander, and St. Paul tell us corrupt good manners. He has texts for most of the Greek moral

---

[26] *Cf.* Hesiod, *supra*, p. 243, and Pindar, *infra*, p. 250.
[27] *Cf.* Hesiod, *supra*, p. 243.

commonplaces. He has much to say of vicissitude, hope, wealth, and poverty. He protests to Father Zeus against the visitation of the sins of the fathers on the sons.[28] He declares before Sophocles that not to be born is best of all, and next, to die as soon as may be.[29] I have given a compact summary of his teaching in the article "Theognis" in Hastings' *Encyclopædia of Religion and Ethics*.

Simonides owes his place among Arnold's four prophets of the religion of the imaginative reason to the glorious epigrams or epitaphs on the heroes of the Persian Wars, which still remain the inevitable and unapproachable models for all modern utterances of this kind, and also to a few noble and resigned passages on the frailty and ephemeral lot of mankind. Such as, for example:

> Remember thou art mortal and forbear
> To boast how on the morrow thou shalt fare;
> And deem no happy man secure of earthly span.
> As is the fleet fly's filmy-winged brood
> So swift vicissitude.

But the Greeks, or at any rate Plato, hardly thought of him as an ideal moralist, and Schmidt's *Ethik der Griechen* draws very slightly upon him. In a life of nearly one hundred years he became a dominating literary figure and a finished artist who knew how to make his art highly profitable, an interesting and stimulating critic of life, art, and morals. But the chief passage which Plato quotes from him, the poem interpreted with excessive ingenuity by Socrates in the dialogue "Protagoras," though it contains the line from which Dante got through Aristotle his

> Ben tetragono ai colpi di ventura

and Tennyson the 'foursquare to all the winds that blew''

---

[28] 735, first mentioned in Hesiod, *Works and Days*, 185-186, then in Solon, and sometimes thought to be implied in Homer.

[29] 425. *Cf. Œdipus at Colonus*, 1224.

of his "Ode on the Death of the Duke of Wellington," is
not, on the whole, a trumpet call of the ideal. It seems
rather a plea for a reasonable compromise of impracticable standards, and its moral, if it has one, is that which
Mr. Drinkwater supposes we have only recently learned
from modern psychology, "that it is quite unsafe to call
anyone just good or bad, and leave it at that."[30]

The vicissitudes of Pindar's fame point to the one law
of literary history—the law of fashion and reaction. The
older lyric was already out of fashion in Euripides' day,
and though Plato was in essential sympathy with the
spirit of Pindar, he makes the young men of his dialogue,
the *Lysis,* satirize the old-fashioned type of the conventional encomiastic ode. To skip the intervening centuries,
in the mid-Victorian literary generation, Pindar, though
of course not a popular poet, was greatly admired by such
leaders of thought as Matthew Arnold, Froude, Ruskin,
and Pater, and among scholars was regarded as the very
quintessence of the Greek spirit by Jebb and Gildersleeve
and Wilamowitz. The more advanced thought of the generation of Murray and Mackail puts him by with smiling
irony or damns him with faint praise. We have not here
to consider his merits as a poet. His interest for us is that
he represents provincial, aristocratic, conservative, ath-
letic, older normal Greek feeling, as contrasted with the
democratic, the sophisticated, the radical thought, that
found expression on the stage of Euripides. All that need
be said of his religion is that he is, like Plato and Æschylus and Sophocles, in the line of the tradition that reverently, and not with Voltairian epigram, deprecates the
less moral parts of the mythology,[31] and that his second
"Olympian Ode" is the earliest text that distinctly af-

[30] See my article on Simonides in *New International Encyclopædia,* 1904.
[31] The liberal or radical Gomperz' way of putting this is that these poets
were unlike Euripides' "trimmers." *Greek Thinkers,* II, 13.

firms immortality and the judgment of the dead.[32] We do not look for a systematic ethics in him. The four cardinal virtues have been read into a passage of the odes where three of them are explicitly named.[33] We need not try to refine away the two passages where, in conformity to ordinary pre-Platonic ethics, he seems to say that anything is justifiable against an enemy.[34] The criticism of life that so endeared him to Matthew Arnold is found partly in the sentences of Greek moral commonplace scattered through the odes, partly in the noble poetic expression and calm acceptance of the brevity, the uncertainty, the tragedy of human destiny, and wholly, perhaps, in the grand style and serene beauty of his expression of what seem to us the essential Greek moods of simplicity, sobriety, measure, reverence, in contradistinction to their opposites in the literature of the hour. Chief among Pindar's conservative commonplaces are the recognition that all is from God and no man can command the future and that therefore the good of the day is all we can count upon; the praise of justice, generosity, hospitality, moderation, and reverence for parents; the warning against envy and insolence—"Violence shall ruin a man at the last, boast he never so loudly";[35] and reckless innovation —"A weakling can upset a state, but to set it on its base again is a hard struggle";[36] the superiority of natural to acquired gifts, and the admonition "Learn what thou art and to thine own self be true.''[37]

By the sheer power of the grand style in simplicity,

[32] There is much on this topic in James Adam's Gifford lectures on *The Religious Teachers of Greece* and in his *The Vitality of Platonism*, both of which are to be used with caution. The chief authority on the whole subject is Rohde's *Psyche, cf. supra,* p. 245.

[33] *Nemean,* III, 72-75.

[34] *Pyth.,* II, 84; *Isth.,* III, 66 (IV, 48).

[35] *Pyth.,* VIII, 15.

[36] *Pyth.,* IV, 272.

[37] *Pyth.,* II, 72.

such reflections are sublimed into great poetry, in Matthew Arnold's favorite lines

> Life unshaken
> Dwelt not with Peleus, Æacus' son, nor Cadmus.
> Sons of gods were they and of men most happy
> Were they counted who heard the golden-snooded
> Muses singing on Pelion's height and down in
> Thebes of seven gates, when Harmonia large-eyed
> Wed the one, and to Peleus golden Thetis
> Came as bride the daughter of wise old Nereus;
> Yet they too knew sorrow and change of fortune.

A thought which Professor Mackail prefers in Simonides' expression of it:

> Not even those heroes of the olden day,
> Sons of our lords, the gods, in times far past,
> Brought life unvexed by fear, pain, toil, decay,
> To happy eld and death at last.

And again in the lines of perhaps Pindar's latest poem on that dream of a shadow—Man, which anticipate and often inspire all that later poets and philosophers have said on the theme, from Shakespeare's "shadow of a dream" to Tennyson's "dream of a shadow" and Præd's chaunt of the Brazen Head.

Nothing less than the eloquence of a Ruskin could do justice to our third point, the contrast between Pindar's manner of speaking of great matters, as, for example, sex, or the mysteries of birth and heredity, and the language of the modish modern criticism of life.

Spirit of beautiful Youth, herald of Aphrodite's loves divine, thou that hovering over the eyelids of boy or girl, dost handle one with the force of a gentle compulsion, but others otherwise. And man must content him if not straying from season and measure in all his endeavours he be given power to attain his nobler desires.[38]

[38] *Nemean*, VIII.

And again:

Eleithuia enthroned on high by the side of the deep-souled Des-
    tinies
Birth-goddess, daughter of mighty Hera, mother of all life, hear
    our prayer.
If we look on the light of the day or the mask of the night, thy
    grace it is
That leadeth us on to thy sister Hebe who maketh the limbs of
    our youth so fair.[39]

And in place of such hymns we teach the adolescent to
chatter of eugenics, and chromosomes, and Mendelian
dominants, and the glands that control personality, and
the procreative urge as the origin of religion, and sex experience and sex "appeal." Is it not pertinent to recall
the warning of Socrates?[40]

Ill words [about the great issues of life and death] are not only
in themselves discordant but they infect the soul with evil.

I do not really intend anything so foolish as the systematic disparagement of modern civilization in comparison
with Greek life in the fifth century.[41] But the contrast of
Pindar's ideals and the expression of them with those of
the most widely advertised literature of our day imposes
itself. "Il n'y a de la poésie," writes Anatole France,
"que dans le désir de l'impossible, ou dans le regret de
l'irréparable." The tonic passages of Pindar are a crushing reply both to the literary criticism and to the implied
ethics of this dictum. For they are at once supreme poetry
and insistent preaching of the opposite ideal. "The love
of the impossible," said the Greek proverb, "is a malady
of the soul"—and many of Pindar's finest lines reiterate

[39] *Nemean,* VII.
[40] *Phædo,* 115e, elaborated in a notable passage of Mill's *Essay on The-
ism* (p. 248). *Cf. Class. Phil.,* July, 1926, p. 267.
[41] *Cf.* my article on the "Age of Pericles" in the *Forum,* April, 1925, p.
495.

the warning. Of a heroine whose willful soul would not heed it, he sings:

She was enamoured of absent things, a malady incident to many. For there is a tribe among men most vain that scorns the things of home and peers after things afar, pursuing phantoms with un- accomplished hopes.[42]

The principle of Anatole France would lead to the art of a Verlaine and an Oscar Wilde and little else. And that, as I have said elsewhere,[43] though it may appeal to our moods of reaction, will never permanently content us as reasonable beings. The soul that speaks to us in Greek art and poetry and philosophy is the soul of form that doth the body make, the informing soul of the imaginative rea- son, of sobriety, measure, harmony, proportion, and vol- untary allegiance to the everlasting laws of beauty. "The mystical in art, the mystical in life, the mystical in nature —that is what I am looking for. It is absolutely necessary for me to find it somewhere!" cries Oscar Wilde hysteri- cally *de profundis*—from the bottom of the pit. "I pray that with God's help I may still love what is beautiful and strive only for things attainable in the days of my youth." That is the note of Pindar, most typical of Greek artists, and it is the ideal of Greek education as described by Plato and Aristophanes.

The theology of Æschylus is open to wide diversity of interpretation according as we dwell upon its mythologi- cal garb or fix our attention on the almost monotheistic religion of Zeus, guardian of justice and author of the law that wisdom comes through suffering, worshiped by the chorus of the Supplices with a sublimity that recalls the prophets of the Old Testament, identified in the *Agamem- non* with the mysterious God of humanity's wistful quest in a hymn that far outsoars the ὕμνος ἄυμνος of Arthur Hugh

---

[42] *Pyth.*, III, 20 ff.
[43] "Age of Pericles," *Forum*, April, 1925, p. 503.

Clough or Watson's "The Unknown God." The main moral of the tragedies may be summed in the two formulas: the law of justice, that the doer must suffer, and the law that wisdom comes through suffering. The justice of Æschylus is—justice, the justice of Aristotle and the Old Testament. It is not generosity, or sweet reasonableness, or turning the other cheek, or social justice, or social compunction, or psychopathic therapeutics for murderers, or any other substitution or evasion of modern idealism and twentieth-century pseudo-science. He does not refine upon the idea or strain it by analogy to cover the entire Sermon on the Mount. And if his teaching retains for us any other than a historical value of curiosity it lies in the solemn intensity of his conviction of the awfulness of sin and the certainty of retribution. It is the moral which Matthew Arnold proclaimed in several volumes, and which the Chicago police are broadcasting to check crime in the form: "You cannot beat the game!" The Eumenides sing:

Hear our warning and obey,
To justice' altar reverence pay,
Let no lure
Tempt thee to spurn it for gain in the scorn of the Lord, for the
    day
Of his vengeance is sure.

.   .   .   .

God's laughter mocks the sinner hot in blood,
Who boasted he should ever find escape,
To see him tossing baffled on the flood
Helpless to round the last shipwrecking cape.
Lost, lost, forever lost, that wealth, that pride,
The reef of Justice touching but his vessel's side
He sinks, unwept, unseen beneath the tide.

It is a simple, primitive, not to say naïve, moral. Do we need it yet? That most popular of teachers, the author of the film of "The Ten Commandments," thinks we do. His last tableau, undesignedly I presume, is almost a direct illustration of the Æschylean imagery. To take a less trivial example, that entirely emancipated, modern, and scientific moralist, George Eliot, is so far from thinking that we have outgrown Æschylus, that she heads the chapters of *Middlemarch* with Æschylean sentences and sums up the lesson of Tito Melema's moral degeneracy almost in the words of a choric hymn of the Eumenides:

His mind was destitute of that dread . . . that awe of the divine Nemesis which was felt by religious pagans . . . and checks the hard bold scrutiny of imperfect thought into obligations which can never be proved to have any sanctity in the absence of feeling. "It is good," sing the old Eumenides in Æschylus, "that fear should sit as the guardian of the soul, forcing it into wisdom—good that men should carry a threatening shadow in their hearts under the full sunshine; else how shall they learn to revere the right?"

More appealing to modern sentiment is the lesson that wisdom comes through suffering:

But Zeus the victor holds eternal sway,
Zeus the wise shall still adore,
Who made us wise in wisdom's deepest lore,
That knowledge comes through suffering evermore.
In sleep drop drop upon the heart distill
The memories of ancient ill,
To chasten the soul and break the stubborn will.
And this too is a dark constraining grace
Of august powers that rule us from that highest place.

But there is perhaps a touch of modern coloring in my version, and the knowledge that we get from suffering may be only that the fear of the Lord is the beginning of wisdom.

It would be idle, and we have here no space, to work out a system of ethics for Æschylus, or to collect every say-

ing that may have some ethical significance. There are
of course some survivals of primitive superstition and
ritual, or of early moral code, as, *e.g.*, the three commandments to revere God, your parents, and the stranger
within your gates. But the overeager quest for such survivals leads to little but unprofitable speculation and mis-
construing of the Greek.[44] The eloquent exposition of the
mysterious Providence that confounds the innocent with
the guilty might be deemed one of these survivals of
primitive thought.[45] But in summing up the lessons of the
World War, Grey of Fallodon writes:

"Learn or perish" is the rule for nations as for individuals by
evident necessity, though the justice of it may seem inscrutable.
One nation or one individual cannot be saved by separate virtue.
A wise individual cannot escape being involved in misfortunes
due to the unwisdom of his countrymen; one nation may learn,
but may yet be involved in the misfortunes of a Continent that
does not learn.

The idea of spiritual evolution in the human or divine
order has been read into the reconciliation of Zeus and
Prometheus in the lost *Prometheus Unbound,* into the
succession of heavenly dynasties that culminate in Zeus,
in the hymn to the unknown God in the *Agamemnon,* and
into the transformation of the Furies into the Eumenides.
It is a pleasing fancy, if not more. The current statement
that another chorus of the *Agamemnon*[46] is an explicit
abandonment of the doctrine of the divine jealousy still
held by Æschylus himself in the *Persæ* is a plausible error, which only a critical examination of the texts could
explain away. Neither Æschylus nor any other Greek
poet clearly anticipates Plato's "envy has no place in the

[44] I may refer to my review of Cornford's *The Origin of Attic Comedy,*
in the *Nation,* Feb. 11, 1915, and my review of Lawson's *Modern Greek
Folklore and Ancient Greek Religion, ibid.,* March 30, 1911.
[45] *Seven Against Thebes,* 597 ff.
[46] 750 ff.

choir divine''[47] or so far transcends ordinary Greek moral feeling as to affirm with Plato, and Christianity, that the good man will not harm his enemies.

But the chief ethical impression made by Æschylus' plays is the unity of moral and religious feeling in each. That is a little disguised in the *Prometheus* because we have lost the reconciling sequel, and Milton's Satan, Byron's Cain, and Shelley's Prometheus have taught us to sympathize with the rebel. In the *Seven Against Thebes* the unity of tone may be felt by contrast with Euripides' *Phœnissæ*. There is much to be said for Polynices, the brother cheated of his promised share in the throne and unjustly exiled. And Euripides spares us no ingenuity of special pleading. For Æschylus it is enough that Polynices is attacking and threatening with destruction his own city, his motherland. The issue is plain. That is wrong. And Æschylus, admitting no discordant note, turns the full current of religious, moral, and patriotic emotion into one channel. The simple moral of the *Persæ* is the nemesis of world-conquering ambition, and the jealousy of heaven. That, too, we might think primitive if we had not been set to learn the lesson again in 1914-1918. The æsthetic sympathy of the modern reader for the glorious criminality of Clytæmnestra might be thought a violation of the moral unity of impression in the *Agamemnon*. And Æschylus himself is swept away by the intoxicating splendor of the rhetoric which expresses her "woman's virile-counselling eager hopeful heart." But his moral judgment never wavers. Her responsibility is fixed. And we are prepared for the retribution that overtakes her in the *Choëphoroe*. There, too, the appalling choral lyrics make us realize the dreadful nature of Orestes' deed. But we no more than he does doubt its necessity. His incipient madness, his persecu-

---

[47] *Phædrus,* 247 A.

tion by the Eumenides, his expiation in the sufferings of exile, further help to reconcile us. And when the final atonement and the conversion of the Furies into the gracious Eumenides comes, no sense of conflict is left in our mind. We have received a lesson and been confirmed in a faith, a mood, not amused or puzzled by the casuistry of a problem play.

The difference in religious and ethical tone between Æschylus and Sophocles is felt by all readers but diversely defined. Æschylus agitates, Sophocles calms and tranquillizes. Ancient as well as modern critics have said this. It is a fact. But to feel it fully one must read the Greek text, perhaps, in the light of some one of the many modern psychological interpretations of the Aristotelian *katharsis*.[48] Æschylus puts the fear of the Lord into our hearts. Sophocles declares the glory of God. For this we must read again the choruses of the *Agamemnon* and the *Eumenides* and compare them with the Sophoclean choruses, cited by Arnold in his essay on pagan and mediæval religious sentiment. Æschylus' dramatic criticism of life portrays man as dominated by some single force of fate, heredity, or infatuation. Sophocles relies more on the play, the clash, and even sometimes the evolution of character. And the lesson that wisdom comes through suffering, in the case of Œdipus at least, seems to receive the interpretation that character is tempered, softened, refined, bettered, in the fires of experience. Yet, though there is much more interplay and conflict of characters in Sophocles, the protagonist of the Sophoclean play, as Professor Norwood points out, is finally governed by an emotion as unswerving and inflexible as Æschylean fate, on which the assaults of reason, persuasion, and the pro-

---

[48] *Cf.* Gomperz, II, 6, speaking of Æschylus: Poetry shares with music the power . . . of creating the inward peace which reigns when the whole personality dominates over its minor elements, and of producing the intense pleasure peculiar to this state of psychical equilibrium.

tests of friends break in vain. We cannot delay to illustrate this by analyzing the actions of Ajax, Electra, Antigone, and less plausibly, perhaps, those of Deianira and
Philoctetes. Nor is there space to collect here and classify
all Sophoclean passages into which it is possible to read
ethical significance, whether historical or absolute. At the
head of such a list would stand Antigone's contrast of the
eternal unwritten laws of God with the decrees of Creon
—a chief text in all modern ethical culture, collective
scriptures. Mr. W. H. S. Jones' useful but forgotten little
book on *Greek Morality in Relation to Institutions* offers[49] a convenient index of all ethical and religious passages in the Greek drama under the headings "Religion,"
"Politics and Society," "Family," "The Individual."
Some of the subheadings for Sophocles are: "Friendship"—a friend may become an enemy, an enemy a
friend;[50] "Lex Talionis";[51] even a slave may be noble;[52]
money the cause of evil;[53] suicide not condoned as a moral
offense; the good are noble; chastity, truth, beauty of
morality, work, value of awe.

Such references, valuable as helps and guides, are
worse than useless if taken over slavishly by the modern
essayist and moralist. One must always observe for himself the true probable intent of the author in the light, not
only of the entire context, but of the whole body of his
work. A startling example of modern misuse of classical
texts will make this plain. The normal Greek, and for that
matter the normal man, has always felt, in spite of the
protest of Christian and Platonic idealism, that punishment, retribution, revenge, if we must employ the invidi-
ous term, is indispensable to the maintenance of moral

[49] Pp. 167-181.
[50] *Ajax*, 679-683.
[51] *Œdipus at Colonus*, 229-236, 271, 272, 1191.
[52] *Maidens of Trachis*, 61-63.
[53] *Antigone*, 295-299.

law and faith. In that temper Electra says of her murdered father (in effect):

> For if these dead must rot
> And be as souls forgot,
> And those assassins shall not pay
> The price of blood upon some judgment day—
> Away with right and law!
> With reverence and awe!
> No more to any god bend knee or pray.

Mr. Jones pigeon-holes this under the rubric "Immortality," with which it has little or nothing to do. During the great war I quoted this passage to an American audience with obvious application. The next week, a pacifist orator rebuked me and quoted, "A nobler message from Greek Tragedy." It was Professor Murray's beautiful translation of Euripides' *Bacchæ*[54]—the favorite text of all pacifists, advanced liberal thinkers, and radicals in our day, and perhaps more frequently quoted in the past ten years than any other saying in Greek literature. The lines run:

> What else is Wisdom? What of man's endeavour
> Or God's high grace so lovely and so great?
> To stand from fear set free, to breathe and wait;
> To hold a hand uplifted over Hate;
> And shall not loveliness be loved forever?

The actual meaning of the Greek words in Euripides' text is:

> What is wisdom? What fairer gift
> On man can the gods bestow?
> Than his victorious hand to lift
> Over the head of his foe?

Instead then of attempting an impracticable and unintelligible enumeration and systematization of all the ethi-

[54] 877 ff.

cal sayings of Sophocles and of that Euripides in whom
a plausible sentence can be found for anything, I will
conclude with two Sophoclean thoughts which mark the
highest point reached by non-philosophical Greek poetic
ethics and which still possess more than a merely historical significance for our own spiritual life. The first of
these ideas is the symbolism of Wordsworth's "Ode to
Duty":

Thou dost preserve the stars from wrong,
And the most ancient heavens through thee are fresh and strong.

The assimilation of the moral law of our own self-control
to the eternal laws of God and nature makes resignation,
submission, endurance, easier. "Henceforth," cries Ajax
(half petulantly, it is true, but soon becoming the mouth-
piece of the poet), "henceforth, I shall know how to yield
to heaven and teach myself to honor the powers that be.
They are our masters and we must obey. How not?

> The world's most dread and potent powers yield
> One to the other, Winter's snow-strewn plains
> Give place to Summer's fair and flowering fields.
> The weary round of dreadful night makes way
> For Dawn's white steeds to flood the world with light.
> Fierce winds die down and lull the moaning sea
> To rest again, and all-composing sleep
> Unbinds its fetters and holds us not for aye.
> Shall I not yield and learn to know my place?"[55]

This is the moral of Ulysses' great speech on degree in
Troilus and Cressida (I, iii):

> The heavens, themselves, the planets and this centre
> Observe degree, priority and place.

Sophocles and the Greeks were distinctly conscious of it.

[55] Here, by the way, is one of the three or four equivocal meanings of
sophrosyne, which essayists on the Greek spirit fail to discriminate. *Cf.* my
note in the *American Journal of Philology*, vol. XIII, p. 362.

The chorus in the *Trachiniæ* console Deianira with similar symbolism:

> Slay not fair hope to thy soul's annoy,
> Our mortal portion is sorrow and joy.
> Pain follows pleasure and pleasure pain
> As the stars that wheel in the northern wain.

More often it is the sea that furnishes an image of human destiny:

> Sophocles long ago
> Heard it on the Ægean, and it brought
> Into his mind the turbid ebb and flow
> Of human misery.

Matthew Arnold is here thinking of such passages as *Antigone,* 585; *Œdipus at Colonus,* 1240; *Ajax,* 351; *Maidens of Trachis,* 111. A notable passage of Plato's *Republic* develops the general thought: Can he who has grandeur of soul and is the spectator of all time and existence think much of our little human life? Will he not rather lift up his eyes to the things which abide and are eternal, and, seeing that they neither wrong nor are wronged by one another but move to perform their tasks in order and according to reason, try to imitate them and assimilate his own spirit to them as far as may be? Plato's lesson is repeated in his own style by Plotinus.[56] The Platonic lecturer, Dio Chrysostomos, makes it the text of his admonition to the turbulent democracies of Asia Minor.[57] Look upward to the vast spaces of the heavens, behold how those mighty orbs roll on in their everlasting course without conflict or clash in unbroken harmony, and cannot you, the dwellers in one little hamlet in a corner of Asia Minor, keep the peace? This commonplace of later Platonism was transmitted by Boethius to Dante:[58]

[56] 1, 8. 5.

[57] XL, vol. 2, Teubner, p. 199.

[58] *Cons.,* III, 8: respicite cæli spatium, firmitudinem, celeritatem et aliquando desinite vilia mirari.

The heavens call you and o'er your heads revolving
Reveal the lamps of beauty ever burning;
Your eyes are fixed on earth and goods dissolving,
Wherefore He smites you, He, the all-discerning.

Modern radical critics credit to Euripides this natural-
ism, as they call it, which refers morality to natural law.

Elsewhere, and this is our second thought, the lesson of
charity, patience, acceptance, or renunciation, rests not
on the appeal to natural law, but on the mere recognition
of human frailty and transience. It is a commonplace of
criticism that the Greek poets frequently recur to this
theme of mutability and the frailty and uncertainty of
mortal life and mortal hopes.[59] The moral lesson, which
they rarely fail to associate with the thought, is too often overlooked. From Homer down, the slightest suggestion of boastfulness, pride, arrogance, and vainglorious
self-reliance, recalls a Greek poet to the admonition—
walk humbly with God, think mortal thoughts, and speak
not the "big word." We may call this "knocking on
wood" if we please, a survival of the superstitious belief
in the jealousy of the gods. It is more truly as well as
more fairly described as the mood of Kipling's "Recessional":

If drunk with sight of power we loose
Vain tongues that have not Thee in awe.

In *Iliad*, XX, 242, Æneas adds to his speech the words:
"But it is Zeus that increases or diminishes the virtue [value, worth] of men as he pleases." An eminent
modern scholar comments: "This evidently alludes to
Achilles' sarcasm[60] about Æneas' flight at Lyrnessus."
That misses the point. In the previous line, Æneas had
concluded the story of his race triumphantly—"of this

[59] *Cf.* among the many essays on Greek melancholy Butcher's *Aspects of the Greek Genius*.
[60] Some forty lines above.

blood and lineage I boast [declare] myself to be." Greek
religious and ethical feeling calls for a recessional from
this display of pride.[61] Pindar frequently qualifies the
praise of his heroes by the recognition that it is all, in
Emerson's phrase, only more or less of power supplied
from the eternal. And both Pindar and Herodotus say in
effect of Salamis and the rout of Xerxes, "It is not we but
the gods who have done this thing." In Æschylus' *Seven
Against Thebes* the vaunt of the champions on the patriotic side is tempered in the same way: "We may have
confidence in our defenders' strength—but (414) Ares decides the battle." And again (675): "We may deserve to
win—but success is the gift of the God."

The thought is purified from all sediment of superstition when the lesson of human frailty is that men should
be kind to their fellow men, sharers in a common lot. This
idea, though sometimes too faintly indicated for modern
interpreters to perceive, recurs too frequently and too explicitly to be an accident. "I know that I am but a man,"
says King Theseus in his pride to the beggared and exiled
Œdipus:

> I am a man and my assurance is
> No more than thine in what the morrow brings.

And later, when Œdipus hints at possible conflicts between the allies, Thebes and Athens, Theseus wonder-
ingly asks, in the words which Edward Fitzgerald could
never read without tears, and which surely have not lost
their poignancy for the world today:

> Dear son of Ægeus, to the gods alone
> The changeful years bring neither death nor change;
> All else doth all-subduing time confound:
> The good soil's strength decays, the body's might,
> Faith dies, and Unfaith flowers on its grave,

[61] Somewhat similar is the feeling of *Iliad*, VII, 102.

And veering gusts of passion now blow love,
Now hate from man to man and state to state.
And late or early pleasure turns to pain,
And from the bitter the sweet is born anew.
If now fair weather smiles for Thebes and thee,
Yet endless time in endless course begets
Innumerable days and nights wherein
The sword on the dissension of a doit
Shall sever the affiance of your plighted hands.

This is more than the sensualist's or the epigrammatist's foreboding of mutability and decay chilling hot passion. It lifts the soul to a plane where human pettiness has no power upon it. Matthew Arnold felt the religion of these lines, and brings it out in more explicit modern fashion in the paraphrase of his "Merope":

O Merope, how many noble thoughts,
How many precious feelings of man's heart,
How many loves, how many gratitudes,
Do twenty years wear out and see expire!
Shall they not wear one hatred out as well?

The moral that thus finds consummate expression in Sophocles can be traced throughout Greek literature. A noble speech of Odysseus develops it in *Odyssey*, XVIII, 130-142: It is the reflection that stays the hand of Cyrus, when about to burn Crœsus on the pyre. "Never upbraid a man with his poverty," says Theognis, "for Zeus turns the scale now this way, now that." "Be helpful and generous," says Pindar, "for the hopes and fears of toiling men are common." "Laugh not at another's misfortune, for fortune is common," is a saying attributed to Chilo, one of the Seven Wise Men. "Taunt no man with his wretchedness," says Isocrates, "for fortune is common and the future unforeseen."

I am not insolent in others' woe,
Fearing that I may suffer even as they,

cries Euripides' Perseus. "I count that man a fool who casts another's fortune in his teeth," says Demosthenes, "for no man knows that the happiest fortune will endure for a day." And, to return to Sophocles, Philoctetes supports his despairing appeal to Neoptolemus by the plea:

> That mortal life is all a dreadful hasard,
> Of good, or good's appalling opposite.

Greek philosophy soars into the ether of speculation, and leaves little more for modern disquisition to discover or divine about the origin and meaning of good and evil, the sanctions of right, and the justification of the ways of God to man. The teaching of Greek poetry culminates in the simple lesson:

> Life is mostly froth and bubble,
> Two things stand like stone;
> Kindness in another's trouble,
> Courage in your own.

Or, in Matthew Arnold's more dignified version of the Sophoclean lesson:

> Let us be true to one another; for the world
>
> .   .   .   .
> Hath really neither joy nor love nor light,
> Nor certitude nor peace nor help for pain.

THE ETHICS OF THE GOSPELS

ERNEST FINDLAY SCOTT

IX.

The ethical teaching of Jesus has always been normative for Christianity. Differences arose, almost from the beginning, with regard to doctrines, institutions, forms of church government; and it can plausibly be argued that our religion in its later phases has little in common with the original gospel. But its moral standards have always been those of Jesus. They have been maintained, with no essential change, in all ages and by all sections of the church.

Critical analysis has made it certain that the Gospels were compiled from a variety of sources, and that material dating from the earliest years has been blended in our record with later additions and interpretations. This is true of the ethical teaching attributed to Jesus, as well as of the history. There is reason to believe that a brief collection of the Lord's sayings was drawn up soon after his death, and was gradually expanded by the insertion of further sayings and of maxims which had commended themselves to the general mind of the church. The collection was finally arranged in something like literary form, and was combined, in the Gospels of Matthew and Luke, with the narrative of Mark. Another collection, consisting for the most part of parables, has been incorporated in Luke's Gospel, and forms a priceless addition to our knowledge of Jesus' ethical teaching. Apart from written sources the evangelists doubtless had access to a number of sayings, more or less authentic, which had been handed down by word of mouth. For historical purposes these various strands of tradition which have been woven together in our Gospels must be carefully discriminated, but such analysis can help us little in the study of the ethical teaching. The sayings ascribed to Jesus are undoubtedly of very different degrees of authenticity. It is

possible that in almost every case the form of the saying
has been modified in the process of transmission, and that
the original teaching has gathered into itself many of the
results of later reflection. But the ethic as a whole bears
the same unmistakable character. All the additions are
fully in harmony with the mind of Jesus as we know it
from the sayings which are beyond dispute. Instead of
confusing our impression of what he taught, they serve
to define and strengthen it, witnessing, as they do, to
a conception of the moral life which now dominated the
minds of his followers. Nothing is more striking in the
New Testament books than the absolute agreement of all
the writers in their ethical judgments. It may fairly be
said that even if none of the original sayings of Jesus had
come down to us we should still have been able, from this
consensus of early Christian testimony, to determine the
nature of his ethic.

From the ethical point of view the evidence of the
Fourth Gospel is hardly less valuable than that of the
Synoptics. It may now be regarded as certain that this
Gospel was written under the influence of Hellenistic
speculation, and presents a conception of the life and
message of Jesus which is not strictly historical. The
ethical sayings contained in it, if they were uttered by
Jesus at all, can hardly be preserved in their original
form. None the less they reflect the temper and outlook of
Jesus, precisely as we know them from the Synoptic record. In one respect, indeed, the fourth evangelist brings
out the nature of the new morality more clearly than the
other three, for he never fails to emphasize its close dependence on the purely religious message. It becomes apparent, on closer examination of the Synoptic Gospels
themselves, that in this light the ethic of Jesus must be
interpreted.

In the so-called Sermon on the Mount the chief elements of the ethical teaching are brought together in such a manner as to present them as a systematic whole. The discourse in Matthew is based on a similar one which is preserved in Luke, and it may be inferred that from a very early time the need was felt of a coördinated account of the new rule of life. Criticism, however, has made it certain that the discourse was pieced together from a number of remembered sayings which were spoken at different times and in different connections. Jesus himself does not seem ever to have attempted to systematize his teaching. He contented himself with giving utterance from time to time to maxims and parables, suggested often by chance questions and incidents, and from these detached sayings we have to understand his mind on the great moral problems. The summary of the teaching in the Sermon on the Mount has tended, in one way, to give a false impression of its nature. Jesus is made to appear in the character of a lawgiver, who set himself to replace the ancient code of morals by a new and superior one. His precepts are arranged as if they were so many definite rules for conduct in the various relations of life. It is not difficult to show that the teaching, when thus understood, is impracticable, that it covers only a small part of man's moral activity, that it cannot be applied, without many reservations, to altered times and circumstances. But the conception of Jesus as a lawgiver is a radically mistaken one. He was not concerned with rules but with principles, which are capable of manifold application, and which men must learn to interpret for themselves. What seem to be formal precepts are in almost every case illustrations. Intent on establishing his principle Jesus takes up one concrete instance and another, and shows how it may be carried into action. That this is the character of his teaching is evident from the fact that so much of it is conveyed in parabolic form. Few of the parables can be so construed as to yield a set rule for conduct. Their purpose is rather to quicken the moral instincts, so that we may discern, in their actual working, the true principles of the higher life.

It follows that Jesus often expresses himself with a certain degree of paradox and exaggeration. Taken as they stand not a few of the precepts appear unnatural and even grotesque; and the attempt to follow them out literally has sometimes led to strange perversities. But they have to be understood in the light of their central idea. In his effort to make it absolutely clear Jesus goes out of his way to state it in an extreme form. Much in the teaching that seems to remove it from the world of real conditions must be attributed to this desire to lay all the stress on ultimate issues. A legal ordinance must be guarded with many qualifications, but Jesus purposely avoids this precision, for he does not seek to lay down definite laws. His one concern is with the guiding principle, and he asserts it in its ideal scope, without compromise.

It has been recognized of late years, and cannot now be seriously questioned, that the message of Jesus has to be understood against the background of the apocalyptic hopes current in his day. John the Baptist had given a new vitality to the belief that the Kingdom of God—the new age when God would assert His sovereignty—was just at hand. Jesus took up this hope of the coming Kingdom, and made it the framework of his gospel. How is the ethical teaching to be related to the apocalyptic hope? It has been held by some modern scholars that since Jesus expected the present order shortly to disappear he must have confined himself to proclaiming an "interim ethic." Before the advent of the Kingdom an interval was to elapse in which men might prepare themselves for the great change, and his aim can have been nothing more than to prescribe a rule of action for this interval. His ethic, therefore, laid no claim to an absolute validity. If the apocalyptic view is pressed to its logical issue, an interpretation of this kind is almost necessary. Everywhere the teaching presupposes the world in which we now live—a world in which hatred, oppression, self-seeking, anxiety about the future, are always with us. In the coming age these conditions will obtain no longer. There will be no place for the exercise of patience, forgiveness, care for the poor and miserable; and such precepts as are laid down in the Gospels will cease to have any meaning. But this theory of an "interim ethic" may be confidently put aside. (1) It rests, for one thing, on the false position that the intention of Jesus was to prescribe set rules for action, and his precepts, as we have seen, are rather to be regarded as illustrations of great principles, which are in their nature absolute and eternal. Love, trust, holiness, cannot but be the highest things in the coming age as in this. The man who gives effect to them even in the cramping circumstances of the present is not contenting himself with a makeshift morality. He is following out the will of God as it must always be. (2) Again, while the apocalyptic element in Jesus' teaching must be frankly acknowledged, it cannot be pressed in any rigid and one-sided way. The more we examine his attitude to the current beliefs, the more we realize that he did not allow himself to be fettered by them. Indeed, it would hardly be too much to say that while he took over the traditional apocalyptic ideas his thought was in inward conflict with them. Apocalyptic was the outcome of a mood of despair. It assumed that in the present age God had withdrawn from the world, and that all faith must find its object in the future. It assumed, likewise, that when God at last acted it must be suddenly, by way of miracle, since in the present there are no regenerating forces. The religion of Jesus is

opposed in its very essence to these two root-conceptions
of apocalyptic. So far from believing that God will only
interpose in the future, he calls for a living faith in God,
whose providence is over His people from hour to hour.
So far from staking all his hope on a sudden miracle, he
is confident that the good is always triumphing, by its
own inherent might, and that nothing else is strong and
real. Jesus himself does not appear to have thought out
the radical difference of his own beliefs from those which
underlay the apocalyptic hope. He accepted it as it was
cherished among pious Jews in his own day, and made it
the starting-point of his teaching. Yet he made use of it
only in so far as it helped him to envisage more clearly
the great religious truths in which he was primarily interested. The Kingdom meant for him that condition of
things in which the will of God would be done on earth
as in heaven. He sought to understand God's will as it
would manifest itself in the Kingdom, and to impress on
men how they must act if they desired to have part in that
higher order. With the apocalyptic theory for its own
sake he troubled himself little, and we cannot suppose
that out of deference to it he allowed a mere temporary
value to his ethic. His whole object was to mold men's
lives into harmony with the absolute will of God.

It has often been maintained that the teaching of Jesus,
in practically all its main features, was borrowed. Paral-
lels to many of the typical sayings have been found in the
religious literature of India, Persia, Egypt,—not to
speak of the Greek moralists; and in this there is nothing
remarkable. The great principles of the moral law have
been apparent to earnest minds from the first. They have
been stated in different lands and times almost in identical terms, and if Jesus had not repeated them his teaching
would have been original only in the sense that it was ec-
centric and unmeaning. Of late years attention has been

directed, more particularly, to the many striking agreements between the Gospel sayings and the maxims of the
rabbis; and the inference has been drawn that the ethic
of Jesus was simply that of Judaism, set free from its
legal entanglements. In this view there is certainly a large
measure of truth. Jesus set out from the Hebrew morality
as it had been proclaimed by the prophets and elaborated
under the Law. Probably in more instances than have yet
been ascertained he availed himself of current maxims
which expressed his own judgments forcibly and con-
cisely. But while the elements of the teaching are thus, in
great part, borrowed, they have been recast and touched
with a new significance. The originaltiy of his ethic must
be sought in its formative ideas and not in the separate
precepts.

(1) Morality is made to spring directly out of the new
relation to God. It was the aim of Jesus to inspire his followers with his own absolute trust in the Father, who is
altogether just and good. As children of God they are to
subordinate their wills entirely to His will. Their action as
moral beings is to be nothing but the outcome of this con
formity to the will of God. At a later time union with God,
in the sense of a mystical participation in the divine nature, was the watchword of Christian piety. Jesus' own
thought was not mystical; or rather, if we might so express it, he taught an ethical mysticism. The essential nature of God, as he conceived it, was love, goodness, truth;
and in so far as men have these things in themselves they
become one with God. The morality of Jesus is grounded
in the requirement "That ye may be children of your
Father who is in heaven." By doing the will of God men
are to grow like Him, and so enter into fellowship with
God.

(2) A new emphasis is laid on the value of the individual soul. For Jewish religious thought it was always

the nation which was the object of God's care. Individuals could lay claim to His favor and protection only as members of the nation which he had chosen. For Jesus, it is men and women in their separate lives who have worth in the sight of God. "It is not the will of your Father who is heaven that one of these little ones should perish." This change of emphasis from the group to the individual involves a new attitude to all moral problems. For the first time man is conceived as a personality, and all his action, whether it regards himself or his fellow men, is fraught with a new and profounder significance.

(3) The moral quality of an act is made to consist in the thought or intent that lies behind it. In his criticism of the "old commandments," as set forth in the Sermon on the Mount, Jesus is concerned from first to last with this conception of the *inwardness* of morality. He shows that the good or evil of a deed consists wholly in its motive, and that the moral task is nothing else than the right ordering of that inward life which alone is within a man's control, and out of which all his action proceeds. So in all his teaching he occupies himself wholly with the *will*. He reduces the countless precepts of the Jewish code to a few great requirements, and ultimately to the two demands of love to God and love to men. He insists that everything depends, in the final issue, on the right direction of the will. Everywhere he aims at creating in men this new disposition, which will flow out of its own accord into all noble thought and action. Here again it is evident that the ethic of Jesus cannot be separated from his religion. Everything is traced back to the renewal of the will, and this can be effected only by a "change of mind,"—by entering into a right relation to God. The Johannine doctrine of the new birth is bound up with metaphysical ideas which were foreign to Jesus, but the meaning that lies at the heart of it is fully in harmony with his thought.

(4) Resting as it does on the demand for a new will the ethic of Jesus is *positive*. It insists not so much on the avoidance of what is wrong as on the willing choice of what is right and good. The familiar maxim of Jewish and pagan morality—"Do not to others what you would not have them do to you"—is changed into the positive injunction of the Golden Rule. And since moral action is thus voluntary, no limit can be prescribed to it. Men are to do God's will not because of a commandment which need only be obeyed to the letter, but because their own will has become one with it and urges them from within. They are to forgive, not seven times, but seventy times seven. They are to do good hoping for nothing again, because goodness is the law of their own nature. The gospel morality thus sets up an infinite ideal; and from one point of view this is its weakness. It offers counsels of perfection which are incapable of fulfillment under the given conditions of human life. But this is also the secret of its abiding vitality and power. The ideal which it holds up is one that can never be attained, and which therefore can never be exhausted.

(5) Morality is purified of all extraneous and accidental elements. Jesus was himself "born under the law," and there is no indication that he ever consciously broke with it. Yet he draws a clear distinction between the essential commandments and those ordinances of custom and ritual with which they were entangled in the religious practice of his time. His great saying, "Not that which goeth in but that which cometh out defileth a man"[1] marked a new stage in the moral consciousness of the race. It now became possible to apprehend the moral law in its purity. The ceremonial ideas which had served for its protection, and which had finally overlaid and obscured it, could now be thrown aside.

[1] Mark 7: 21; Matt. 15: 17-20.

(6) By his own character and example Jesus gave a new reality to the moral law. He was no mere abstract thinker who worked out an ethical theory. All that he taught he exemplified in himself, so that he stands out as the ideal type of the higher life. It is this, above all else, that has enabled the Christian morality to impress itself on the world. The nature of right action can never be taught by precepts and formulæ, any more than an art can be understood by a study of its rules. Moral principles have meaning only when we see them in their working, as the attributes of a living personality. At all times the Christian ethic has resolved itself into the imitation of Christ. His gift, as the fourth evangelist perceived, was nothing else than the communication of his own life to those who accepted him as Lord.

The governing idea of Jesus was that of the Kingdom of God, and his ethical teaching must be viewed in its relation to this idea. Formally, as we have seen, he takes over the apocalyptic hope, but in substance he breaks away from it. The Kingdom means for him that condition of things in which the will of God will absolutely prevail. Throwing his mind forward into the ideal order which he expects shortly to be realized, he asks himself what it will require of men, what sort of character will best conform to it. By means of the hope of the Kingdom he is enabled, in a vivid and concrete fashion, to apprehend the moral ideal. In one respect, however, his thought is limited by the apocalyptic theory from which he sets out. Again and again his ethic appears to bear a marked *ascetic* character. Those who desire to enter the Kingdom are required to surrender everything,—their earthly possessions, their old activities, even the ties of friendship and family. Unless they are prepared to make these sacrifices they are declared unworthy of the name of disciples. Now it cannot be denied that this call for renunciation forms a very real side of the ethic of Jesus, and cannot be separated from its essential demands. He requires that men must look first to the higher interests and think of them as paramount. Whatever may interfere with them, however good and necessary in itself, must be sternly relinquished. It was in this conviction that Jesus himself abandoned everything for the service of God, and he demanded that his followers likewise should take up the cross. Not only so, but he recognizes that sacrifice in itself has a value for the development of man's higher nature. "He that findeth his life shall lose it, he that loseth his life shall find it." Yet this call for renunciation has nothing in common with asceticism. It is never suggested that the earthly things are in their nature evil. On the contrary, they are acknowledged as God's gifts to His children, and are described in many beautiful sayings as the evidence of His goodness and His care for human needs. "Your heavenly Father knoweth that ye have need of these things." If they are to be sacrificed it is not because they are in themselves harmful, but because they stand in the way of other things which are still more necessary.

To some extent, however, the call for renunciation must be explained from the apocalyptic hope of the nearness of the Kingdom. The time was just at hand when the existing order and everything that belonged to it would pass away; why should men waste their labor in gathering up treasure that would presently be worthless? By their care for earthly things, moreover, they bound themselves to the old order. They rendered themselves unfit to participate in the new age in which all would be different, and could not even honestly desire that it should come. On this side of his thought we can indeed recognize an "interim" element in the ethics of Jesus. His teaching is influenced not so much by absolute considerations as by the demands of apocalyptic theory.

At various times, and more particularly in mediæval types of piety, the Christian rule of life has been wholly colored by these ascetic conceptions which appear to form a real part of the gospel teaching; but the corrective to them is supplied by the teaching itself. It is only when the thought of the nearness of the Kingdom is strongly present to his mind that Jesus condemns the desire for earthly possessions. In his own characteristic thinking he regards it as natural and even praiseworthy. Many of his sayings are concerned with the right use of wealth, and in the parables he assumes, as a matter of course, that buying and selling, care for one's belongings, prudence in daily business, are among the most important duties of life. So far from denouncing the earthly things he speaks of them continually as the appointed means for discipline in God's service. They are evil only in so far as they are turned to base and selfish purposes. By right employment of them men are to train themselves in charity, wisdom, self-control, obedience. They can make friends by means of the unrighteous mammon,—so disposing of the earthly treasure that it will secure an enduring treasure in heaven.

As a result of its close connection with the idea of the Kingdom the teaching of Jesus is eminently social. It contemplates a new order, a new society, in which God is King and men coöperate with one another in His service. They are to live even now as the destined members of this society, and to carry out its requirements in all their intercourse with their fellow men. To this side of his thought Jesus gave concrete expression by gathering around him a band of disciples. They were not merely his helpers in the mission but the nucleus of the community that should inherit the Kingdom, and in their fellowship together they were to exemplify the new human relations which in the Kingdom would be normal and

universal. The teaching of Jesus was mainly addressed
to this band of disciples, and had reference not only to
their individual duties but to their communal life.

Since the will of God is the sole law in the Kingdom,
men are to seek, in their intercourse with one another, to
take their example from God. Like Him they must return
good for evil, forgive those who trespass against them,
show kindness even to the unthankful, protect and save
the weak. It will be noted that here also the ethic of Jesus
is bound up with his religion. We have grown accustomed
to think of the social teaching of Christianity as of something that has nothing to do with Christian doctrine. In
many of the movements of our time it is detached altogether from its religious setting, and presented in the
form of humanitarian theory. But the social morality of
the Gospels is based throughout on a given conception of
God and of man's relation to Him. It is an integral part
of this conception, and depends on it at every point for
its sanction and validity.

While he has much to say about immediate duties to
our neighbors, Jesus hardly touches on the wider social
relations. He held completely aloof from the national
movement which was agitating Palestine in his day, and
when asked to pass judgment on the vexed question of
allegiance to Cæsar he gave a noncommittal answer.[2] In
his own behavior he seems to have been duly observant
of laws and ordinances, and he takes for granted that
men should obey constituted authority and discharge the
obligations laid on them by the state. Yet he never inculcates the duty of active citizenship. Apparently he accepted the state as indispensable, but was willing to leave
its interests in the hands of the appointed rulers and
magistrates. It is nowhere suggested that ordinary citizens should make service for the state a real part of their

2 Mark 12: 17; Matt. 22: 21; Luke 23: 2.

service for God. This attitude was no doubt due, in large measure, to the peculiar conditions that obtained in Palestine under the rule of a foreign power. It may also have been partly due to a studied avoidance on the part of Jesus of all teaching that might give a political complexion to his work. But his detachment is chiefly to be explained from his preoccupation with the hope of the Kingdom. He looked for a time even now at hand when all artificial divisions of classes and nations would be done away. All men would be gathered into the Kingdom in which God alone reigned, and in which they would recognize each other as brethren. In the meanwhile their relation to the state was to be one of passive obedience. They were to submit to it even when it was tyrannous and unjust, knowing that it would shortly disappear and give place to the true society. Even now, although they acquiesced in the existing order, the law to which they inwardly conformed was to be that of the Kingdom of God.

In the Gospels, therefore, we are not to look for any political or social program. Attempts have been made, at every stage of Christian history, to make out that some particular type of government or some industrial system was that which was contemplated by Jesus; but such efforts are necessarily futile. What is true of his ethic generally is more especially true of his social ethic. He laid down no definite enactments. He was concerned not with the mechanism of society but with the inner principles which ought always to control it. Men are so to order their life together as to ensure justice for all, and to afford help to the weak and suffering, and to fulfill God's will on earth. The particular laws and institutions through which they may try to realize these ends are not prescribed. To the man who asked him to adjudicate on a question of inheritance Jesus answered "Man, who made me a judge and a divider over you?"[3] and he observed a like reticence as to all the specific arrangements of the social life. To this rule there is only one exception. The three synoptists are agreed, and Paul bears out their testimony,[4] that Jesus enacted a definite law on the matter of divorce. The precise terms in which he expressed himself are difficult to determine; but critical analysis of the various passages appears to leave little doubt that he forbade divorce altogether, affirming that while it was permitted by the Mosaic code it was only granted as a concession to human perversity.[5] According to the original divine plan, man and woman were made for each other, and entered by marriage into a union that could not be abrogated. The ruling on divorce is therefore no real exception to Jesus' general attitude. He recognizes that marriage stands on a different plane from all other contracts. It belongs not to social legislation but to the natural order. Man and woman were so created as to form one flesh, and to belong indissolubly to one another. Their union must give effect to this divine intention.

That the morality of Jesus is profoundly social there can be no question. It can only be realized in a society in which men are bound together in the most varied relations, and all monastic seclusion is completely alien to it. Reformers in every age have rightly insisted that it has its inevitable outcome in a remodeling of all forms of civic and industrial and national life. But there is no indication that Jesus thought of the perfecting of society as the ultimate moral goal. Many modern writers have assumed that this is implicit in his proclamation of the Kingdom of God. They maintain that his primary interest was the advancement of the Kingdom, and that he

3 Luke 12: 14.
4 1 Cor. 7: 10.
5 Mark 10: 5 f.; Matt. 19: 8.

therefore made the gradual building up of an ideal social system the grand object and inspiration of moral endeavor. This view, however, rests on a misunderstanding of his conception of the Kingdom. It is indeed possible that he believed that men might hasten its coming by repentance and earnest prayer and obedience to God's will. One of his chief aims, it may be, was to initiate a movement whereby the Kingdom might be brought nearer. But he takes for granted always that the consummation is wholly in the hands of God. The most that men can do is to move God's will and prevail on Him to "shorten the days." The idea that men themselves can bring about the Kingdom, and make this the end and motive of all their effort, is a wholly modern one, which we cannot legitimately ascribe to Jesus.

In the last resort, it was not the community with which he was primarily concerned. As we have seen already, one of his chief advances on earlier morality was that he broke away from the conception of the group as the governing factor in human action. Men had value in the sight of God not as units in a society but as individual beings. This is the constitutive principle in the social ethic of Jesus, and it is this which in all times has made it a revolutionary power. Christianity has no political program, and the attempt to identify it with one given system or another has always ended in disaster. But it never ceases to demand that the communal life must be so organized as to allow full play to those rights of personality which are always in danger of being over-ridden by the interests of the group.

The social teaching of Jesus has thus its ultimate motive in his assertion of the worth of the individual. (1) On the one hand, he requires that each man in all his dealings should acknowledge the value of his neighbor. Our conduct toward others must ever be determined by the sense

that they are God's children,—responsible to Him and
under His protection. No man has the right to employ another as a mere tool for his own ends. Against all forms
of oppression Jesus directs his sternest denunciations.
He declares that it were better for a man to perish utterly
than to take advantage of the weak.[6] He makes God's
mercy to us conditional on our mercy to our fellow men.
He forbids men even to pass harsh judgments on their
neighbors, since God is the one Judge to whom all must
give account.[7] So in our intercourse with others we must
be guided by the thought that they belong to God and are
therefore entitled to reverence and to full opportunity to
do service to God. (2) On the other hand, men are to find
in the common life the chief means for their own development as personal beings. It is true that Jesus insists constantly on the need for service and sacrifice. He requires
that as he came himself not to be ministered unto but to
minister, so his followers should look solely to the good
of others.[8] This call for the suppression of all personal
interests in service to the larger life of humanity belongs
to the very essence of his moral demand. Yet the idea
which underlies it is that by denying himself for others a
man most fully realizes himself. ''He that would be greatest let him be the servant of all.'' ''He that loseth his life
shall find it.'' Since the one end of life is to fulfill the will
of God, he who most obeys that will has most attained to
life. He possesses in himself in largest measure the nature of God. And it is through our intercourse with others
that we can best fulfill God's will. His highest attributes
are love, goodness, justice, free bestowal of all His blessings. In our relations to our fellow men we have the op-

[6] Matt. 18: 6; Luke 17: 2.
[7] Matt. 7: 1.
[8] Mark 10: 42-45.

portunity of acting as God acts, and so of realizing our
own true life.

This, for Jesus, is the ultimate moral motive; and he
often speaks of it under the figure of *reward*. Men are exhorted to suffer privation and make sacrifices in view of
the recompense that awaits them in the Kingdom. They
are to humble themselves that they may be exalted, to forsake friends and possessions that they may receive them
back an hundred-fold.[9] It has often been urged as one of
the gravest criticisms of the gospel morality that the motive of reward is thus made prominent. In this respect it
seems to fall below the level even of the loftier pagan
ethics. But that Jesus does not think of reward in any
literal sense is evident from many sayings in which he condemns as worthless the righteousness that springs from
this motive. His conflict with the Pharisees turns on nothing else than the Pharisaic assumption that the service
of God is of the nature of a contract, and that any performance beyond that which is bargained for must have
a recompense. In the parable of the Laborers in the Vineyard he plainly declares that the idea of reward can have
no place in man's relation to God, who has a right to our
service and can do what He will with His own.[10] Indeed,
there can be little doubt that when he dwells on the reward in store for God's servants, Jesus only seeks to impress a new meaning on a current religious term. He
declares that the one reward which men are to seek after
is participation in the Kingdom. The end of their being is
to do the will of God, and in the new age when they can
do it perfectly they will attain the goal.

So far from making reward the motive of right action
Jesus desires that his followers should act in a spirit of
self-forgetfulness. Unlike the Pharisees, who calculated

9 Mark 10: 30; Matt. 19: 29.
10 Matt. 20: 15.

the result of every good work, they are to do good uncon-
sciously, out of the fullness of their love to God and
man.[11] Their right hand is not to know what the left is
doing. They are to earn God's approval unawares. We
have here one of the most striking differences of the morality of Jesus not only from Jewish and pagan ethics but
even from that of the later church. Christian moralists
have laid stress on the duty of self-examination—on the
deliberate building up of character. Jesus himself sets
little store on a goodness which is the product of a set
design. He asks for moral action which shall not only be
right but spontaneous—the natural outflow of the renewed will.

For the greater part of his teaching Jesus is occupied,
more or less directly, with the duties of men to their fellows. He recognizes that life is disciplined and tested and
enabled to realize itself in its social relations. But in
many of the sayings he deals with the duties which more
immediately concern the individual.

(1) Of purity, in the narrower sense, he says little.
This may partly be due to his revolt against the current
Jewish morality, which laid all the stress on avoidance
of the grosser sins. At a later time, when Christian missionaries were thrown into contact with the corrupt
heathen society they had to protest, often exclusively,
against those sins; but in the Jewish code they were sufficiently condemned. Jesus sought to impress on his hear-
ers that the sins of the spirit, of which they were hardly
aware, might be even more harmful. Publicans and harlots would pass into the Kingdom of heaven before
scribes and Pharisees.[12] But the reticence, at times it
might almost seem the tolerance, with which he touches
on sensual sins is chiefly to be explained from the posi-

11 Matt. 6: 1 ff.
12 Matt. 21: 31.

tiveness which is an unfailing note of his teaching. He took for granted the need for personal purity. He condemned not only the impure action but the lustful thought and look.[13] But he sought to combat the baser desires by so purifying the will and charging it with loftier purposes that they should die down of their own accord.

(2) One of his outstanding demands is for *sincerity*. His followers are to cultivate an entire simplicity of speech and action,—making their yea, yea, and their nay, nay. Again and again he expresses his utmost scorn in the word "hypocrite"; and he thinks of hypocrisy not merely as an inconsistency of the act with the thought or intention. Men must make sure that their inward thoughts are themselves absolutely true. The worst hypocrisy is that of self-deception: "if the light that is in you is darkness, how great is the darkness."[14] This exercise of a perfect sincerity is to be based on the knowledge that God is present everywhere. From Him nothing can be hidden, and men are to feel at all times that He is aware of their secret thoughts, and requires them to be in harmony with His will.

(3) In like manner Jesus insists on the need of *fidelity*. Several of the most impressive parables turn on the idea of stewardship. Men are to feel that the duties to which they are called have been laid on them by God, to whom they owe an unlimited obedience. They are to be faithful in small things as in great, with a constant sense that the highest issues may depend on their loyalty.[15] The chief emphasis is thrown, however, not on the value of the actual work but on the inward strength which accrues from faithful discharge of duty. The man who is faithful has won for himself the approval of God. He has fitted him-

13 Matt. 5: 28.
14 Matt. 6: 23.
15 Luke 16: 10.

self for higher responsibilities. He has given proof of the character that is in him and has confirmed and deepened it. Fidelity in the ordinary duties of life is thus the pledge of a man's worthiness to enter the Kingdom.

(4) One of the distinctive features in the ethic of Jesus is the central value which is attached to *humility*. Here again we have to reckon with the protest which he was constrained to make against the current morality. The cult of the Law had its outcome in a self-righteous temper, which vitiated actions that in themselves might be praiseworthy. The service of God was made a means of ministering to human self-sufficiency and pride. But the emphasis on humility is more than an accidental note in Jesus' teaching. It was inseparable from his profound sense that our life is lived in the presence of God, who sets before us an infinite ideal. It is never possible to feel that this ideal has been attained. When such a feeling takes possession of a man the moral sense is paralyzed. All the motives that serve to advance and quicken it lose their power and the man is morally dead. The true attitude must be one of constant humility. Filled with the sense that their task is an endless one, men must act always as if they had achieved nothing and have the true fulfillment still in front of them.

(5) Closely related to the mood of humility is that of unfailing *trust* in the goodness and providence of God. Men are to be humbled by the knowledge that God is over them and requires of them a service which they can never fully render. But the same knowledge is to inspire them with a confidence which is proof against all earthly peril and anxiety. They have the assurance at all times that God is with them,—protecting, guiding, supporting. They can live from day to day without care for the morrow, and can bear all trouble patiently, knowing that by means of it God is working out His purposes. This trust in God is

fundamental to the morality as it is to the religion of Jesus; and the attitude he enjoins has often been called in question, as fatal to the forethought and resolution which are necessary elements in the moral life. The Christian ethic, it has been urged, involves a fatalism—a passive submission to circumstances instead of valiant effort to master and direct them. But it must be noted that the demand for trust in God's will presupposes an honest endeavor to understand it and carry it into action. The injunction to take no thought for the morrow is addressed to those who have been striving to follow God's direction, and who may therefore leave all consequences in the hand of God.

(6) Jesus himself sums up his ethical teaching in the requirement that men should live always with a view to the highest end. "Seek first the kingdom of God and his righteousness."[16] It is implied that when the ultimate goal is kept steadily in sight the path that leads to it will disclose itself. All other interests will fall into their due place when they are subordinated to the one sovereign interest. The task which Jesus set himself was to impress on men the nature of this goal which they were to keep ever before them. He sought to make them realize it as he himself did, so that the pursuit of it should be their one controlling passion. Here, as everywhere, his ethic merges in his religion. As Paul perceived, his purpose was not to formulate a system, analogous to that of the Law, but to communicate a Spirit, which should issue of itself in all right thought and action.

It has often been objected to the gospel teaching that at the best it is one-sided. Judging of life solely from the religious point of view, Jesus left out of account much that is necessary to its richness and harmony. He has nothing to say on those questions of civic and national duty which are so perplexing and so all-important. We

16 Matt. 6: 33.

examine his words in vain for any clear guidance on the
problems of labor and commerce. He never in explicit
terms condemned war or slavery. Art and science and culture, with their manifold bearings on morality, lay quite
outside his horizon. It is maintained that his rule of life,
intended as it was for a peasant community in a remote
age, cannot be applied to our complex modern conditions,
and that the effort so to apply it must be futile, where it
is not positively misleading. Criticism of this kind, however, rests on a misunderstanding of the whole character
of Jesus' teaching. He never professed to offer definite
solutions for all the problems which confronted his own
time, much less for those which were to emerge in the distant future. He did not even attempt, like other ethical
teachers, to make an inventory of man's varied activities
and lay down directions, in each case, for their right employment. His concern was with the governing principles
of the moral life, and he purposely refrained from discussing their application in detail. This had been done
already in the Jewish code of the time, with the result
that the whole nature of the moral law had been obscured.
Jesus recognized that no formal prescription is possible.
The conditions under which men are called on to act are
infinitely variable, and the moral problems, while fundamentally the same, present themselves in ever new forms,
and require new solutions. If Jesus had imposed a definite code, however salutary for his own time, it would
long ago have become a burden. But he was content to set
forth the principles which must always determine right
action. He sought, above all, to create in men the moral
temper which would enable them to judge and act for
themselves. For this reason his ethic is permanently
valid. It is adequate to all changing circumstances and
new modes of activity, for it makes men their own lawgivers by imparting to them the right will.

THE ETHICS OF THE PAULINE EPISTLES

C. HAROLD DODD

X.

NOTE. The Pauline Epistles are here taken to include Romans, I and II Corinthians, Galatians, Ephesians, Philippians, Colossians, I and II Thessalonians, and Philemon. The measure of doubt attaching to the authorship of II Thessalonians and Ephesians is not important for the present purpose. The Pastoral Epistles, though containing Pauline elements, are too alien from the main body of Paul's thought to be profitably used in an account of his ethical teaching.

INTRODUCTION: THE PRESUPPOSITIONS OF ETHICS

MAN, according to Paul, is a being of twofold nature. He has a lower nature, "the flesh,"[1] in which he is akin to the material creation and the beasts. But a more tragic fate than theirs has fallen upon him, for, by whatever means, "the flesh" has fallen under the dominion of sin.[2] Sin for Paul is not identical with conscious and deliberate moral transgression;[3] it is a condition of mankind—a condition social and racial in its scope—in which man "falls short of the glory of God,"[4] and is exposed to that retribution[5] which in the nature of things follows upon a failure to realize the true end of one's being. But there is also the "inward man," whose characteristic faculty is the reason.[6] The reason has a native knowledge of God[7] and, even apart from revealed religion, some apprehension of good and evil; and it utters itself in conscience in approval or condemnation.[8] Yet in the bulk of the human race sin against the light of the knowledge of God has perverted the reason itself[9] and left man in the bonds of

[1] I Cor. 15: 50. The whole passage, 15: 35-57, throws light on Paul's metaphysics.

[2] Gal. 5: 17; Rom. 7: 7-25.

[3] Rom. 5: 12-14.

[4] Rom. 3: 9-23.

[5] Gal. 6: 7. Paul's term for the natural laws of retribution is "the wrath (of God)," Eph. 4: 6; Rom. 1: 18-2: 11.

[6] II Cor. 4: 16; Rom. 7: 22-23.

[7] Rom. 1: 19-20.

[8] Rom. 2: 14-15.

[9] Rom. 1: 21-25, 28; Eph. 4: 17-19.

sinful flesh.[10] In this evil case not even the clear light of
revelation in the Law brings man any help. The Law can
bring knowledge of good and evil, but not power to overcome the flesh and do the right.[11] Thus the guilt of sin becomes deeper, and man's freedom is the more hopelessly
destroyed.[12]

Paul's religious teaching is based upon experience of
the way in which this miserable condition is overcome
and man given the power to live and act as a fully moral
being.[13] Christianity is not for him primarily a moral
code. It is an inward power to change the heart and give
freedom to the will.[14] It does so by the communication of
a Spirit, the Spirit of Christ, given to all who through
him have faith in God.[15] "Where the Spirit of the Lord
is, there is liberty," and there at last man attains to full
moral personality.[16] Paul often speaks as though in the
one act of faith full righteousness had been attained.[17]
On the religious plane, indeed, there is such finality about
the experience of salvation that the work of grace seems
complete. But Paul well knew that upon the moral plane
the long task was only begun.[18] "The power not to sin"
("*posse non peccari*") is given, and through the working
of the Spirit and the presence of Christ final victory will
come.[19] Paul's ethical teaching is addressed to those who
know something of the power of Christ, and it describes
the forms in which the new life of the spirit manifests
itself in actual thought, word, and deed.[20] The basis of

[10] Rom. 8: 7-8.
[11] Rom. 3: 20, 5: 20, 7: 14-21, 8: 3.
[12] Rom. 7: 8, 13.
[13] Rom. 8: 1-2.
[14] Rom. 1: 16.
[15] Gal. 3: 2-6, 4: 4-7; Rom. 8: 9-11.
[16] II Cor. 3: 17; Gal. 5: 1, 13, 16-18.
[17] I Cor. 6: 11.
[18] Phil. 3: 12-16.
[19] Rom. 8: 31-39; I Cor. 15: 57.
[20] Rom. 12: 1-2.

Paul's ethics is in his religion, and the one cannot be fully understood without the other.[21]

PART I: ELEMENTS OF CHARACTER

1. *Moral Insight.* Where morality is conceived as simple obedience to a code, the first requisite for the individual is docility and a submissive spirit. What Paul expects of the free man who is "servant of Jesus Christ" is a clear and independent insight into moral values. The Christian, if he has truly entered into the new life, is able to "ascertain by experience what is the will of God" and to judge for himself what kind of conduct conforms to that will.[22] Paul expects to find such moral insight in simple and ordinary lay folk. He knew the risks of this demand, but he was sure that to make the demand was the way to that fullness of character which is the Christian ideal.[23] On moral questions "Each individual must be fully convinced by his own reason."[24]

Now there is no clear insight into moral values apart from a sane estimate of oneself. A fantastical estimate of one's own worth, powers, and importance is one of the most radical, and certainly one of the commonest causes of moral failure and unhappiness. It is those who take themselves most seriously and fix their ideal highest who are most exposed to this danger. We can, therefore, understand why Paul gives so prominent a place to self-knowledge. To "think soberly" of oneself is the beginning of wisdom.[25] In this Paul is in the line of the wisest Greeks. Only with him the religious background gives a deeper meaning to the precept "Know thyself," while it also points the way to its attainment.

[21] See further, C. H. Dodd, *The Meaning of Paul for To-Day* (Doran).
[22] Rom. 12: 2; Phil. 1: 10; Eph. 5: 10, 17.
[23] I Thess. 4: 9, 5: 21; I Cor. 10: 15.
[24] Rom. 14: 5.
[25] Rom. 12: 3; *cf.* I Cor. 11: 28; Rom. 14: 22.

2. *The Presentation of the Moral Ideal.* Unlike many moralists, ancient and modern, Paul does not attempt to find one single all-embracing formula for the ethical End, from which all particular ethical precepts may be deduced. He approaches the ideal from more than one standpoint and describes it in terms belonging to different planes of thought

A. *Rational Concepts of the Ethical End.* In Romans 12[26] Paul interprets the religious concept of the "will of God" into ethical terms as "that which is good, acceptable and perfect." The first of these terms is the most general expression for what is of absolute worth in and for itself, and as such is common to all philosophies. The second term, not previously used, it would appear, as a technical term of ethics, has in ordinary usage the sense "satisfactory." It emphasizes the *effect* of moral action in giving satisfaction to the agent and to others. The third term is borrowed from the vocabulary of the Stoics. The "perfect" man is defined by them as the man whose character is complete on all sides, possessing all the separate virtues as elements of a fully developed personality. We may recall that our psychologists regard the impulse toward completeness as "the most compelling motive of life,"[27] and often find in it the basis of "natural" ethics.

To these terms we may add those which are implied in two expressions found in Romans 1-2: (a) the expression "they do by nature the things of the law" (2:14); and (b) the contrary expression "things which are not fitting" (1:28). These two also have as background the Stoic conception of the "law of nature." Nature itself, the Stoics held, gives to each being the ideal which it must strive to fulfill, and virtue is that which belongs to

---

26 Τὸ ἀγαθὸν καὶ εὐάρεστον καὶ τέλειον. These adjectives are not to be taken as epithets of θέλημα, but substantivally in apposition.

27 Hadfield, *Psychology and Morals*, ch. viii.

or "befits" the nature of man. Paul's (often misrepresented) doctrine of "original sin" did not prevent him from believing (as his fellow rabbis taught in Judaism) that man is a good creature of God, made in His image, with the capacity for knowing what he ought to do, even though this capacity may have been weakened and frustrated in various ways. Consequently that is good which is truly "natural" to man.

Finally, we may associate with these terms the untranslatable expression *to kalon*—"that which is fine, honorable, noble or beautiful."[28] No single one of these words adequately translates the very characteristically Greek term that Paul uses. The concept of *to kalon*, which hovers between the rational and the æsthetic, is most deeply rooted in Greek thought. It is admirably illustrated for English readers by what R. L. Stevenson[29] says of the marines of the *Wager*, who when marooned to die on an island because there was no room in the lifeboat, gave three cheers and cried, "God bless the King!" Says Stevenson, "They were giving their lives, there was no help for that; and they made it a point of self-respect to give them *handsomely*."

On this side of it, then, Paul conceives the moral ideal as that of a life which gives satisfaction to the person living it and to his fellows, because it has about it the "handsomeness" of a thing complete and rounded-off, befitting human nature in its essential nobility, and so deserving to be called, in the fullest sense of a much-abused word, "good." All that is very Greek, which is as much as to say, very humane and very reasonable.

[28] Our translations disguise the fact that this term τὸ καλόν is one of Paul's most constant expressions for the word ideal; it is used in Rom. 7: 18, 21; II Cor. 13: 7; Gal. 6: 9; I Thess. 5: 21; while the adjective καλός is similarly used in other connections. Our versions usually render it "good," which disguises its special shade of meaning.

[29] *Virginibus Puerisque*: Essay on *The English Admirals*.

B. *The Religious Concept of the Ethical End*. The definitions of the moral ideal, however, which he shares with the Greeks are perhaps not after all the most characteristic of Paul's thought. He is a religious man through and through, and the fundamental thing in all religion, as we have recently been taught anew, is "the Idea of the Holy."[30] That idea is not one which reason forms for itself. It is simply that before which one feels an instinctive "awe"—a mystery beyond our knowing and yet potent to kindle our deepest emotions. In all theistic religions this awe is felt for God; and persons and things are "holy" which belong to Him and share His nature. Now for Paul, as for other early Christian teachers, the Christian man is a "holy" person, because he belongs to Christ, his "Lord," and possesses the "Holy Spirit," which is the Spirit of God. The ethical value of this idea is wholly dependent on the moral quality attributed to the divine personality. Already by his Jewish training, and certainly not less by his Christian experience, Paul was compelled to think of God's holiness in ethical terms, and where this is so, the enormous weight of instinctive emotion which attaches to the idea of the holy is placed at the disposal of the moral ideal. Thus the Christian is exhorted to lay his "body" (that is, his individual personality as an acting concrete whole) on the altar of God as a "living sacrifice";[31] or in other terms he is bidden regard this "body" as a temple of God.[32]

C. *The Moral Ideal as Embodied in Christ*. In spite of all he had learned from the Greeks this emphasis on the idea of the holy might well have thrown Paul's ethics over to the side of the irrational. The Pharisaism in which he had

[30] See Rudolf Otto's book *Das Heilige,* translated into English under the title quoted in the text.

[31] Rom. 12: 1; *cf.* 15: 16.

[32] I Cor. 6: 19; in I Cor. 3: 16, Eph. 2: 21, and probably II Cor. 6: 16, the "temple" is not the individual but the community.

been bred did not wholly avoid a taint of irrational superstition in its ethical code. It proscribed certain foods, for
example, not because the eating of them could be clearly
seen to be inconsistent with "the good and acceptable
and perfect," but because of an obscure sense that they
were "unholy." Paul was in fact saved from this not so
much by Greek rationalism as by the fact that he identified the "Spirit of Holiness" with the Spirit of Christ,[33]
and so had a ready point of reference in a figure standing
in the clear light of history with the concrete solidity of
a powerful human personality; and one whose morality
in word and deed was reasonable and humane, with no
taint of taboo in its ideal of holiness. That Christ loved
us and died to save us is the most moving fact in Paul's
universe. And he so died "that those who live should no
longer live for themselves."[34] His love puts a moral con-
straint upon us. Accordingly the stamp of Christ will be
upon the whole of the Christian's daily activity.[35] The
"law of Christ" is binding upon him in all things.[36] That
law is apprehended inwardly by the activity of the indwelling Spirit of Christ, for it is the Spirit that gives us
the "mind of Christ."[37] But it would be a mistake to divorce this thought from a direct reference to the historic
teaching of Jesus Christ. Paul, in fact, not only allows
that teaching to mold and color his own thought to a
greater extent than is commonly realized, but he also
definitely cites the words of Christ as morally authoritative.[38]

Further, Christ is to be imitated.[39] "The grace of the

[33] Rom. 1: 4.
[34] II Cor. 5: 14-15. The second of these two verses has been too much ignored by those who have tried to interpret Paul's teaching about the cross.
[35] Col. 3: 17.
[36] Gal. 6: 2.
[37] I Cor. 2: 12-16.
[38] I Cor. 7: 10, 9: 14, perhaps also Rom. 14: 14.
[39] I Cor. 11: 1; I Thess. 1: 6.

Lord Jesus'' is held up for an example to be copied. That grace was exhibited in his condescension to poverty for our sakes, and the Corinthians will imitate him by contributing to the point of sacrifice to the needs of their brethren.[40] Similarly the selflessness, humility, and obedience of Christ are made an example to the Philippians of those qualities which are needed to preserve the unity of the church,[41] and the fact that ''Christ did not please himself'' constitutes an appeal to the Romans to act graciously to difficult members of their community.[42] In such passages Paul tends to hold up for contemplation not any particular aspects of the life of Jesus on earth, but the moral qualities involved in the incarnation and determining his whole activity as Saviour of men. Yet it is wrong to suggest that Paul is setting up a purely ideal figure. The appeal to the Philippians would have no force if Jesus were not known to have died a servile death. The reference to his poverty would be frigid in the context unless the Corinthians knew that Jesus of Nazareth really had been a poor man. It would be wholly unreal to represent the ''gentleness and sweet-reasonableness of Christ''[43] as attributes of an ideal Messianic figure existing only in a pious imagination. Paul fully identified the Christ in whose fellowship he lived with Jesus of Nazareth. He is trying to avoid the dangers of a merely slavish imitation of a life once lived in the past, and yet to preserve all the reality of a personal life and character as the inspiration and the norm of Christian conduct. It is instructive to observe how in Colossians and Ephesians a continuous reference to Christ is made to give definite character to an outline scheme of common duties which in

40 II Cor. 8: 9.
41 Phil. 2: 5 *sqq.*
42 Rom. 15: 3, 7.
43 II Cor. 10: 1.

itself is largely conceived in the form of current ethical teaching.[44]

D. *The Eschatological Motive and its Transformation.* In Paul's thought, as in that of other early Christian teachers, the eschatological motive plays a not unimportant part. To think eschatologically means (according to strict etymology) to take into account the Last Things— death, judgment, and the future life. The ethical value of such an outlook consists in the fact that it contemplates human life apart from all accidents of time and place in the light of the "great white throne" of divine judgment, and refers all human action to that ultimate justice as an absolute standard. For Paul, especially in his earlier phase, the thought of the awful imminence of the Day of the Lord provides a purgation of the conscience and a spur to watchful self-discipline.[45] But in two ways the cruder eschatology is modified by his Christian beliefs. First, he holds that the Christian belongs to the age of miracle in which the divine justice is already being unveiled. He is a citizen of a new and absolute world-order— a "son of the day,"[46] and must live with the moral seriousness of one who not merely looks forward to a last judgment, but lives in the very presence of the "great white throne."[47] Secondly, the vague outline of the holy Judge in popular eschatology is for Paul filled in by a vivid realization of Christ as a concrete personality. The great tribunal is "the judgment seat of Christ,"[48] and while the final estimate of our character and conduct awaits the coming of the Lord,[49] his presence as Judge within the redeemed community, and in communion with

[44] Col. 3: 18, 20, 22, 23, 24, 4: 1; Eph. 5: 22-23, 6: 1, 5-8, 9.
[45] I Thess. 5: 1-10; I Cor. 15: 58; Rom. 13: 11-14. In an exaggerated form, I Cor. 7: 29-31.
[46] I Thess. 5: 5; Eph. 5: 9.
[47] Rom. 1: 18. The present tense is to be taken seriously.
[48] II Cor. 5: 10, and perhaps Rom. 14: 10.
[49] I Cor. 4: 5.

the individual believer, provides a present inward standard of absolute moral valuation.[50] Thus not only is the conception of the moral ideal saved from the subjectivity which might lurk in Paul's emphasis on the spiritual autonomy of the individual, but the motive for moral seriousness is presented in a new and compelling form—"We are ambitious to be well-pleasing to him.''[51]

3. *The Discipline of Character*. It is evident that to some of Paul's converts his proclamation of an achieved salvation seemed to place them "beyond good and evil," while the "manifestations of the Spirit" were too much akin to the less moral emotional elements in contemporary cults for their ethical significance to be immediately evident. This fact gave Paul occasion to make it very plain that in his view the new sphere of life into which faith in Christ translated the believer was a sphere of strenuous moral effort. Salvation is indeed the free gift of God, but we must "work out our own salvation with fear and trembling, because it is God who works in us both will and deed.''[52] The moral life is one of stern self-discipline. It is like a battle,[53] like a race or a boxing contest.[54] Such are Paul's favorite illustrations. Moral self-discipline, therefore, is to be regarded as the sublimation of the instinctive impulses of pugnacity and emulation— the "equivalent for war in the moral sphere" of which William James spoke. The most illuminating passage on this point is I Corinthians 9:24-27, where Paul makes confession of his own intense struggle to maintain the full

---

[50] I Cor. 4:4; *cf.* Rom. 9:1, where the Holy Spirit (which is identified with the indwelling Christ, II Cor. 3:17) gives validity to the judgments of conscience; Col. 3:1-4.

[51] II Cor. 5:9; *cf.* Col. 3:23-25.

[52] Phil. 2:12-13.

[53] I Thess. 5:8; Eph. 6:10-17; Rom. 13:12; I Cor. 9:7; II Cor. 10:3-6; Phil. 2:25; Philemon 2. (Also I Tim. 1:18, and II Tim. 2:4, but these are probably not Pauline.)

[54] Phil. 3:14; Gal. 2:2 (II Tim. 4:7, probably Pauline).

ethical standard of the Christian life "lest after preaching to others I should myself be a castaway."

This attitude to life readily passes into asceticism. The ascetic is properly one who "goes into training" for the attainment of virtue. But asceticism generally implies a certain condemnation of the natural enjoyments of life as in themselves evil. In this sense Paul is not to be reckoned an ascetic. For him "the earth is the Lord's and the fulness thereof"[55] and one can "eat and drink to the glory of God."[56] To live in fear of some taint of evil in material things is to be "weak in the faith,"[57] and to submit to prohibitions and taboos is to sink back into that life of "the world," under the dominion of the "elemental spirits," from which Christ has redeemed his people.[58] "All things are yours and you are Christ's"[59] is a charter of emancipation from a superstitious asceticism.

On the other hand, a man should have such self-control as to remain independent of external goods while making use of them.[60] In his earlier phase, indeed, Paul was inclined, under the pressure of an ardent expectation of the end of the age, to advocate an exaggerated detachment from all earthly interests.[61] But to be afraid of being entangled in the things of this world, and to despise them for that reason, is not after all to be fully emancipated or truly independent of them. Such independence is, in fact, the fine fruit of experience in Christian living. It is not until his last letter, that to the Philippians, that Paul is able to claim for himself that he has received the "initiation" which makes him content and self-sufficing what-

[55] I Cor. 10: 26.
[56] I Cor. 10: 31.
[57] Rom. 14: 14; cf. 14: 1-6; I Cor. 8: 8.
[58] Col. 2: 20-23; cf. Gal. 4: 9-10.
[59] I Cor. 3: 22-23.
[60] I Cor. 7: 31.
[61] I Cor. 7: 29-35.

ever his outward condition.[62] This ideal of content or self-sufficiency[63] was the ideal of the Stoics (from whom, in fact, Paul borrows the word he uses). It bears, doubtless, a certain tinge of asceticism, but it is essentially humane and not superstitious. In even the finer Stoics, however, this self-sufficing attitude is mingled with a proud consciousness of superiority which is in strong contrast to the quiet self-forgetfulness of Paul's last phase. The mellow, tranquil spirit of the last chapter of Philippians, with its happy contemplation of all things lovely and of good report, all virtue and praise among men, leaves us in no doubt that Paul really had at last surmounted the "fightings and fears" of his earlier days and attained the secret.

4. *Forms of Moral Evil.* The ethical life is represented, as we have seen, on one side of it as a fight against evil. In several of his epistles Paul gives a more or less explicit and detailed list of the forms of evil to be fought.[64] No two such lists of vices, however, exactly correspond, so that we cannot find in Paul a systematic treatment of individual forms of wrong conduct such as many moralists have given. Nevertheless, an inspection of his lists, especially the more comprehensive ones, reveals the fact that the vices he has in view tend to fall into two groups, (1) sins of the flesh, such as drunkenness and sexual immorality, and (2) anti-social sins, such as anger, malice, lying, pride, injustice. That this grouping is not fortuitous becomes clear when we recognize a similar classification in other ancient moralists. Thus, certain Pythagorean moralists traced all vices to two principal tendencies, "intemperance" or lack of self-control, and *"pleonexia"* or grasping "self-assertion" at the expense

62 Phil. 4: 11-13.

63 αὐτάρκεια

64 The most comprehensive lists are in Rom. 1: 24-32; I Cor. 5: 10-11; II Cor. 12: 20-21; Gal. 5: 19-21; Col. 3: 5, 8; Eph. 5: 3-5.

of others.[65] Paul agrees in a general way with their diagnosis of moral evil, and arrays against "intemperance" the Christian ideal of "holiness" and against "self-assertion" the Christian principle that no man lives to himself.

5. *The Virtues.* If Paul gives no regular scheme of vices, still less does he offer a detailed and classified treatment of the virtues, such as most ancient moralists deemed necessary. He has no "cardinal virtues," for the triad "faith, hope, love" is nothing of the sort. It is indeed of the essence of his system that character is not formed by the adding of virtue to virtue, but by the permeation of the personality with a Spirit. Accordingly those dispositions of the soul which might otherwise appear in lists of virtues are presented collectively as "the fruit of the Spirit." In Galatians 5: 22-23 a list of typical qualities which come under that general heading is given. Of these the first, love, is not strictly a virtue among other virtues, but the principle of all true morality.[66] Then follow joy, peace, and patience, which are rather indications of the temper in which the Christian life is lived than particular virtues. Kindness, goodness, faithfulness, and gentleness are the reverse of the anti-social sins, and the last on the list, self-control, is the reverse of the fountain vice of intemperance. Clearly there is nothing systematic or exhaustive about this list. A similar short list in Ephesians 5: 9 gives the "fruit of light" as goodness, justice, and truth. Elsewhere we have short lists like "purity, knowledge, patience and kindness,"[67] "humility, gentleness and patience,"[68] "pity, kindness, humility, gentleness and patience."[69] A characteristic term of Greek

[65] ἀκρασία and πλεονεξία ("greediness" in our A.V.). See Iamblichus' *Life of Pythagoras*, XVII, 18.
[66] For the meaning of ἀγάπη see below.
[67] II Cor. 1: 6.
[68] Eph. 4: 2.
[69] Col. 3: 12.

ethics appears in II Corinthians 10:1, where the A.V. makes Paul speak of "the meekness and gentleness of Christ."[70] The rendering "gentleness," however, would be more appropriate to the first term, while the second is the almost untranslatable Greek word which Matthew Arnold proposed to render "sweet reasonableness." It is certainly a stronger virtue than "gentleness." To complete the picture we must note the emphasis laid on sincerity[71] and singleness of mind.[72] That the Christian will be sober-minded and alert we have seen. He will have a strong sense of responsibility for the use of time and opportunity.[73] If the virtue of courage is not specifically named, yet the Christian will be firm, steadfast, and ready to endure,[74] and the frequency of military metaphors in the sense of an aggressive warfare against evil sufficiently brings into relief the importance of the hardier and sterner virtues.

At best the picture is a mere outline of the elements of individual character. But it demands the social background if it is to have any force or vividness. Almost the whole of the positive content of Paul's ethics is, in fact, supplied from his conception of the Christian society. The virtues that count in the upbuilding of character are social virtues.

PART II: SOCIAL ETHICS

1. *The Body and the Members.* Paul is not original in thinking of the community on the analogy of a living organism.[75] But he works out the idea very effectively, and by connecting it with religious experience gives it a pecul-

[70] πραΰτης and ἐπιείκεια.

[71] ἰλικρίνεια, II Cor. 1: 12, 2: 17.

[72] ἁπλότης (*not* "liberality"), Rom. 12: 8; II Cor. 11: 3; Eph. 6: 5; Col. 3: 22.

[73] Eph. 5: 16; Col. 4: 5.

[74] I Cor. 15: 58; Rom. 5: 4, etc.

[75] See for example, Livy, II, 32.

iar significance.[76] In a living organism the all-important
fact is the interdependence of the organs, and their harmonious functioning in subordination to the ends of the
whole. The same is true of society. But in societies known
to Paul, as to us, this organic unity frequently breaks
down. What will guarantee a permanent and effective
unity? Paul replies, the sharing of all the members in a
common religious experience which is in its nature destructive of selfishness. Such is the redemptive experience
of the gospel, through which the Spirit of Christ controls
the believer.[77]

As the mark of a true organism is perfect unity in diversity, so in the Christian community diversity is provided by the varied endowments or "gifts of the Spirit"
which appear in individuals, and the unity is found in the
unity of the divine Spirit itself.[78] The primitive church
had recognized the working of the Spirit in such "miracu-
lous" phenomena as "speaking with tongues" and the
healing of disease by other than physical means. Paul indeed accepts such phenomena as indicating spiritual
endowment, though he prizes "tongues" but slightly,
greatly preferring "prophecy" as the inspired and inspiring utterance of truth.[79] But his conception of the
range of the Spirit's gifts is very wide, including, for
example, intellectual gifts of wisdom and insight, practical gifts like "helps and governments," and moral endowments, of which the greatest is love.[80] We should, in
fact, not be doing him wrong if we brought into this category all qualities and capacities which are recognized as
enhancing personality. They are the gifts of the divine

[76] I Cor. 12: 12-26; Rom. 12: 4-5.
[77] I Cor. 12: 12-13; Eph. 4: 4-5.
[78] I Cor. 12: 4-11.
[79] I Cor. 14: 1-5.
[80] I Cor. 12: 8-10, 28, 13: 1; cf. Rom. 12: 5-9.

Spirit; and further—this is Paul's great point—as such they are to be regarded from beginning to end as endowments for service in the community. To exploit any spiritual gift for individual ends is rank misuse. And as for the gifts themselves, their value is to be assessed by the one principle, "unto edification" (*i.e.*, "for building up").[81] The perversion of the meaning of the term "edification" in modern religious language leads to most serious misunderstanding of Paul. What he means by "edification" is the upbuilding of the community. That is "edifying," which is socially constructive, and nothing else.

2. *Love as the Creative Principle of Social Ethics.* The "gifts of the Spirit" by which the ends of the community are served through diversity of function in its members are, as we have seen, infinitely varied. But in order that the diversity may be contributory to a real unity, there must be a universal principle governing them all. This principle Paul finds in "charity" or love.[82] The postulate of a Christian society is the maxim, "Love builds up."[83] The body of Christ grows by the harmonious functioning of every individual "towards its upbuilding by love."[84]

The word which is here inadequately rendered "charity" or "love" is the Hellenistic Greek *agapé*, a word which scarcely exists in pre-biblical Greek, and whose specific meaning must be gathered from the Christian literature which first gave it real currency. For Paul, *agapé* is primarily the distinctive activity of the Divine Nature— the redemptive goodness of God exhibited towards the undeserving.[85] It is not strictly definable, nor, indeed, can it be fully comprehended in intellectual concepts; yet it

81 I Cor. 14: 26.
82 Love is the "bond of completeness," Col. 3: 14.
83 I Cor. 8: 1.
84 Eph. 4: 15-16.
85 Rom. 5: 8.

can be known in religious experience.[86] Moreover, that religious experience in which we know the love of God also implants love in our nature as an indwelling energy.[87] Thus love is the supreme and all-inclusive gift of the Spirit.[88] Conformably with the teaching of the Gospels, the objects of such love are God[89] and our neighbor;[90] but it is upon the latter that the emphasis falls, other terms being used by preference for our attitude to God. Love directed toward men is the central principle of ethics— "the full content of the Law."[91] Without it no action has fully ethical quality, not even the most extreme forms of self-sacrifice.[92]

In I Corinthians 13 *agapé* is described in a series of aphorisms. It is the source of the patience and gentleness which are characteristic Christian virtues. It excludes jealousy, being thereby sharply distinguished from some other forms of "love." Where it is present any form of egotism is excluded, whether a fantastic estimate of oneself such as would lead to lack of respect for one's fellows, or any form of self-seeking such as would lead to *pleonexia* and its kindred vices. It saves a man from those irrational outbreaks of resentment which are (as modern psychology can assure us) chiefly the result of an affronted self-fantasy. It breeds a generous oblivion of the wrongs one suffers. Not only so, but it fixes the attention upon the highest values in personality,—right and truth, and produces a sense of joy in their presence which excludes any mean satisfaction in the moral defects of others. In the presence of the imperfections of humanity it

[86] Eph. 3: 19.
[87] Rom. 5: 5.
[88] I Cor. 12: 31, 13: 1.
[89] Rom. 8: 28; I Cor. 2: 9, 8: 3—or Christ, Eph. 6: 24.
[90] Rom. 13: 8-9; Gal. 5: 14; *cf*. I Thess. 4: 9.
[91] Rom. 13: 10. Not the "fulfilment" of the Law, which, in modern English at least, would have a different meaning.
[92] I Cor. 13: 3.

preserves a belief in human nature and an indefeasible hope of its perfection even in the fallible folk one knows.

There is obviously here no attempt to give a logically exhaustive description of *agapé*. The passage is, in fact, poetical rather than scientific. This fact enables us to add that *agapé* is suffused with emotion. Yet it is not simple emotion. It is, in the language of recent psychology, a "sentiment," within which various instinctive impulses and emotions are organized and sublimated. It may from this point of view be described as *the sentiment for humanity as identified with its highest values,* right and truth. All sentiments, we are told, have their appropriate duties. Accordingly, in the comprehensive sentiment of *agapé* the whole idea of duty is carried up into a higher category. A duty is something "owed." Your duty to your neighbor is that which you owe him, or your obligation to him. "Be under obligation to no one," says Paul,[93] "except the obligation to mutual love, for whoever loves another has exhausted the content of the moral law." He goes on to show that the precepts which define our duty to other men forbid acts which are impossible to one whose conduct is determined by the sentiment of *agapé*. In place of them all we may set the precept "Love thy neighbour as thyself." That precept is quoted, as Jesus quoted it, from the Old Testament, where it is given as a simple categorical imperative. But for Paul, as for Jesus, it ceases to be a mere categorical imperative because it is directly related to the religious experience of God's love for us.

3. *Social Ethics as based on Love*. The fullest treatment of *agapé* as the mainspring of practical conduct in social life is to be found in Romans 12-14 and in Ephesians 4-6. In neither passage is there a fully systematic treatment, but in a brief and allusive way the writer gives

[93] Rom. 13: 8-10.

an adequate impression of the general character of the ethical direction he gave to his newly founded Christian societies. For our present purpose it will be most convenient to take Romans 12 as the text.

Here we start with a brief exposition of the theory of society as a living organism with differentiation of function within an overruling unity of purpose (4-8). Then the writer passes on at once to the principle which gives such unity—the principle of *agapé* or love. Love must be absolutely sincere (9) and it must be related to the ideal values of right and truth (10). This is his first general charge. He then deals with the implications of such love, first within the Christian society, and afterward in relations between Christians and outsiders. The division is not made quite clear, but verses 9-13, 15-16, belong to the former section, and verses 14, 17-21, to the latter.

A. *Ethics of Love within the Christian Community.* Here *agapé* takes the special and narrower form of *philadelphia,* the love of brothers. It is accompanied by warm feelings of affection (10). The "tender emotion" primarily associated with the parental instinct is thus taken up into the exalted sentiment for humanity. There is naturally a ready sympathy with joy and grief in others (15), and a strong impulse towards unanimity of thought and feeling (16). The instinctive craving for superiority is, within the dominant sentiment, so redirected that instead of desiring superiority for himself, a man desires his associates to excel (as a parent finds fullest satisfaction in the success of a child) (10). Personal vanity is excluded[94] by a high estimate of the worth of others, and a readiness to serve the whole in the humblest ways (16). Within a family of brothers, there will be a full sharing of needs and resources (13). With all this will go a particular emotional tone—one of joy, fervor, hopefulness, dili-

94 *Cf.* Gal. 5: 26.

gence (11-12). Such are the marks of conduct which is not
dictated by mere obedience to precept, but produced by a
sublimation of instinctive energy within a dominant sentiment.

Here we may pause to consider briefer passages in
other epistles which cover much the same ground, especially I Thessalonians 4: 9-12, 5: 13-14, and Galatians 6:
1-5. In these passages we observe especial emphasis on
the theme of mutual responsibility, with particular reference to differences of moral capacity and attainment
within the community. In the Roman epistle this theme
receives separate treatment at considerable length in 14:
1-15: 6, and this treatment in turn depends on the attention which Paul had been obliged to pay at Corinth to certain questions of casuistry bearing upon the attitude to
be taken to particular kinds of ritual taboo.[95] The interest
of these discussions for our present purpose lies in the
light they throw on Paul's conception of the implications
of "brotherly love" in a community where differences of
ethical attainment were marked. Love demands genuine
respect for the other man as a moral agent, a respect
which does not permit you to pass judgment on his con-
scientious conduct, and which is in no way abated if you
cannot accept *his* judgment on certain points. It is fully
granted that not all members of the community have attained an equal level of freedom and enlightenment. The
attainment of a relatively high level is not to be allowed
to minister to self-esteem. It entails a heavy responsibility
for the moral well-being of the weaker. Such responsibility limits the practice of the liberty which the Christian
enjoys. The necessary balance of liberty and subservience
is well summarized in Galatians 5: 13: "For liberty you
were called; only do not make liberty an opportunity for
the lower nature, but through *agapé* be slaves one of an-

[95] I Cor. 8-10.

other.'' This mutual responsibility is put to the most severe test in cases of actual moral failure of a gross kind. Such failure does not destroy the essential relation of *philadelphia*. The stronger must bear the burden of the weaker.[96] If his sin has offended or injured another member of the community, the offended will forgive "as the Lord forgave you.''[97] Only a scandalous and contumacious defiance of the moral sense of the community may lead at the worst to a withdrawal from communion.[98] The excommunicate is not to be treated as an enemy, nor does excommunication imply a judgment on his ultimate fate. It is the last resource of a fellowship which desires that at all costs "the spirit may be saved at the day of judgment.''[99] Repentance is to be followed by complete restoration.[100]

In Ephesians 4: 17-5: 2 we have a section which may be compared with Romans 12. It begins in the same way with a call for the renewal of the spirit, and the author continues: Be true in all your intercourse, because we are members one of another (4: 25). Do not sin by cherishing anger (26-27). Work honestly in order to make your contribution to the economic needs of the community (28). Watch your speech and test it by its value for the building up of true social relations (29). Be kind and pitiful, forgive as God forgave you (31-32)—in a word, love one another as Christ loved you (5: 2). This may serve as a final summary of what *agapé* means in its aspect of *philadelphia,* within the Christian community.

B. *Ethics of Love Beyond the Limits of the Christian*

[96] Gal. 6: 1-3; Rom. 15: 1.
[97] Col. 3: 13. We may add that he will endeavor to overcome the sinful temper which occasioned the offense by extra kindness, since the precepts of Rom. 12: 17, I Thess. 5: 15, though they have outsiders mainly in view, apply *a fortiori* to fellow Christians.
[98] II Thess. 3: 14-15; I Cor. 5: 9-11.
[99] I Cor. 5: 5.
[100] II Cor. 2: 6-8.

Community. With the latter part of Romans 12 we pass beyond the limits of the Christian community. The order of the exposition is somewhat confused. We may start with the general demand (17b) for respect for the moral standards of non-Christian neighbors. This point is repeated in almost every epistle, and in some with even greater emphasis than here.[101] The danger of a revolutionary movement in ethics, such as early Christianity was, is that in claiming independence of convention in the interests of a higher morality, unstable characters are liable to lose the support which comes from public opinion, and to abuse their independence in the interests of a lower morality than the conventional. That this actually sometimes happened in the Pauline communities is clear from I Corinthians 5:1-2. Such a danger would be obviated if Paul's precept (borrowed from the Old Testament with a significant modification) were followed: "Plan for yourselves a course of conduct which shall be honourable in the sight of *all* men." *Agapé* demands that no one shall affront the conscience of another unless directly and necessarily in the interests of a higher good for that other.

The assumption is that there is a certain moral standard common to Christians and pagans—doubtless the "law written on the heart," which good pagans follow "by nature"[102]—and *agapé* requires the Christian to make the most of this as a basis for harmonious relations. One of the social manifestations of *agapé* is peace. Peace among men was for Paul one of the most desirable of all things: Christ had died to make it possible.[103] Accordingly the Christian must always strive for peaceful relations with his pagan neighbors. If collisions occur, as they al-

101 I Thess. 4: 12; I Cor. 10: 32; Col. 4: 5; *cf.* Phil. 4: 5.
102 Rom. 2: 14-15.
103 Eph. 2: 14-18.

most inevitably will, the provocation must not come from the Christian side: "if it be possible, so far as it lies with *you,* keep the peace with all men" (18). The difficulty of keeping such a precept in the conditions of the first century is evident. The limits of possibility contemplated are of course the higher demands of the Christian conscience.

On the question, how far intimate social relations between Christians and non-Christians should be cultivated, Paul speaks with a somewhat uncertain voice. In II Corinthians 6:14-7:1 (which is perhaps a fragment of a letter to Corinth prior to our I Corinthians) he takes a strongly puritan line. There can be nothing in common between light and darkness, and any intimate relation with a non-Christian is an unnatural union of opposites.[104] In I Corinthians, however, a strict separation from non-Christian society is not recommended. On the contrary, the advice given respecting "eating food offered to idols" clearly contemplates the freest possible social intercourse short of actual participation in idolatry.[105] One cannot even attempt to avoid intercourse with pagans who fail to live up to their own moral standards. In fact, though a Christian must take cognizance of sins of his fellow Christians, the sins of outsiders are none of his business.[106] This goes perhaps farther than Paul would ordinarily have been prepared to go in the way of tolerance for pagan sinners. At any rate Ephesians 5:11-13 enjoins Christians not only to abstain from any share in "the barren works of darkness," but to "show them up"; but the implication is that they are to be shown up by the light of a superior moral practice rather than by words of condemnation.

[104] The word ἑτεροζογεῖν, in view of ἑτερόζυγον in Lev. 19:19, might be held to have special reference to mixed marriages, which were certainly a difficulty in the early Church. *Cf.* I Cor. 7:12-16, 39.

[105] I Cor. 10:25-29.

[106] I Cor. 5:9-13.

The treatment is obviously unsatisfactory, but it offers a rough practicable scheme for Christians in the peculiarly difficult situation of the first century. In any case, *agapé* demands that one shall not only refrain from offending or shocking one's pagan neighbors, but also endeavor positively to do them good. This is implied rather than stated in Romans 12:17, but it is made quite explicit in I Thessalonians 5:15, and Galatians 6:10. The special difficulty in the application of this rule arises when the neighbor in question is an enemy. If one suffers injury, what is to be done? First, there are to be no reprisals (Romans 12:17, 19). The specious plea that if injuries are overlooked the moral order will suffer is met by the counsel "Give room to the wrath"—"the wrath" being Paul's designation for the principle of retribution inherent in a moral universe. In other words, the moral order will look after itself without the crude attempt of the individual to "get even with" people who have done him wrong.

But mere abstention from revenge is not yet fully Christian. Quoting his Master, Paul says "Bless your persecutors" (14). To bless is to wish well and to turn that wish into a prayer. If the wish and the prayer be sincere, they will lead to action as opportunity offers. So, "if your enemy is hungry, feed him; if he is thirsty, give him drink: that is the way to make him burn with shame" —for that, whatever the passage in Proverbs (25:21-22) originally meant, is doubtless what Paul understood by the "coals of fire." The principle which is here at work is the law that evil can never be overcome by evil, but only by a greater good. This is by far the most important thing that Paul has to say about *agapé* in its wider application. *Agapé* is, as we have seen, in its essence that property of the divine nature by which God is good to the undeserving, supremely expressed in that "Christ died for the

ungodly.'' Where the divine love is ''shed abroad in the
heart,'' there evil will be met with an unwearying beneficence which in the end will wear out the evil. That such
will be the ultimate result can only be believed if human
nature is fundamentally good, and evil only an abnor-
mality. This Paul held, in spite of ''original sin.'' The injunction ''Do not let evil conquer you, but conquer evil
with good'' is an admirable summary of the teaching of
Jesus in the Sermon on the Mount about what is called
''non-resistance,'' and it expresses the most creative element in Christian ethics.

4. *Social Institutions.* In the application of his ethical
doctrine to social institutions Paul's thought underwent
an important development. In his early phase (represented by the epistles to the Thessalonians and the first to
the Corinthians) he was strongly under the influence of
the illusion that the end of the existing world order was
actually imminent, and in the writings of this period his
attitude to all organized social life is one of extreme detachment. In I Corinthians he puts forward a curious
theory that the outward relations of a man's life should
remain as far as possible unchanged during the short interval before the end.[107] With such a view, any serious
doctrine of social institutions is almost impossible. As
the imminence of the end gradually ceased to be an urgent
necessity of his thought, Paul showed a greater interest
in such matters. The tables of social duties in the epistles
to the Colossians and Ephesians are a sign of this growing interest.

A. *Property and Industry.* Paul's ethical ideal, as we
have seen, demanded a certain independence of external
goods, but not an ascetic rejection of their value. It is in
harmony with this standpoint that he rebukes the religious fanaticism which was leading some of his converts,

[107] I Cor. 7: 17-24.

in view of the expected "End," to neglect the drudgery of ordinary labor. By precept and example he set forth the necessity and value of working honestly for a living.[108] He was severe on the "shirker" and laid down the rule "if a man will not work, neither shall he eat."[109] This injunction clearly has in view abuses of the system by which the early Christian communities made themselves responsible for their poorer members. The experiment in communism at Jerusalem indeed had had by no means encouraging results: the Jerusalem community was wretchedly poor. Paul, however, accepted without question the principle which underlay that experiment. In fact, it is he who first provided it with a formula—the formula that fellowship in spiritual goods should carry with it fellowship in material goods.[110] A new motive for labor is suggested by the precept, "He who used to steal must steal no more, but rather labour, putting in good work with his own hands, *in order that he may have something to share with the man who is in want.*"[111] The dignity which Paul's teaching, in line with the best Jewish tradition, attributed to labor, was a most salutary influence in the early Gentile churches, established in the midst of a society in which the foolish Greek prejudice against trade and industry was still strong.

B. *The Household.*—1. *Marriage and the relations of the sexes.* In Paul's view, the Christian life transcends the distinction of sex, as it does those of nationality, culture, and civil status.[112] Nevertheless, the difference of function exists, and for Paul, with the outlook of his time, that involved in some sense the subordination of women.[112a] His resentment of some aspects of "feminism" in the

108 I Thess. 4: 11-12.
109 II Thess. 3: 6-12.
110 Rom. 15: 26-27; *cf.* I Cor. 9: 11.
111 Eph. 4: 28.
112 Gal. 3: 28.
112a I Cor. 14: 33-35, 11: 1-16.

church was not without good grounds in the social conditions of the Empire. Nevertheless, it is mingled with superstitious ideas regarding sex which are not really reconcilable with his repudiation of asceticism. It is interesting to see him struggling out of this level of thought. After reaching the lowest depth of his argument in I Corinthians 11:10, he proceeds,—''and yet, man and woman are mutually dependent and in the Lord they cannot do without one another; for just as woman came out of man (according to the myth in Genesis), so also man comes into being through woman, and God is the source of all.'' Nothing could be more instructive as a picture of the Christian spirit making its way in a man's mind through a tangle of prejudice, even though as a positive contribution to ethics it does not come to very much.

This deposit of unsurmounted superstition is probably partly responsible for Paul's earlier view of marriage, though the reasons he gives for that view are various. Celibacy, he has no doubt, is the ideal state, first, because the time is short and detachment from the things of this age is required, and secondly, because marriage diverts man and woman alike from the pure service of God.[113] Accordingly he approves in principle mutual vows of celibacy between men and women. Yet he is aware of their dangers, and his regulations in I Corinthians 7:25-38 are chiefly intended to mitigate these. Marriage, he admits, is often the lesser of two evils. True to his principle of continuing as things are until the End, he accepts such marriages as exist, and regulates them.[114] Husband and wife are to be exclusively faithful to one another; marriage is to be a real and complete thing; and perfect

[113] I Cor. 7:1, 7-9, 25-35. He confesses quite frankly that all this is merely his personal opinion, and does not come ''from the Lord''—as is indeed obvious.

[114] I Cor. 7:10-24, 39-40.

equality of rights is here to be maintained.[115] Marriage between Christians is indissoluble: if for any reason separation takes place, remarriage is forbidden. This, Paul adds, is not his personal opinion, but the commandment of the Lord. He supplements it with some corollaries of his own, adapting the Christian rule of monogamy to cases of mixed marriage between Christians and pagans.[116] Here we have a Christian law of marriage shaping itself in a pagan environment. Its basis is the teaching of Jesus, which Paul honestly tries to apply; but he has handicapped himself by yielding to prejudices which are not part of his Christianity as well as by a one-sidedly eschatological outlook.

In Colossians and Ephesians he has to some extent at least shaken himself free of these hindrances to clear thought. The subjection of woman remains, but some attempt is made to bring it under the category of the *mutual* subordination of Christians for the ends of the Body.[117] There is further the command "Love your wives,"[118]—a command which is significantly absent from I Corinthians. In Ephesians this precept is strengthened by a doctrine that the love of husband and wife is a "mystery" or sacrament of the most perfect spiritual love that it is possible for the mind of man to conceive—the love of Christ for His Church.[119] Such a doctrine lifts the whole idea of marriage to a new level.

2. *Parent and child.* The children of Christian parents (even of one Christian parent, and *a fortiori* where both are Christian) are "holy"[120]—*i.e.,* they belong from birth to that redeemed order of life into which their parents en-

115 I Cor. 7: 3-6.
116 I Cor. 7: 12-16.
117 Col. 3: 18; Eph. 5: 21-22.
118 Col. 3: 19.
119 Eph. 5: 25-33.
120 I Cor. 7: 14.

tered at baptism. This suggestion of the spiritual solidarity of the Christian family plainly offers itself for development, but within the Pauline writings no such development is found. In Colossians and Ephesians there is a brief summary treatment of the relations of parents and children.[121] That children should obey their parents is, for Paul, a clear consequence from their being "in the Lord." It is a more original thought when he demands that parents shall not irritate their children or discourage them. In this recognition of the rights of the child's personality we see once again the Christian spirit beginning to remold family ideals.

3. *Domestic slavery.* For Paul the relations of master and slave are part of the life of the household. With industrial slavery—which has provided most of the examples of inhumanity that shock the conscience—he does not deal. In his early period his indifference to all social arrangements extends itself to the question of slavery, but with a significant modification. Social status is indeed a thing indifferent: the Christian slave is the Lord's freedman, and the Christian master is the Lord's slave. Yet freedom is so great a natural good that if the slave has a chance to become free he should take it—even though this involves upsetting arrangements which should otherwise be kept as they are till the End. On the other hand, no Christian would think of selling himself into slavery.[122]

In Colossians and Ephesians the thought is more developed.[123] Slavery is here accepted as a part of the social order which is to be Christianized. The slave is to make his daily service a service of Christ. The master is to remember that he too is a slave—the slave of Christ. He is to act by the slave as the slave is instructed to act by him

121 Col. 3: 20-21; Eph. 6: 1-4.
122 I Cor. 7: 20-24.
123 Col. 3: 22-4: 1; Eph. 6: 5-9; and see Philemon for an application of principles to a particular case.

—*i.e.,* he is to show the same "good will and singleness of heart." He is not to invade the personal dignity of his slave by threats, but to treat him in all things with impartial equity. The slave thus becomes not a chattel but an essentially free personality, whose dignity as a person is not to be outraged merely because in the structure of society he discharges subordinate functions. If this principle is worked to its conclusion, slavery fades out of existence, though it took the Church long to draw this conclusion and to give full weight to the Pauline principle "in Christ there is neither bond nor free."[124] Paul no more than the Stoics (who also believed in the essential freedom and equality of all men) thought of inaugurating a movement for the general emancipation of slaves: to have done so could only have had the result of provoking the horrors of another Servile War, and no one in the Roman Empire with any historical memory or imagination could wish for such a repetition.

C. *The State.* In II Thessalonians 2: 5-7 we find adumbrated a view of the Roman Empire as the power which by the divine Providence restrains the threatened outbreak of absolute evil in the person and dominion of that enigmatic figure "the Man of Iniquity." Whatever may have been the precise meaning of this doctrine, at least it inclined Paul's followers away from that barren anarchism which lay all too near to some forms of eschatological belief,[125] and towards a positive valuation of the great state under whose protection they all lived. Such a positive valuation is propounded in Romans 13: 1-7—a passage standing in the closest relation to the discussion of the wider applications of *agapé* or love for one's kind in chapter 12. If we love our neighbor, we shall discharge

124 Gal. 3: 28; Col. 3: 11.

125 The splendid poetry of the Revelation of John is marred by a rancorous hatred of Rome. See in particular chs. 17 and 18.

with all good will every obligation to him. Now many of our obligations to our neighbors are defined in terms of the demands which the state makes of its subjects. To pay tax and tribute therefore with a good grace is clearly a part of Christian conduct.[126] Further, the state is a part of that natural moral order in which the principle of retribution works toward righteousness. The injured Christian is exhorted to refrain from private revenge and "leave room for retribution."[127] Now in the civilized world the primary means of retribution is the sword of the state. In this sense, therefore, the magistrate is an "agent of God for righteousness," and "the existing authorities are ordained by God."[128] They are of divine institution in much the same sense as the unalterable operations of nature are divine, and not as forming part of that redeemed order of things, that "new creation," to which the Christian belongs. He will submit to the state for the sake of its righteous purpose in the divine scheme of things, while he will himself seek to practice the higher righteousness revealed in Christ. His attitude to the state remains one of detachment. Paul discouraged even the use of the imperial law courts by Christians for the settlement of disputes regarding their worldly affairs, recommending instead (if they could not live up to the full ideal of Christianity which would make all such disputes impossible) the setting up of arbitration courts within the Christian community.[129] Such courts, perfectly regular as private procedure under Roman law, formed the germ of the later ecclesiastical jurisdiction.

D. *The Christian Commonwealth*. The idea of a Christian state lay beyond the horizon of Paul's thought. Yet

126 Rom. 13: 7.
127 Rom. 12: 19: the clear connection of thought is disguised by the chapter division.
128 Rom. 13: 1-5.
129 I Cor. 6: 1-11.

in his conception of the Christian society or Church his positive political ideals are to be sought. It is an organic unity moved by one Spirit.[130] It unites mankind on a level beyond all distinctions of sex, class, race, and culture.[131] In it that ancient and typical antipathy of Jew and Gentile—an antipathy which, perhaps in the very year of Paul's death, broke out into most atrocious war—is transcended by the creation, out of both, of "one new humanity."[132] Therein lies the promise of the final reconciliation of all hostilities in a true commonwealth. Built up by the harmonious functioning of all its members, the commonwealth must grow until it expresses in itself the whole meaning of Christ's own humanity.[133] Here Paul's social doctrine passes into his mystical faith. The rest is vision and prophecy.

[130] See above, p. 309.
[131] Gal. 3: 28; Col. 3: 11.
[132] Eph. 2: 14-17.
[133] Eph. 4: 11-16.

MOSLEM ETHICS

JOHN CLARK ARCHER

XI.

THE true Moslem is not so completely the "slave of Allah" that he enjoys no measure of freedom to will and to do. Essential Islam is not so thoroughly a religion of "submission" or "acceptance" that it has imposed upon its followers themselves no moral responsibility for the issues of life. On the contrary, we find Islam recognizing and encouraging moral freedom. Although the history of the movement and the mind of the Moslem masses show the prevalence of determinism, there is in essential Islam no irreconcilable conflict with human freedom. The Moslem is not fundamentally different from other men in that, owing to the pressure of his faith, he is less a free agent than they. He, too, has been conscious of his own free will. If "fatalism" has dominated the life of the Moslem masses it has been due more to circumstantial emphasis than to critical evaluation. Hardship and danger have prevailed in their environment, and loom large in their consciousness of historical unity. These masses have made little or no distinction between the faith and the circumstances which have gathered about its propagation. Among the leaders of the movement, however, determinism has by no means been the unbroken rule, nor have they given uncritical assent to a doctrine of the absolute, divine ordering of all things. And the masses will discover as world progress makes its insistent demands upon them that a fuller, freer life is possible for them within the realm of the faith they hold. We have before us an inviting and fruitful field of ethical inquiry. Even were Islam wholly deterministic in theory, problems of an ethical nature would arise in actual practice.

It is significant and not surprising that within the broad range of Mohammedan literature so small a place is occupied by treatises on ethics. Indeed, it is scarcely a distinct place at all, but rather a treatment of things ethical in connection with other matters, chiefly religious. Practical ethical problems have been faced and dealt with as incidental to the spread and maintenance of the faith. We have, therefore, in the main, treatises on religious morality[1] and not a discussion of ethics in the true sense. But Islam is certainly not lacking in valuable materials for the building of a true science of ethics. New moral values may be found in the great trinity of the Islamic future: Mohammed, the Prophet and the ideal; *Ijma'*, the principle of agreement or consensus of opinion; and al-Ghazāli, the wise doctor, mystic, and "restorer" of the faith. We set ourselves now the task in a brief illustrative survey of indicating some of the major materials in the field of Moslem ethics.

The whole field might not unprofitably be divided into three major portions, the national, the imperial, and the international. Or, since the second and third have much in common, we might observe two divisions, namely, the original ethical deposit within the Arabian borders, and the body of ethical theory and practice which held under the influence of new culture contacts incidental to Moslem expansion into the larger world of Greek philosophy, Roman law, Persian religion, and beyond.

The Arabian epoch is simple in comparison with the subsequent history of the movement, but is in the nature of the case of primary importance. He "errs with palpable error" who would minimize the value of the original deposit or of the place Mohammed holds of right in the ethical development of Islam. Arabia was Mohammed's world. His was an almost exclusively Arabian conscious-

---

[1] *Adab*, one of the five sections of the Law, denotes the field of which morals are a part. It is without strict ethical significance, including as it does music, art, and other branches. It is only the loose, general field of which the aphorism says "Adab equals two-thirds of the field of religion," and not an indication of the Moslem's idea of the ratio of ethics to religion.

ness. He was a prophet to his own people, the Arabs (3: 158),[2] to whom Allah sent down through him an Arabic Koran (43:2), and the Caliph Omar was doubtless expressing the Prophet's own mind when a few years after Mohammed's death he called a halt to conquest at the borders of the Arab world. Mohammed scarcely anticipated the problems of experiment and adjustment in the larger world into which the vigorous Moslem tide surged. He had to do with Arabs for the most part, for whom he laid down the saving way (45:17; 5:52). Nevertheless, Islam thereafter took its impetus and direction from him, and he must be the end of appeal in whatever adjustments Islam may yet make.

Original Islamic morality was not only a product of Arabia, but more particularly of pagan Arabia. Jewish and Christian elements entered in,—more of the former than of the latter, if we take Mohammed's own account,— yet the influence of Christianity was very great. The crushing fire (104:4), the resurrection (99:2, 6), the day of reckoning (1:3), these Christian elements loomed large in his early preaching before the great Jewish factor, the Unity of God, became unyielding dogma (112: 1-4). And the Christian monk exerted a certain very profound influence upon him.[3] But Mohammed was first of all a pagan, and the child of pagan times, and the very Ka'ba, the central shrine of Moslem devotion, is a perpetual symbol of the peculiarly Arabian character of early Islam. Let us compare the moral teachings of Mohammed with the pagan morality of his time.

It may be well to keep in mind some distinction between "the people of the wall" and "the people of the tent," for Mohammed's moral reformation affected the former more than the latter. Mohammed spoke of "the Arabs of

[2] Numerals appearing in this manner refer to chapter and verse of the Koran.
[3] But cf. 9:31, 34; 5:85.

the desert'' (9: 98-102) as stout in dissimulation and hypocrisy, and yet we may assume that the desert Arabs of
his day were not unlike those of our day, with a comparatively high customary morality. The fourteenth-century
historian Ibn Khaldun claimed for the nomads moral
superiority over the dwellers in cities. Mohammed really
condemned the Bedouin for their resistance to *Islam!* The
Arab of the inner desert has ever been a hardy man, an
incorrigible individualist, a confirmed democrat, and sus-
picious of overtures from the city and the outside world.
He has loved the desert and its hardness, and has seldom
been willing to exchange permanently his desert home for
a city dwelling and its softer living. We may be sure that
it was not the attraction of a sensual Paradise alone
which induced him to move with his tribe upon ''the path
of Allah.'' War has been a common occupation, and violence and death familiar sights to him, but his individualism has not made him raise his hand against every man.
Equality, fraternity, and cheerful hospitality have been
the finest traditions of true Bedouin. Courage has been an
indispensable virtue and the desert has been no place for
weaklings. The women themselves were brave and were
wont to deny their love to the base and cowardly. The
very hardness of desert life determined to a large extent
the morals of both men and women. Laxity in the relations of the sexes was curbed if not prevented by rigid
custom and lack of opportunity for promiscuity.[4] It may
be, as Wellhausen says, that in pre-Islamic days ''the
fear of God had no thoroughgoing, practical influence,''
and yet religion played its part in the current morality,
for the desert dweller had a sense of God as an encompass-
ing, overruling, and inexorable power which made him
find his life in obedience to his environment. His thought
may not have rested much upon the next life, but he

[4] *Cf.* also Lady Anne Blunt, *Bedouin Tribes,* II, 226.

vaguely felt that life to be something better than this. We
may question whether the morality of the Arabian desert
today is at base any more Islamic than original pagan.

The morality of Mohammed's immediate pagan background, on the other hand, was thoroughly hedonistic. De
Percival says, "the Arabs were much addicted to wine,
and . . . took pride in both gaming and drink." Wellhausen quotes them as saying, "We journey hence to an
uncertain destiny, from which we turn our thoughts by
eating and drinking." There was extreme laxity in the
relations of the sexes. Other qualities will be cited (see
below) in connection with Mohammed's reform. We are
attempting no full description of the pure desert Arab,
the nomad on the desert's edge, or the city Arab, but only
to show some reason for distinguishing between Mohammed's immediate environment and the more remote. This
will throw into clearer perspective the work which Mohammed accomplished.

As the sense of mission developed in Mohammed he became aware of a serious conflict of standards of conduct.
In his conversion from paganism ethical considerations
were coincident with theological. He was at last stirred
by conditions about him, the poor were oppressed (89:18-
21; 107:2), the rich displayed anxiety for wealth (100:8;
104:2), dishonesty in trade (101:6; 83:1-3) and inhumanity toward both man and beast were manifest; and, in
the words of Goldziher, men showed "insolent unconcern
for the higher interests of life." Goldziher says that Mohammed was "impelled by a resistless impulse to become
the teacher of morals to his people." We may say in a
general way that Mohammed introduced personal morality in the place of tribal, save that in Medina there was
a community with the tradition of orderly government
and a semblance of community morality; and he provided
materials out of which Islamic morality, both national

and imperial, was to grow, indicating to some extent the form which it should assume.

At the beginning of this chapter we observed that the true Moslem enjoys a measure of freedom of will and action. Do the consciousness and teachings of Mohammed support this observation? During his mission he was, of course, burdened with the desire to convert all men to Islam (68:52; 21:107). He at least judged them to be free to accept his teachings, and held those who refused to be responsible for their disobedience (6:110; 7:177). He certainly felt that his "warnings" were "worth while" (87:9; 80:4; 51:55). But aside from that aspect of the case, he does indeed seem to have had for himself a sense of freedom, and to have taught that man is not merely a non-resistant, inactive creature in the hands of a distant, all-powerful God. In spite of the Prophet's extraordinary God-consciousness and sense of the divine control of the affairs of men (21:23; 47:18; 17:14; 87:2, 3), he declared that men "follow their own inclinations" (47:18), that "each man acts according to his own way" (17:86), and that God allows men to wander in their own disobedience (6:110; 7:177; 17:99). Labīd, a poet contemporary with Mohammed, must have caught the Prophet's idea when he wrote, "Whom God guides in paths of right is well-guided and happy-hearted; whom he wishes he allows to stray." It seems fair, then, to assume that Mohammed considered himself to be truly a moral reformer, and to be imposing upon men a moral responsibility for their welfare as servants of Allah.

There is no moral code in the Koran, but the nearest approach to one might be paraphrased as follows:

Set not up another god with Allah. Thy Lord hath ordained that ye worship none but him, that ye be kind to your parents as long as you live, speaking to them respectfully, and deferring to them humbly. Give all relatives their due, and turn not away from the poor and the wayfarer. Be not extravagant in thy gifts, nor yet niggardly; give according to the need and thy substance. Let not poverty cause you to kill your children. Have naught to do with adultery. Put no man to death without just cause, and beware of private vengeance. Let the guardian treat his ward with justice. Be honest in trade. Walk not proudly on the earth. Give glory to God. (17 : 23-39, 45.)

And this covers by no means the whole of Mohammed's moral teachings. Among the evils against which he gave explicit legislation were—in addition to those cited above —suicide, robbery, inhumanity, usury, gambling, slander, perjury, the sale and consumption of intoxicating drink, and plurality of wives beyond four at one time. Among the good acts—in addition to several named above—which he enjoined as a rule upon all Moslems were humanity to slaves, justice to the orphan, marriage, and propagation of the faith.

It is not easy to distinguish the essential from the circumstantial, yet with a view to finding the essential in the moral teachings of Mohammed, let us look more closely at three elements which received at his hands unique treatment. Take first the case of woman and marriage. In pagan Arabia both polygamy and polyandry were practiced, and both were unlimited by social custom. Both were to the Arabs as truly forms of marriage as is monogamy to the American. Mohammed did not recognize polyandry at all. He recognized polygamy, but restricted it (4 : 3). There can be no doubt that his limitation of polygamy tended to correct a lower practice, and was therefore a step in advance. Where, however, Islam has introduced polygamy amidst monogamous surroundings it has wrought harm. Mohammed changed the standards of marriage in the interest of morals, in the interest of modesty and respectability.[5] Certain it is that he wrought

5 Houdas et Marçais, *El-Bokhari*, 67-2-0.

improvement in sex relations in Mecca and Medina. Yet his system of marriage was at bottom practically the old pagan marriage of purchase and dominion, with less freedom to the woman than she had enjoyed in pagan days and less protection to her person than the tribal system had afforded, for marriage under the old order in no way severed the prior ties of kinship, nor took the woman beyond the practical watch care of her own brothers. Furthermore, he recognized the institution of divorce and allowed to men especially great freedom therein (4:24; 2:229; 65:1, 4), although he hedged it about with minute restrictions (2:228-242; 4:1-39; 65:1-7). And he placed no limit upon the number of concubines which a man might legally have in his family. This must have been due in part at least to the circumstance of war, which affected also to some extent the questions of marriage and divorce. On the whole, Mohammed looked at things from the point of view of the free male Arab, but that he consigned woman to a permanent place of inferiority would be too difficult to prove. It is possible for Islam to introduce monogamy and to prohibit polygamy in obedience to the mind of the Prophet himself, for he said, "If you fear that you will not act equitably [toward several wives], then [marry] only one" (4:3).

Another institution which has been characteristic of Islam is slavery. Mohammed accepted it from his times. There was then no voice raised against it, nor did he raise his except to reform the practice in the interest of humanity. In fact he saw certain values in it, for it helped to solve a condition brought on by war and want. It related the captive and the pauper to Mohammedan families and tended to better their lot. In incorporating slavery into Islam he unquestionably raised it to a higher moral level. There is reason to think that had the real wishes of Mohammed been always observed by his followers slavery in Islam would never have been a legal abuse and so great a reproach, but that the slave's condition might always have been tolerable and often happy, for Mohammed thought of slaves as "poor brothers" and "God's wards." Slavery is not so ineradicably embedded in Islam that it may not be abolished. The task of abolition would seem to be no harder in theory than that which Christians faced not long ago. And sanction from the Prophet might be found in his exhortations to his followers to free their slaves as an act of merit,[6] a means of atonement for sins (5:91), and as an act that God most likes.[7] Islam might agree to abolish slavery in the interest of humanity and find itself quite in harmony with a principle and a practice of Mohammed.

Mohammed's greatest moral achievement was the establishment of the Islamic brotherhood, in spite of his toleration within the order of what Tylor calls "the greatest of all divisions," that between master and slave. All Moslems were not freemen, but in a very real sense all Moslems were brothers. Slaves might be freed—the male by manumission, the female by bearing her master a son—and then equality within the House of Islam became complete. In view of the Koranic records we may take as authentic the Tradition which says that "Moslems are brothers in religion." The institution arose not merely from theory but also out of a concrete situation. When Mohammed and his "Companions" had been "driven from their homes and their substance" (59:8; cf. 8:72) and had taken refuge with the "Helpers," their brethren in the faith in Medina, there was created by Mohammed between the fugitives and their hosts a temporary relationship by which the latter shared their houses, their goods, and—according to a possible Tradi-

[6] *Mishcat ul Masabih*, II, 147; cf. 53:4, 5.
[7] *Ibid.*, II, 120.

tion—their wives. The Helpers accepted their guests as relatives. This arrangement was abrogated within a couple of years, but it had furnished a concrete example in the building of a larger, permanent institution. In establishing the Islamic brotherhood Mohammed cut effectively athwart the old pagan order and broke down the tribal system of kinship (*cf.* 8:72). After a time of testing, in the battle of Badr, for instance, when Meccan pagans hesitated to strike their blood relations in the ranks of the Medinese Moslems (*cf.* 8:2 f.), the order became fixed in the consciousness and life of the new religious community. The old order passed away, and justice, kinship, and equality were reinterpreted in terms of the new brotherhood, the most revolutionary of all Mohammed's moral reforms.

Now back of all his moral reforms stood a great fact,—the fact of God. It was God in his own experience which inspired Mohammed's program of reformation. We detect this in one of the earliest *suras* of the Koran,

Did he (God) not find thee an orphan and take thee in as his guest, . . . erring, and give thee guidance, . . . poor, and give thee wealth? (93:6-8.)

As Mohammed conceived of the creation of the world something of moral purpose underlay it (45:21), and he thought of the end of all things as conditioned by the same quality that shared in their origin (45:31). To God who created, who preserves, and to whom all return, Mohammed directed men's thoughts as reason and incentive for righteous living (17:19-22; 18:110). God is righteous, or good (3:104), and a pattern for men (3:100, 106, 110). As God is forgiving, so men should forgive (42:41; 33:35). He requires repentance of men (25:71; 4:20; 24:32), and scrupulously rewards those who do well (4:123). He is not mere numerical unity, but moral, and therefore capable of inspiring men to desire and practice good conduct. It is clear that although as an Arab and a Moslem Mohammed's mind was disposed to accept arbitrary divine decrees, he often acted and spoke as if man's destiny were alterable and much in his own hands. By nature men possess both good and evil qualities, so the Prophet thought (91: 7-9; 16: 95; 7: 177; 13: 33). He was no moral pessimist, thinking of man as born in sin and into a world that is altogether evil. He speaks of disease that is in men's hearts (33: 32; 47: 22), of impatience (70: 20), insolence (96: 6), and pride (16: 25), but in Mohammed's mind sin is more an attitude than it is a disposition which came to all men, for example, through Adam. It is man's duty to overcome his natural faults (*cf.* 70: 19), and to develop his heritage of good (91: 9).

Before we leave this part of our theme, we may ask, What of Mohammed himself as a moral factor in the life of Islam? Ibn Ishāk, early biographer of Mohammed, records that Khadija, the first and for a long time the only wife of the Prophet, loved her husband for the beauty of his character, his honesty, and his truthfulness of speech. She became his first convert and supporter, testifying thus to her estimate of his sincerity. His fellow townsmen, before the time of his mission, frequently applied to him the appellation of "the trusty." And later in the heat of jealousy and strife the charges against his personal character are few and unconvincing. Even among his own followers there was never any long-sustained criticism of his conduct (*cf.* 23: 26, 37; 2: 214). He himself never laid claim to moral perfectness. He considered himself a warner and a herald (74: 2; 35: 22), without any sophisticated notion, however, that the ordained priest when he speaks for the church is to be heard regardless of the speaker's own moral qualities. Mohammed mentions in one place his "earlier and later

faults'' (48:2). He was ''only a man,'' albeit the agent
of revelation (18:110). While he himself overstepped
the bounds of his own limitation of polygamy—on political and economic grounds, it may be—he seems to have
regretted it (33:52), in spite of Allah's word that ''no
blame attaches to the prophet where God has given him
a permission'' (33:38). Clearly Mohammed left it possible for Islam to develop independent of himself as a man,
although utterly dependent upon the essential message
which he proclaimed.

We turn now to the larger, or imperial, field of Moslem
ethics, and select at first a period of five hundred years
to survey. We shall indicate the most significant develop-
ments and variations in this period which extends roughly
from the time of Mohammed to that of al-Ghazāli (d. 1111
A.D.), the greatest of Moslem ethicists, and from Spain on
the west through a wide belt to the borders of India and
China on the east. During this period and throughout this
area there is evidence of a constant struggle between
moral strictness and moral laxity, between the moral
teaching of Mohammed and the insufficiently developed
moral consciousness of Islam in reaction on the one hand
toward pagan standards, and development, on the other
hand, under the influence of new culture contacts.

Imbued with religious enthusiasm by their Prophet, the
Arabs were soon upon the road to vast empire. This
brought them into contact with peoples over whom the
Byzantine and the Persian Empires had held sway, who
were possessed of ideas and traditions which soon bore
much weight in Moslem circles, who by their very presence, whether as conquered or as converted, exerted a
profound influence upon Islam and by their capacity rose
to places of leadership in the development of Islamic institutions. It was inevitable that in the days of expansion
and empire the moral complexion of Islam should un-

dergo modification, even though, in the figure of Yazīd, it were but the water taking on the color of the receptacle in which it is.

It was a time of war. In the early days, especially, the Arabs fought fiercely, far from home and family, and often against great odds. Throughout the half-millennium, warfare, whether that of the foreign campaign or of internal strife, was common. We, with our recent experience of war, need not dwell upon the general evil or the general good which war produces. On the whole, the conduct of the Arabs "upon the path of Allah" compared quite favorably with that of their opponents. The Arabs did not use poisoned arrows nor did they pillage and burn enemy villages indiscriminately, as the Byzantines did.[8] Theoretically, surprise attacks were not allowed against those who had not first received a call to accept Islam, nor was it ever allowed to kill hostages. Their armies were composed of volunteers rather than conscripts. Conquest brought spoils into the coffers of the Moslem state and into the hands of the common soldier, and the effeminacy which Omar had foreseen began to creep upon the Moslem victors. Wealth flowed into Medina, Mecca, Damascus, and Baghdad, and with luxury came dissolute living. With war and conquest and foreign settlement came slavery and intermarriage and a consequent lowering of the moral level below that which Mohammed had set. Al-Mughira, governor of Basrah in 638 A.D., was guilty of most flagrant breach of the limitation upon polygamy, although a flaw in the evidence when he was tried allowed him to escape stoning to death for adultery. The poet Omar ibn Abi Rabia, a convert to Islam and governor of Junad in Yemen, openly preached and practiced the gospel of love and the worship of female beauty. In Mecca,

---

[8] Nor did the Turkish armies in the East during the Great War use poison gas.

Damascus, and Baghdad a veritable cult of woman sprang up, to such extremes did misconceived gallantry run. The ideal female was not the chaste Umayma, but any adventurous, ill-guarded Layla, ever ready to "pass merrily from eve to dawn" in the embraces of her secret lover, unrestrained by the "Watcher who keepeth ward over our souls." In his notes on *The Arabian Nights* Lane mentions "an Arabic work of some celebrity," written by a judge, a guardian of religion and morality, which, he says, is "characterized by wit and humor plentifully interlarded with the grossest and most revolting obscenity." He further asserts that it may be taken as an index of the state of morals of the time. The Abbasid prime minister Yahya could write to his son Fadl,

> Many there be, esteemed of life austere,
> Who nightly enter on a strange career,

and could commend to him the policy of keeping his pleasures veiled by the sable curtain of night against the eyes of "spying rivals and censorious foes." Abu Nuwas, author of *The Arabian Nights* and a poet of extraordinary genius, who drank and jested with the Caliph Harun al-Rashid, could write

> Curst and poor is every hour that sober I must go,
> But rich am I when e'er well drunk I stagger to and fro.

Lane says that the frequent stories in *The Arabian Nights,* "describing parties of Muslims as habitually indulging in the use of forbidden beverages" and "similar anecdotes interspersed in the works of Arab historians . . . could not have been offered to the public by such writers if they were not of a nature consistent with the customs of a considerable class of the Arab nation." We may take the piety of the Omayyad Omar II of Damascus and that of the Abbasid Muhtadi of Baghdad as protests against a very general condition of moral laxity in their dominions. For the most part both dynasties were worldly, as dynasties usually have been. Omayyad ethics were far less Islamic than those of Medina and of Mohammed. The Omayyads were Arabs first and Moslems afterward, and during their century of rule (661-750 A.D.) there was, for good as well as for ill, something of a resurgence of Arab ideals. The Abbasids were no less Arab in race when they set up their capital in Baghdad, but within a few generations the Arab element lost its predominance and Persian influence took control. And the Persian moral sense was weak. It was upon a wave of Persian treachery that the house of Abbas was borne to the throne. In Abbasid days (750-1258 A.D.) the doctrine of *taqiya* gained sway (*cf.* 16:108), by which the means is justified by the end, and *mut'a* or temporary marriage became legitimate and orthodox. In Persia the doctrine of the Hidden Imam ("leader") grew strong, and opened the door not only to vagaries of religion but laxity in morals and treason against the state.

What then prevented the unhesitating moral decay of the Islamic order? Mohammed was ever the great name, and at least a nominal allegiance to the Faith was always maintained. Mosque services were not dispensed with even when caliphs themselves were absent from the daily prayers. Among the masses everywhere was unquestioning devotion to Allah, Mohammed, and the rites of the Faith. The Koran was taught and discussed in the mosque schools and something of moral leaven was thus disseminated among the populace. But in addition several great and significant movements were under way, looking toward the correction of prevalent evils, the renovation of moral doctrine, and the unification of the moral consciousness in behalf of progress. We pass to a consideration of these movements, the legal, the philosophical, and the mystical, although we attempt no detailed precision with respect to their chronological relationships.

During the first century of Abbasid supremacy (750-850 A.D.) legalistic ethics developed in the form known as Canon Law. Or, rather, Canon Law developed and included within itself the field of ethics. *Fiqh,* the "knowledge" or "science" of law, included religious, ceremonial, civil, and moral laws. This development of law came to hallow some things and to prohibit others, and in both aspects did not hesitate to set itself at times against Koranic and Traditional ethics. In reality, the field of ethics was narrowed and minutely divided. Courts were established and judges installed and a system of earthly punishments instituted. Regulations were made with regard to local and temporary interests. Altogether there developed amidst the Moslem people an elaborate system of moral oversight. In fact, in Baghdad and elsewhere a special officer was provided as overseer of public morals, along with other duties. He was charged with the maintenance of good morals, the prevention of acts which the law forbade, and the arrest of all offenders against the law. Among other duties he was commissioned to find husbands for widows, to protect slaves from the cruelty of their masters, to prevent the public sale of intoxicants and dishonesty in trade.

It will be remembered that the Moslem had at first for his guidance in matters of morality, the words of Allah and the example of Allah's prophet, that is, the Koran, which was codified soon after Mohammed's death, and the Traditions which were linked back to Mohammed. However, with the growth of new conditions and the rise of new occasions, opportunity and necessity were offered the jurists for the exercise of new factors in the regulation of conduct, and certain new principles came into play by way of the extension and modification of the original materials. At times judgment was based partly upon legal opinion (*ra'y*),[9] or rendered from analogy (*qiyas*), or determined by the agreement (*ijma'*) of the Moslem community, and all because cases arose which were not covered by the Koran and by Tradition. Naturally some confusion crept into the situation, and the need of a legal canon became increasingly apparent. Indeed, four orthodox ''schools'' of canon law arose, all accepting both Koran and Tradition, but differing with respect to the value placed upon the newer principles of moral theory and practice, and varying from the extremely conservative and reactionary Hanbalite code to the comparatively liberal code of Abu Hanifa. The orthodox Moslem, *i.e.*, the Sunni, could have—as he may still have—his choice, therefore, of tradition, liberal tradition, practical liberalism, and a more or less theoretical liberalism. In theory, at least, all four schools agreed in their division of moral acts into the following five categories: (1) acts forbidden and unconditionally punishable, (2) acts disapproved but not punishable, (3) acts which are permitted, (4) acts which are recommended, which are rewarded if done, but not punishable if omitted, and (5) duties whose performance is rewarded and whose omission is punishable. But specific acts are variously classified and the rewards and punishments vary, according to the school. For example, the Hanbalite would kill a man for not saying his prayers, counting the omission equivalent to apostasy; the Hanifite would only chastise him. The Hanifites say that the command, ''When you encounter the unbelievers, strike off their heads'' (47:4) refers only to the battle of Badr which Mohammed fought against the Meccans; others think the command a universal obligation. Ibn Hanbal was for enforcing the severest Koranic penalties

---

[9] *I.e.*, what a judge might think best, or deem for the good of the community.

(*cf.* 5 : 42), but Abu Hanifa would mitigate their severity as far as possible. The Shafiites and Malikites likewise had their own peculiar views.

These schools of law grew secretly under the hands of the pious during the reign of the Omayyads. During the Abbasid days they became firmly established, although their geographical distribution was not then determined. Each sought to correct the evils of the time, and to renovate and unify the popular moral consciousness. Each truly made its contribution, and that each was deemed an orthodox school is evidence of the fact that it answered the needs of a considerable body of the Moslem population. But they all confused the ceremonial and the moral, and reduced and confined ethics to a mere legal code.

There were other influences and tendencies at work in the interest of public morals, one of which we may call rationalism. Many felt and taught that morality was grounded in reason. They would distinguish between ceremonies and morals. They would impose upon man as a free agent the responsibility for his own conduct. God, they said, had given men power over their actions, or ability to produce actions, and men were, therefore, morally responsible. Men, they said, had reason as the means to the knowledge of the moral nature of things. This current of rationalism began early and has continued down to the present day, but it never attained great volume. It was not confined to any particular party, but appeared alike in the ranks of the main body of Islam, the Sunnis, and among the members of the great sect, the Shi'as. Its contribution to the development of Islamic morality was slight and secondary, for whatever name it bore, whether Qadarite, Mu'tazilite,[10] or other, it was looked upon by the great mass of Moslems as impious and a flouting of God and all things sacred. Its greatest influence was as a

[10] According to these, God was not the author of evil.

foil for the development of Islamic scholasticism. It
forced to the front issues which Islam could not ignore. The Mu'tazilas especially "leavened Muhammadan
thought to a considerable extent,"[11] for they did not reject Islam and acknowledge only the moral law. As a
party they had their day[12] and ceased to be, but long
afterward leaders of thought, like Ma'arri (d. 1057 A.D.),
could safely urge men to "think about things," could
teach them that "there's no Imam but Reason," and that
virtue consists not in fasting and prayer, but in casting
all evil away and sweeping the breast "clear and clean
of malice, envy, and spite."

Next to law, however, the most potent factor in the development of Moslem ethics was mysticism. As was true
of the rational element so also the mystical was inherent
in the original Islamic heritage. That there were mystical
elements in Mohammed is beyond question.[13] During the
centuries under review these elements were seized upon
by Moslems who had come under certain foreign influences which may have suggested their use, and utilized
as means toward the full realization of Islam.

There were soon all types of mystics, from the conservative ascetic to the free-thinking liberal and the antinomian who in being "without law" was virtually outside
the "House of Islam." Many of the ascetics—and asceticism was confined to no one party or sect—felt themselves
to be most truly Moslem in their renunciation of the
world, but for the most part they were much in error in
the extremes to which they carried their practices. To
Mohammed the ascetic ideal was valuable, but, on the
other hand, asceticism was not valuable in itself; rather,
it was of value, most of all, for the sake of the mystical,

[11] Nicholson, *Literary History of the Arabs,* p. 370.

[12] Rising to official prominence, even to the dignity of the state faith in
the early ninth century.

[13] See the writer's *Mystical Elements in Mohammed.*

and both the ascetic and the mystical were avenues to higher and more than personal ends. It is not surprising, however, that conditions being as they were hosts of men should seek escape from the ills of the world by the path of renunciation. They were sincere, if mistaken. There was much sincerity also in the more philosophical type of mysticism which sought through speculation, contemplation, and ecstasy to unify life and realize the highest good. All honest mystics sought to triumph over the world about them and to find union with God in one way or another, but during the early centuries Islam was much in danger from them as they carried their various theories into practice. The ascetic was too individualistic. Indeed, all mystics lacked any truly social conception of religion and morals. The Sufis especially—Sufiism was the great ascetico-mystical movement of the times—observed as the main features of their creed "self-abandonment, rigorous self-mortification, fervid piety, and quietism carried to the verge of apathy."[14] On the whole, the way of the mystic was scarcely accepted as altogether orthodox, having within it, as it manifested itself then, features antagonistic to essential Islam. Mysticism, however, was to become orthodox, but its attainment of orthodoxy belongs to the story of al-Ghazāli.

It is not so much what al-Ghazāli accomplished in his day—he was considered a heretic then[15]—but the place his teaching acquired subsequently that makes him of great importance in the history of Moslem morals. He was a profound moralist, the greatest of the Islamic few, both on the ground of his own experience and of his interpretation of the essential morality of Islam. He stands about the year 1100 A.D. at the geographic center of Islam and at a most significant point in the history of the Moslem

14 Nicholson, op. cit., 231.
15 His books were burned by the Mohammedan theologians in Spain.

moral ideal. From the latter part of the tenth century
the caliph ruled little more than his own palace in Baghdad. Moslem rivals sat upon the thrones of ten other
dynasties, ruling in Spain, Morocco, Egypt, Arabia,
Persia, and the East. Turks and Mongols had appeared
within the eastern borders. Moral uncertainty matched
the political confusion. The Seljuk Turks were destined
to bring back again some unity of empire, and to the
Persian Ghazāli fell the task of "delivering from error"
both religion and morality, and of welding both theory
and practice into one whole again. Islamic asceticism
had carried Koranic prescription and the example of
Mohammed to grave extremes, developing undue emphasis upon works as the means to the highest life. Ascetics
had everywhere impressed the masses with their saintliness and had acquired such influence that they were
looked upon as the very overseers of morals and proper
examples for all the people. The whole Sufi movement,
whether it expressed itself in asceticism, pantheism, or
eroticism, had become a moral menace to Islam. Ghazāli
himself was a mystic, but a moral mystic seeking to correct extreme self-abandonment, to restrain pantheism, and
to curb the sensual. The doctrine of the "inner witness"
had led many into gross error, making man's will a law
unto itself, since by his will had the man come to know
his Lord. Ghazāli, who had himself come into a safe and
full experience of God's inner witness to man's soul, declared unto men a way in which both religious and moral
practices were necessary to save them (*cf. sura* 107).
Philosophers had taken science as their guide and felt
themselves released from submission to a religion of authority. They declared religion to be intended as a restraint upon the passions of the vulgar and not for themselves. Ghazāli properly attacked them both on religious
and moral grounds, for their example had led many to

practice religion merely as a "useful exercise" and a "safeguard," and to private indulgence in wine and the commission of "other shameful actions." Some religious sects, especially the Ismailians, gave currency to the notion that God is entirely without attributes and cannot be known and that men have in an Imam[16] the infallible judge and guide. Ghazāli said that God could be known, that this world, the world of the senses, exists by his power (*qudra*) and not by divine Reason, that God had revealed himself and his qualities in a way to all people, and that he had revealed through Mohammed and the saints all necessary ethical laws and theories (*cf.* 9:98). Ghazāli set himself also against the scholastic theologians who contended for authority, who knew no such thing as order in nature, or regular development in the life of man, —it was all a matter of miracle, in fact,—and advanced the position that the world, including man's life,[17] is in constant orderly change, and that acceptance on authority is modified by immediate experience of God, for, as Professor Macdonald observes of Ghazāli, "there is a likeness between the spirit of man and God in essence, quality and actions."

The ethical element bulks very large in Ghazāli. He was a preacher of righteousness after the manner of the Prophet himself, a warner also against anger, envy, and fleshly lust, against covetousness and desire of the world, a herald of the wrath of God, and an expounder as well of God's love. He calls men to fight for character by spiritual warfare against passion and pride. In his moral teaching he reintroduced the element of fear, not "shallow fear," he said, but "fear that forbids sinning against

16 "Leader," among Ismailians an incarnation after Ali of the divine Reason, through whom alone truth may be arrived at.

17 The soul of man, however, according to Ghazāli, "belongs to the spiritual world and not to this world of sensible things." Macdonald, *Development,* p. 231.

God and instills obedience to Him.'' It was in part the
fear of hell fire (*cf*. 74:55) which Ghazāli stressed. He
said a man would be led into it by the devil in him unless
he overcame the temptations of the devil by the thought
of God (58:20).

Ghazāli was subject, of course, to many of the moral
limitations of his day. For example, he views marriage as
a proper subjection of the woman to her husband,[18] although he recognizes the institution as of fundamental
importance in Islam, a means of health to the soul and an
abomination to the devil.[19] Nevertheless he saw that a
man's life must be a continual moral struggle and that the
believer's happiness here and hereafter depends not so
much on what he believed or on what religious duties he
strictly performed, as on what he had been in himself, on
the purity of his life and his realization of spiritual truth.
It is this teacher whom the Moslem world finally pronounced orthodox, putting its seal of approval upon his
interpretation of Islam, and, incidentally, by its acceptance of him and his teaching, offering strong proof of a
certain inherent plasticity in Islamic life and institutions,
and of a power of moral adaptation in the midst of changing conditions.

With most of our survey now behind us we may conveniently and with better understanding turn to a division of our theme which we appeared to discard at the
outset, namely, the field of international ethics as distinct
from imperial. Even before the fall of the great Moslem
capital, Baghdad, in 1258 A.D., great changes were under
way throughout the Moslem world. The line of Arabic—
or, as we of the West say, Saracenic—succession was
breaking, and converts to Islam from beyond the edge of

[18] Hans Bauer, *Von der Ehe*, 111. By his likening a wife to a slave Ghazāli
means that she is a person and not a chattel.
[19] *Ibid.*, p. 2.

the Moslem world were on their way to supremacy at the center of the political stage—first, the Seljuk and then the Osmanli Turks, not to mention the Moghals of India. During the centuries since the time of Ghazāli the Islamic world has grown extremely complex and Islamic morals in practice become difficult indeed to evaluate. It becomes less easy than ever to discriminate between conduct and character that are determined by race and culture and what is appropriately connected with the Islamic faith. Islam spread into India in part by invasion and settlement, but the vast majority of Indian Moslems are indigenous. During five hundred years Islam acquired and maintained political suzerainty, but this does not altogether explain the conversion of Indians to the foreign faith. Apart from the throne a popular movement began in which Islam both gave and took somewhat after the policy which Babur, the Moghal, commended in Persian verse to his son Humayun,

If you are fettered by your situation, submit to circumstances,
If you are independent, follow your own fancy.

Moslems in South India propitiate local Dravidian deities. Moslem convert women of all classes in India go unveiled. Polygamy is rare, and widows view remarriage as an outrage of the memory of the former husband. In Bengal especially Islam has been influenced greatly by caste. On the other hand, Islam has stood against caste but has benefited from this peculiar Hindu social organization to the extent of forming a new caste, admission to which gave all converts a real equality. Indian Moslems as a rule have objected to infant marriage. But on the whole Indian Moslem morality has been of lower grade than that of Hindus.

To return to the traditional center of Islam, we may refer to Turkish morality. In popular Western thought the term "Turk" is one of ill repute, and that on moral grounds. And the Turk is taken as the typical Moslem, in spite of the fact that he is the least Islamized of all Moslems and least willing to make his final appeal to Mohammed. With special reference to race relations he is depicted in words far from flattering, "with no charge for the colouring." We must discriminate, however, between the characteristic morality of the real Turk and the impression made through prejudice and propaganda since the very days of the Crusades and extending through the period of European meddling with the Near Eastern Question.

Alexander Ross,[20] who called the Koran "a hodg podge of Contradictions, Blasphemy, Fables, and Lyes," attests the zeal of the Turks in piety and charity, their love to each other, their care of strangers, their exercise of "Justice, Temperance, and other moral Vertues." He may have been prejudiced in favor of the Turks as he was against the Koran, although he knew the former better than the latter. Finlay's assertion,[21] however, of the "moral superiority of Othoman society" is sound. In comparison with other peoples of the Near East both the Arab and the Turk would seem to have a better record of honesty and trustworthiness. It is difficult, however, to make a just appraisal on the administrative side when one considers the fact that the blood of Greek, Slav, Italian, and Russian has flowed in the veins of "Turkish" rulers. But we may note without hesitation a remarkable display of toleration. Qualitatively the Turk has treated all non-Turks alike, whether for good or for ill. On the other hand, his theory of state has excluded the possibility that adherents of other faiths could enjoy equal rights with Turks in the Turkish dominion. This political

[20] Quoted by Arnold, *The Preaching of Islam*, p. 170.
[21] *Ibid.*, p. 171.

theory more than any other cause has lain behind the inhumanity of Turkey in dealing with non-Moslems over whom she had the power. A confusing identity of religion and patriotism has prevailed in the Near East.

The Turk as a Moslem is a Hanifite. This means, as we have seen above, that in religion and morals he is a liberal. He has given his support to the enforcement of prohibition. He has drawn no color line. He has consented to and encouraged the tendency to eliminate polygamy and slavery, and to curb the social evil. But the Turkish administrator has permitted corruption through a false distinction between presents and bribes. This has affected judges and courts and worked hardship for the common people. It has encouraged crime. The Turkish peasant has been patient and frank, and, if undisturbed, kindly. He has lacked educational facilities save those provided by mosque discussions of the rudiments of Islam. His morals have been no better and no worse than the mass morals of all Mohammedan peoples. To say that the Moslem masses everywhere stand in need of moral development is not to state a unique case. It is more important to ask what the essential morality of Islam is which they may advance toward, granted they remain Moslem. We have already attempted to answer this question, but must stretch our space for the sake of a few words more in conclusion.

We mentioned above the great trinity of Moslem morality, Mohammed, al-Ghazāli, and the principle of *Ijma'* or Agreement. By them Islam has lived and will continue. Mohammed may be idealized, Ghazāli the ''Revivifier'' is orthodox, and *Ijma'* has remained strong in spite of Canon Law and notwithstanding a Sunni theory that *Ijma'* has not been possible since the days of the four great doctors. The Shia's believe they still have *mujtahids* capable of interpreting the Law. All Moslems may appeal to a Tradition ascribed to Mohammed which says, "My people will never agree upon an error." Necessity, practice, and the Prophet's warrant all seem, therefore, to combine to make *Ijma'* a potent factor in Islam. Indeed, it is not inconceivable that Islam may go even beyond *Ijma'* as a technical legal principle, for there is evidence of a popular Islamic moral consciousness. As Ghazāli deposed the "science of law" from the place it had usurped, so public opinion may transcend and transform the legal as a factor in moral development. There is a Moslem state of mind and a sense of historical continuity. The name itself of Mohammed is potent throughout the Moslem world. Mecca is the Islamic capital and center of pilgrimage. In the absence of national boundaries Islam is the Moslem's native land. The Moslem has and exercises full pride of race and religion, for he has learned from his Prophet that there is only one "true faith," and from the doctors of the law that Moslems are fundamentally superior to all other men. And there is no little indication of a common mind in the general opposition to strong drink—Islam is the world's greatest prohibition society—and in that regard for life, or dependence upon destiny which has made the suicide conspicuously absent. Even where religious lines divide, as between Sunni and Shia', for example, there may still be found something of a common basis of theory and practice.

The differences, however, are very great, and the inertia of the common consciousness very profound. Islam is complex, not uniform. It is not the faith and code of one people, land, or time. Agreement in the interest of moral advance can never operate by a sudden, widespread and complete unanimity. A universal result can be obtained only through the leavening influence of concensus (*Ijma'*) gradually formed in progressive communities. Then the legal sanction gained for reform will represent

in reality an achievement of the popular moral consciousness, touched from within and from without by the spirit
of enlightenment. Among the reforms which Islam stands
greatly in need of making are the abolition of slavery in
every form and of polygamy,—Albanian and Turkish
Moslems have already abolished polygamy, and monogamy has been the rule for generations among the
Berbers,—the exaltation of womanhood to an equality
with man in law, education, and social esteem, the breaking down of the double standard of morality implicit—
and most explicit in time of Holy War—in the distinction
between "The House of Islam" and "The House of
War," and the organization of an effective program of
moral education for the young to supplant mere Koranic
instruction and to counteract the harmful influences of
harem and street conversation. Happily, Islam is in possession of inherent life and vital principles which allow
her, if she will, to address herself to these problems with
the hope of success. Historically the Institution has over-
shadowed the Individual, but we feel sure that there is
within Islam an opportunity for that development of the
Moslem which will not destroy whatever of permanent
value the Institution represents. Moral progress is possible and may be achieved with benefit to the Faith.

THE MORAL VALUES OF RELIGION

E. HERSHEY SNEATH

XII.

ONE cannot study the history and psychology of religion without being impressed by the fact that it is an exceedingly complex phenomenon. In it nearly all of the primary modes of human functioning are manifest. This is especially true with respect to the intellectual, social, æsthetic, and moral forms of behavior. This gives rise to different conceptions of values within this sacred sphere. There is a tendency on the part of some to exalt the intellectual values in the form of dogma and creed. Others emphasize the social values. Indeed, there is a decided opinion among certain students of the phenomena of the religious consciousness that religion in its very essence is the functioning of the social nature. Others tend to make the æsthetic values paramount, as is manifest in the significance attached to rite and ceremony. Still others attribute sovereignty to the moral values. With them religion in its ultimate nature is righteousness. It is highly important both in our theory and practice of religion that we develop a true sense of values. Those who have read the preceding studies in the ethics of the great religions cannot fail to recognize what a tremendous emphasis the moral values receive in the sphere of religion. This is especially true of the Hebrew and Christian religions. In them, particularly in the latter, it is not dogmatic to say that the moral values are supreme. And they are thus recognized to be supreme because, as a matter of fact, they are so. We ultimately subject all other imperatives—the bodily, intellectual, social, economic, political, and æsthetic—to the moral. Even religion itself is subject to the moral standard. If a religion demanded immorality of us, even though it claimed to be the word of God, we would reject it as unworthy. The highest values of true religion are ethical, and all other forms of the religious life have value only as they contribute to the realization of the real objective of religion, which is righteousness. As the late Professor Bowne said: "Whatever our theological faith, whatever our religious practices, and whatever our religious pedagogics, their sole use and value consist in helping us to live lives of love and righteousness before God and man."[1]

The temptation to a wrong evaluation in religion is at least threefold: First, to emphasize the intellectual at the expense of the moral; secondly, to emphasize the emotional at the expense of the moral; and thirdly, to emphasize the emotional and volitional in the form of rite and ceremony at the expense of the moral.

The presence of the intellectual factor in religion gives rise to attempts at a rational interpretation or construction of religious experience,—to a philosophy of religion, a theology and creed. Those who have carefully reflected on the matter will hardly be disposed to find fault with this. Criticism becomes justifiable, however, when we improperly judge the value of doctrine and creed in its relation to the religious life,—when men exalt it at the expense of the moral values of religion. For such men, as Professor Stratton says, "The essence of religion is to have right conceptions and beliefs; and they often picture to themselves the Divinity as far more anxious about men's thoughts than about their feelings and intents. The Scotch, from whom so many disputants have sprung, have always been religious in an intellectual way. Their old-time Sabbaths, with an unbroken line of argumentative sermons, clearly show this element in their devotion. America, which Scotland and its ways of thought have greatly influenced, reveals the type less clearly; for the moving of home, with all its cares, has encouraged activity at some drain upon reflection. Yet, among the New

---

[1] Bowne, *The Essence of Religion*, Boston and New York, 1910, pp. 75-76.

England Puritans religion was, in a large measure, unquestionably an intellectual attachment to the Good, it was largely a matter of contemplation, of reasoning, of creed. In the earlier days, too, of Christianity there could be found those for whom religion was largely a way of thinking. The Gnostics were notable among them, with their claim to clearer mental light, and their zeal for attacking in philosophical spirit the doctrinal problems which Christianity had started."[2] In similar vein the late Henry Drummond stated that several decades ago the Scottish clergy of that period had become so possessed of and obsessed with the idea of the Christian life consisting chiefly in a belief in a theological system, that the nature of every minister's sermon from Sunday to Sunday could be anticipated, for their sermons were merely presentations in their order of the doctrines contained in Dr. Charles Hodges' Systematic Theology. That conception of religion which regards it as chiefly "a way of thinking" represents a mistaken sense of values. It exalts intellectual belief at the expense of righteous feeling and will. Character and conduct are subordinated to intellectual conception and belief in things religious.[3]

This subtle temptation to a wrong sense of values manifests itself in another form. Not only intellect, but feeling, functions in religion, and it functions powerfully. It does not require a profound knowledge of either the history or the psychology of religion to recognize this fact. In its higher forms, at least, religion involves love, and in Christianity love is supreme. Now, love seeks communion with its object, and such fellowship is productive of the highest and most exquisite enjoyment of which the human soul is capable. But just because of this, the soul is subject to a most subtle and dangerous temptation in

[2] Stratton, *Psychology of the Religious Life*, London, 1911, pp. 195-196.
[3] *Cf.* Sneath, *Shall We Have a Creed?* New York, 1925.

its estimate of values—a temptation to subjectivism that seriously dulls the moral spirit. Psychologists speak of a mutual opposition between the fundamental powers of the mind. A man of profound thought is often lacking in emotional capacity. On the other hand, a man of profound feeling is often lacking in clearness of thought, which, in turn, causes doubt and doubt inhibits the will. Unfortunately this mutual opposition seriously affects our religious life. Feeling, which is so operative in religion, tends often to deaden volitional effort. It begets a tendency to quietism—to lose ourselves in pious feeling. Feeling rather than doing, then, characterizes our religious life. The dean of one of our leading theological schools once said to the writer that there is a good deal of pietism that is utterly lacking in ethical quality. This is lamentably true. Indeed, it is not only wanting in moral quality, but it is often immoral, because of its self-centered character. It is a kind of refined selfishness, and, as Julius Müller, in his work on the *Doctrine of Sin,* says: "Selfishness is the very root of sin." Such pietism makes for moral atrophy. It is a wrong sense of religious values. It keeps the soul in the closet when it ought to be in the highways. It lingers on the Mount of Transfiguration when it ought to be on the plains below. It steeps itself in unwholesome feeling, courting mystical vision, and suffers paralysis of the moral spirit.

There is undoubtedly a quietistic and mystical element in religion, and it is legitimate and potent, for it brings the soul into close touch with God and with things that are eternal—a quietism and mysticism that refresh the drooping spirit, that yield glorious visions of immortal truth, and that often flood the soul with holy peace and joy. But it is only genuine when it is charged with moral power; when it is shot through with ethical inspiration and purpose. Jesus had it in a marked degree. He was in such close relationship with God through frequent and intimate communion with Him that his will became one with the Father's will. But his mystical union with the Father did not degenerate either into an immoral or unmoral pietism or quietism. His soul was aflame with moral purpose and his meat and drink was to do the divine will. As a result, he went about doing good.

Paul, too, was a mystic, but not of the pietistic type. He knew what it was to be caught up into heaven, but only to gain a more glorified conception of duty upon earth. Love translating itself into service was the fruit of his fellowship with the divine. Yes, there is a powerful emotional element in religion,—a mysticism often with its attendant gleams and intuitions of reality and truth, which are of great value in the religious life. Tennyson gives us a remarkable example of it in the *Idylls of the King,* where the king, unlike many of his knights, has developed a true sense of religious worths. He has no time to pursue the Holy Grail, nor "wandering fires." His is the more real and common task of daily duty. His business is to guard that which he rules. But with the daily task accomplished, then come the supreme moments in the life of the soul, when the king gains a vision of the spiritual and eternal realities:

> In moments when he feels he cannot die,
> And knows himself no vision to himself,
> Nor the high God a vision, nor that One
> Who rose again.

The reality of self, the reality of immortality, the reality of God, and the reality of the living Christ—these are the spiritual intuitions that come to the king in his quiet hour of communion after the duty of the day is done. It is the reward of moral service, and the grip on the eternal realities thus gained leads to renewed and more earnest serv-

ice in redressing human wrong and in establishing righteous relations among men. That is the true quietism and
mysticism in religion. It does not lose itself in pure subjectivism and passivity. It is the reward of duty done,
and it leads to further and larger duty.

A third form of temptation to a wrong sense of values
in things religious is often manifest in religious worship.
It is amazing how much of sacrificial rite and ceremony
is to be found in the great religions. Different motives
lie back of it. So far as the motives are moral they represent chiefly a desire to expiate or atone for sin. Such religions err, not in a failure to recognize the ethical nature
of religion, but in a failure properly to estimate the real
nature of the moral obligations which religion involves
and the means by which these obligations are to be met.
Ritual and ceremony are, also, means of expressing certain religious emotions and attitudes, as awe, reverence,
adoration, and love. As such they have a high value for
the religious life. Whether used as a means of religious
expression, or of inducing true religious feeling, they sub-
serve a useful purpose. True worship brings the soul
nearer to God and fellowship with His Spirit endues it
with moral power.

But, here again, the soul often loses sight of the true
values of religion. Form and ceremony, instead of means,
become ends. Æsthetic values, if we may so characterize
them, are substituted for moral values. Externalism sup-
plants the inner experiences of the heart, which should
seek supreme expression in moral rather than in æsthetic
conduct. The history of religion, and, alas, the history of
the Hebrew and Christian religions, illustrate how powerful is this temptation. The prophets inveighed against
the cruder forms of rite and ceremony in the interest of a
higher ethical interpretation of religious obligation. The
impassioned Isaiah waxes indignant at the wrong sense

of religious values developed by the people. He represents Jehovah as being weary of their sacrificial system and religious observances and as calling them to a recognition of the higher moral worths. Jehovah has had enough of their "burnt-offerings," their "vain oblations," their "incense," their "new moons," and "Sabbaths." Do away with these, and "Wash you, make you clean; put away the evil of your doings from before mine eyes; cease to do evil; learn to do well; seek justice, relieve the oppressed, judge the fatherless, plead for the widow." Hosea calls his people away from unrighteousness and the sacrifices offered to atone for it, and represents God as "desiring goodness and not sacrifice." Micah, also, finds this temptation to a wrong emphasis in the sphere of religious values, and tells the people that God's children are not to come before him with burnt offerings, but with a life of service to man and of humility before God. He emphasizes the supremacy of the moral values of religion in his declaration: "He hath showed thee, O man, what is good; and what doth Jehovah require of thee, but to do justly, and to love kindness, and to walk humbly with thy God?" Even in its more refined aspects, as represented in Pharisaism, Jesus becomes impatient with and rebukes it, in the interests of a service that is more truly moral. Yielding to this temptation to an overvaluation of rite and ceremony has been the bane of the Christian Church also through the ages; and is an evil that we have still to contend with. Professor Rauschenbusch says:

Under the influence of non-Christian customs and conceptions Christianity early developed its own ceremonial system. It is, of course, far more refined. Our places of worship have no stench of blood and entrails; our priests are not expert butchers. But the immense majority of people in Christendom have holy places, where they recite a sacred ritual and go through sacred motions.

They receive holy food and submit to washings that cleanse from sin. They have a priesthood with magic powers which offers a bloodless sacrifice. This Christian ritual grew up, not as the appropriate and æsthetic expression of spiritual emotions, but as the indispensable means of pleasing and appeasing God, and of securing his favors, temporal and eternal, for those who put their heart into these processes. This Christian ceremonial system does not differ essentially from that against which the prophets protested; with a few verbal changes their invectives would still apply. But the point that here concerns us is that a very large part of the fervor of willing devotion which religion always generates in human hearts has spent itself on these religious acts. The force that would have been competent to ''seek justice and relieve the oppressed'' has been consumed in weaving the tinsel fringes for the garment of religion.[4]

It often dampens ethical zeal, quenching the fires of humanitarianism, which should be aglow on the altars of a true religion. It degenerates too often into a cold religious conventionalism.

Over against all of these exaltations of the lesser values of religion let us note the evaluation which we find in the teachings and example of Jesus. What answer did he give when John sent his messengers inquiring: ''Art thou he that cometh or look we for another?'' ''Go and tell John,'' he replied, ''the things which ye hear and see: the blind receive their sight; and the lame walk, the lepers are cleansed, and the deaf hear, and the dead are raised up, and the poor have good tidings preached to them.'' Service was the mark of the new order of things in religion. With profound religious insight Jesus regards the very core of religion to be moral. That marvelous discourse which we call the Sermon on the Mount evinces this. Who are the blessed? Are they not those who are meek, merciful, pure in heart, and who hunger and thirst

---

[4] Rauschenbusch, *Christianity and the Social Crisis*, N. Y., 1915, p. 7.

after righteousness, and who are persecuted for righteousness' sake? Men are enjoined to let their light shine
so that others may see of their good works. Their righteousness is to exceed the righteousness of the Pharisees.
They are to be perfect as their Father in heaven is perfect. They are to develop a proper sense of values and
lay up treasures in heaven. They are to seek first the
kingdom of God and His righteousness. They are to be
judged by their fruits. Membership in the Father's kingdom is conditioned on doing his righteous will. Nor
are the parables of Jesus less pronounced in their ethical teaching. Do not the parables of the tares of the
field and of the net filled with fishes illustrate this? In
them Jesus is dealing with righteous and unrighteous
souls and their destiny. Character, according to his teaching, is the only thing that endures. The supreme value of
the soul, because of its moral possibilities, is in the Master's thought. What a profound lesson in the moral values of religion is presented in that solemn question of His,
"What shall it profit a man if he gain the whole world
and lose his own soul?" and he adds that every one shall
be rewarded according to his works. In his reply to the
tempting lawyer he points out the two highest laws of
man's being: The first enjoins supreme love to God, and
the second is like unto it—Thou shalt love thy neighbor
as thyself. The first is exemplified in obedience to God's
expressed will, and the parable of the Good Samaritan
illustrates the meaning of the second great commandment.

In short, in Jesus we have a great teacher who sees
eternal life to consist in character, and in character that
expresses itself in righteous living. His blessings, his exhortations, his explanations, his penalties, and his rewards are all moral in their character. God's kingdom
is a kingdom of righteousness. Religion consists in right

relations with God, with man, and with self. Love is the supreme law of the kingdom and love expresses itself in righteous service. This is the Master's concept of religion. A lofty ethical pragmatism expresses its very essence. There is, of course, a theology implied in his teaching, for he deals with the profoundest spiritual truths and realities. But it is the facts of religious experience that he emphasizes. There was, also, a quietism and mysticism in his religious life. There were sacred moments when he retired from the crowd, and stood apart from his disciples, to commune with his Father, to seek guidance, strength, and sufficiency for his arduous task. These must have been moments of refreshment and illumination, for he returned to his work of patient and persistent fidelity to the Father's will. There was worship also in his life. He went to the synagogue, and showed proper deference for the ceremonialism of the religion of his people. But with keen spiritual intuition he pierced the shell of rite and ceremony and seized the reality of which these were but feeble symbols, and then, with a true sense of values, he flayed the Pharisees because of their externalism and legalism— because of their exaltation of the lower for the higher; because of their substitution of the lesser for the greater. Action, and action for the realization of the highest moral ends,—the execution on earth of the righteous will of heaven,—this was for Jesus the supreme fact, the great objective of religion.

In perusing the preceding chapters it is, of course, very manifest that in the higher religions God is conceived of as a God of righteousness. This is not only an interesting but significant fact as it relates to motivation in the moral life. To believe in a God who rewards virtue and punishes vice proves to be a powerful dynamic in the moral life of the individual and of society, although it does not always result in the highest type of morality. Much of this de-

pends on the nature of the rewards and penalty. In some
of the religions considered these are not of a very high
order.

But in the Christian religion especially, this belief in
a God of righteousness is very significant from another
point of view,—in furnishing a powerful inspiration to
the cause of righteousness. It is the inspiration and help
that come from belief in a righteous God, who is in all
and over all, coöperating with His people for the realization of His kingdom in the hearts of men. The struggle to
establish the kingdom of highest values is a severe one.
Sin is deeply intrenched and has tremendous resources
at its command. Often victory comes to the enemy, with
the corresponding discouragement of defeat to the righteous. Faith and courage in the ultimate triumph of the
kingdom, both in the heart of the individual and in the
heart of society, might fail were it not for the assurance
that we fight with the God of righteousness on our side.
So, however dark at times the outlook may be, we struggle
on, knowing that, with the omnipotent and omniscient
"power not ourselves that makes for righteousness" en-
listed in the struggle, ultimately right the day will win.

Another advantage is theirs who labor for righteousness inspired by religious faith. It lies in the strength
that comes through belief in the immortality of virtue.
According to the teaching of some of the higher religions,
and especially of the Christian religion, the moral values
are eternal. Personal worth survives death and the grave.
We are members of a kingdom of everlasting worths.
Transiency is written on the face of all things, but the
kingdom of right endures forever. It is as imperishable
as God Himself. Such a faith is a powerful support to
those who labor for the kingdom when wrong triumphs
over right,—when the cause of righteousness moves

slowly; when virtue seems of little avail. As Professor McDougall says:

Apart from any hope of rewards or fear of punishment after death, the belief must have, it seems to me, a moralizing influence upon our thought and conduct that we can ill afford to dispense with. The admirable Stoic attitude of a Marcus Aurelius or a Huxley may suffice for those who rise to it in the moral environment created by civilizations based upon a belief in a future life and upon other positive religious beliefs; but I gravely doubt whether whole nations could rise to the level of an austere morality, or even maintain a decent working standard of conduct, after losing those beliefs. A proof that our life does not end with death, even though we know nothing of the nature of the life beyond the grave, would justify the belief that we have our share in a larger scheme of things than the universe described by physical science; and this conviction must add dignity, seriousness, and significance to our lives, and must throw a great weight into the scale against the dangers that threaten every advanced civilization.[5]

As the writer has said elsewhere:

The historian of moral progress would have a far different story to tell had man throughout his history been wanting in this belief. It has been not only an inspiring and sustaining force, but a veritable star of hope leading him through the long conflict between good and evil.[6]

In conclusion, it may be said that the recognition of the supremacy of moral values, and a statement of what these values are, together with belief in a God of righteousness, who rewards virtue and punishes vice; who is in the world working for righteous ends, coöperating with those who are laboring for the realization of life's supreme values; and belief in the immortal nature of those values; —these are the noblest contributions that religion has made to human life.

[5] McDougall, *Body and Mind*, New York, 1911, pp. xiii-xiv.
[6] *Religion and the Future Life*, edited by E. Hershey Sneath, New York, 1922, p. 338.